D1453444

BLAZING ICE

BLAZING ICE

PIONEERING THE TWENTY-FIRST CENTURY'S
ROAD TO THE SOUTH POLE

John H. Wright

Foreword by David M. Bresnahan

Potomac Books
Washington, D.C.

Library of Congress Cataloging-in-Publication Data
Wright, John H.
  Blazing ice : pioneering the twenty-first century's road to the South Pole / John H. Wright ; foreword by David M. Bresnahan.
     p. cm.
  Includes index.
  ISBN 978-1-61234-451-5 (hardcover : alk. paper)
  ISBN 978-1-61234-452-2 (electronic)
1. Antarctica—Discovery and exploration. 2. Antarctica—Social conditions—21st century. 3. Antarctica—Environmental conditions. I. Title.
  G860.W75 2012
  919.89—dc23

                                        2012023729

Printed in the United States of America on acid-free paper that meets the American National Standards Institute Z39-48 Standard.

Potomac Books
22841 Quicksilver Drive
Dulles, Virginia 20166

First Edition

10 9 8 7 6 5 4 3 2 1

for Brian Wheater,
whose cautionary tale of *Linda* kept us on alert,

for the crew,
who toiled on the trail and proved the concept,

and
for all those who helped

Contents

FOREWORD

I felt suddenly alone on the snowy flats of the McMurdo Ice Shelf near Williams Field skiway. Ann had just taken their group picture. Now, the eight of them walked away, back over the snow. Their waiting tractors and sled trains lined up on the snow road, pointed south under a blue sky and a bright sun. I knew they'd do it this time, get all the way to South Pole and back. John was right, though. It wasn't a three-year project. I knew that too, but I had to sell it to others. I had no appreciation at the beginning of what really lay under the red lines drawn on those maps, no idea the level of effort it took to design and assemble the fleet. Support at the National Science Foundation was not undivided, either. But these eight were tenacious. And I was proud of all of us.

Their yellow tractors and red tractors started crawling forward. In a half mile the caravan turned east, directly into the face of the gray blizzard-wall overtaking the Shelf. And that was the point: the weather grounded our LC-130 Hercules aircraft, but the traverse kept going. A perfect start. Damn, I wanted to go with them.

The United States established a strategic presence at the geographic South Pole in 1956. Since that time, we have supplied the Amundsen-Scott South Pole Station from our logistics hub at McMurdo Station on the coast of Antarctica entirely by airlift.

Less than a hundred years ago, no one had even seen the South Pole. These days, World War II and Cold War interests in the unknown continent have quieted. The National Science Foundation now runs the entire scope of American interests in Antarctica through the United States Antarctic Program (USAP). Glimpsing the first thirty seconds after the Big Bang, measuring the annual dilation of the ozone hole, monitoring the front lines of global warming—we do world-class science down there. *That* requires extraordinary logistical support, and *that* was my job.

I'd been intrigued with the idea of an overland supply traverse to South Pole for years. "Traverse" is what we call them in Antarctica—tractor and sled caravans crossing the ice and snow. Some shared the vision, but the concept was not a new idea. A 1962 Operation Deep Freeze report, for example, points out "an overland system for delivering large quantities of bulk fuel to Byrd Station" could substantially reduce airlift costs.

Through the late 1980s and 1990s we advanced the traverse concept in workshops, studies, reports, and field investigations. I was frustrated that others in NSF's Office of Polar Programs couldn't see the future then. But vision is a hard sell in NSF when you want money, not just words. I finally took possession of the traverse development after I spent time in the field exploring a possible route in 1995. When George Blaisdell and I completed our study in 2000, "Analysis of McMurdo to South Pole Traverse as a Means to Increase LC-130 Availability in the USAP," we found the benefits to the program were overwhelming.

Building of the United States' third research station at South Pole was then nearing completion. In 1998–1999 supplying Pole with building materials over and above its normal science support claimed 316 LC-130 sorties, leaving only 182 flights available for remote field science. Since that year, flights for field science dropped to 102, 103, and in 2001–2002 had fallen to only 64. Remote field science, the great strength of the USAP, was dying.

Under these circumstances, we found support for the South Pole Traverse Proof-of-Concept Project. Our study showed the traverse would not only free up LC-130 flights for field science, but that it would be economical as well. Tractors would burn half the fuel to deliver the same payload to Pole as LC-130s. The environment would win in a big way, too: for the same fuel burned, modern tractor engines released merely hundredths of the noxious emissions produced by LC-130 turbo props.

Could we pull off the proof-of-concept? Could we find a route, prove it safe, and show it could be done over and over again?

In an ironic twist, modern technology perfected in the 1990s and available in 2000 enabled this more primitive means of delivering supplies to South Pole. We had GPS for navigation, ground penetrating radar for finding deadly hidden crevasses, Iridium phones with data links for e-mail, and satellite imagery. None of these were available when we'd dropped a bulldozer in a crevasse not far from McMurdo in 1990. The time was right for us now.

Who would lead the project?

At NSF's urging, the USAP support contractor hired John Wright. I knew him, but not well at the time. He had pulled off some challenging jobs in the USAP and had built an impeccable record for safety. I remember pictures of a stunningly accurate hole-through in the South Pole Tunnel Project he ran where two tunnels met face to face in the dark. John always placed his crew in the forefront, while he stood in the background, smiling. For the traverse job, he put together a field team of Ice veterans. They collaborated with the U.S. Army Corps of Engineers Cold Regions Research and Engineering Laboratory, and a host of other contributors. John brought out the best in all his crew. But he sure was hardheaded at the merest shadow of a threat to their safety.

When they came back to McMurdo on January 14, 2006, the nonbelievers stepped aside. They had delivered eleven LC-130 loads of cargo to Pole. They'd done it safely, and with little more impact to the environment than the tracks they left. And they made history. No one had ever traversed from McMurdo to Pole and back. The concept was proved.

Because of that, USAP logistics will never be the same. At maturity, the traverse would give us back ninety flights or more. In 2000, George and I thought it'd take three tractor fleets to do that. These guys showed us it could be done with two. And that's only the beginning of change.

I am pleased to have John, my friend and colleague, tell our story.

DAVID M. BRESNAHAN
SYSTEMS MANAGER FOR OPERATIONS AND LOGISTICS (RET.)
OFFICE OF POLAR PROGRAMS
NATIONAL SCIENCE FOUNDATION
WASHINGTON, D.C.
MARCH 15, 2010

Acknowledgments

To my wife, Samantha, and my friend Ann Hawthorne, I give my deepest thanks for suffering through early manuscript drafts of *Blazing Ice,* and for their encouragement throughout to bring our worthy story to book.

Author William Fox's (*Terra Antarctica*) meditations on rendering geography into landscape through human imprints made him a soul-brother for our undertaking. Tom Sawyer (technology editor, *Engineering News-Record*) recognized both the technical component of our achievement and the dramatic story underlying it. I thank both these writers for their enthusiastic counsel.

Chris Landry, snow scientist, and learned man David Emory, both of Silverton, Colorado, graciously provided critical reads of the manuscript in its middling and later versions. Mountaineer Tom Lyman, intimately familiar with the story by virtue of having lived two years of it, kindly offered his read and comments. And special thanks to Andy Hanahan III for hints on Chicago style.

As pupil, I bow to master Bruce McAllister (mcallistercoaching.com) who helped me wrench *Blazing Ice* out of the technical operations reports it inhabited into the narrative in which the story truly lives. I thank Bruce for ongoing guidance through the forests of modern publishing.

I am profoundly grateful to Anne Devlin of Max Gartenberg Literary Agency for bringing *Blazing Ice* to Potomac Books and arranging this perfect publishing marriage.

Finally, I wish to acknowledge with deepest appreciation Roald Amundsen, Fridtjof Nansen, Ernest Shackleton, Robert Falcon Scott, Vivian Fuchs,

Edmund Hillary, Albert Crary, and John Evans for the legacy documents they left behind. These added immeasurably to our effective route planning, and to ensuring our mission safety and success in the twenty-first century.

Prologue

The white world of snow and ice lay below us now. A frozen cascade, big as Niagara Falls and broken by hundreds of gaping crevasses, draped over the plateau's rim. Downstream, the Leverett Glacier flowed gracefully around the stony buttress of Mount Beazley.

The first of our heavy tractors appeared just below the rim, laboring up the final grade. The place was strangely silent. The snows absorbed all sound. No wind blew.

Finally the tractor topped out. It was a ponderous, stately event.

Today was January 4, 2005. I looked back on the ground we crossed getting here. Seven thousand feet below, icy turbulence had blocked us from the Transantarctic Mountains for a month. Three hundred miles of snow swamp behind that had held us up for a year. And just a day trip out of McMurdo Station, blasting and dozing a path across three miles of hidden crevasses, had taken another year of our lives.

Now, 738 miles out of McMurdo, not one human lived between us and there.

Six hundred miles behind us, on the sea-level realms of the Ross Ice Shelf, lay the frozen flesh of four British explorers and their leader. Robert Falcon Scott, known as Scott of the Antarctic, had been the last one to try for the South Pole and back from McMurdo. They went on foot. They died on their return. Now their scurvied bodies drift slowly toward the Ross Sea, buried under nine decades of snow. We drove right by them.

Only fifteen years ago, not far from Scott's body, a Caterpillar D8 bull-dozer broke through the snow and fell into a black crevasse. My friend went down with that bulldozer. He lived. But the dozer's steely carcass drifts on in that hole toward its own rendezvous with the Ross Sea.

There were eight of us now. We were equipment operators, mechanics, mountaineers, and engineers. I picked them for their years of Antarctic experience. We respected and liked each other. Together we ran five heavy tractors pulling heavy sled trains. We ran a light scout tractor in front of us, rigged with modern crevasse-detecting radar.

When the last of our tractors topped out we had won our foothold on the Polar Plateau. We planted four flags on the plateau's edge and called that point SPT-18.

This was the final year of our three-year project. Between us and South Pole lay three hundred miles of unexplored ground. We wanted to go, but to get back we needed more fuel than we had. The National Science Foundation could give us that fuel at Pole.

Within our warm bunkroom we waited for word. Then sometime during the "night" we felt our shelter rocking in the wind atop its sled base. We would wake to a blizzard.

In his opening remarks at the May 2002 United States Antarctic Program Annual Planning Conference, headman Erick Chiang from the NSF Office of Polar Programs uttered these words: "The National Science Foundation announces its *full support* for the development of the South Pole Traverse." His was a simple, declarative statement.

I spent the next four years figuring out what he meant.

PART I.
GETTING STARTED: MENACE AND HELP

1 | *Linda*

Linda *was thirty-three years old.* She might have been good for another twenty years. On Thanksgiving Day, 1990, *Linda* chugged onto the Ross Ice Shelf. The floating, snow-covered sheet of glacial ice reached endlessly ahead. A gray overcast stole the horizon and robbed the Shelf of all its shadows. *Linda* carried her blade high over the snow. She pulled a twenty-ton sled loaded with thirty thousand pounds of dynamite.

Linda was special, a D8-LGP bulldozer built for Antarctica. Steel spliced into her chopped frame stretched her over twenty feet long. And she was light-footed. Sixty thousand pounds of yellow iron spread over a pair of fifty-four-inch-wide tracks made her a low-ground-pressure machine.

Brian Wheater had just finished his four-hour stretch at *Linda*'s stick. He'd brought her from Williams Field skiway that afternoon. Now he sat off to the side in *Linda*'s spacious cab while his partner took a turn. A diesel-fired heater at their feet kept them warm.

Working only his second season on the Ice, Brian volunteered for anything. Now he staged explosives for a seismic project to the foot of the Beardmore Glacier. This was the glacier that Robert Falcon Scott, and Ernest Shackleton before him, traversed over the Transantarctic Mountains onto the Polar Plateau. To get to the Beardmore, Brian had to cross four hundred miles of Ross Ice Shelf. It had been decades since the United States Antarctic Program (USAP) sent anybody out this way over the surface. From airfields on the ice, near the stony ground of McMurdo Station on Ross Island, the United States flew supplies to its remote outposts on the continent.

The Ross Ice Shelf was a long way from the jungles of Vietnam for Brian. Nothing green here. Nothing growing, nothing wet, nothing warm. Brian kept his vigil no less keen. He was rock solid, a decorated sergeant of the U.S. Marines. Behind his rigid bearing lay an amazing mix of literary erudition and an often-silly sense of humor. He thought carefully before speaking. He chose his words well. But he rarely spoke. Grim-faced, Brian peered through the blank whiteness outside *Linda*'s windows for the other tractors in their caravan.

Linda's sister *Pam* followed a hundred yards behind. *Pam* pulled another twenty-ton sled of fuel drums. Two mechanics from Williams Field alternated at her controls. A four-tracked Tucker Sno-Cat, one-quarter *Linda*'s weight, ran out in front carrying their food, survival gear, and blasting caps. A Kiwi mountaineer ran the Tucker, leading their caravan along the same route explorer Edmund Hillary took in the 1950s.

The orange Tucker disappeared from time to time, and then reappeared. Brian watched it closely, never losing sight of the flag atop its tall whip antenna. He sensed they were on uneven ground, on a lazy ocean of long, slow snow rollers. The Tucker disappeared again. Brian elbowed his partner, pointing. Both stood up, craning for a look. No shadows, no tracks. The last thing Brian saw was the flag on that whip antenna when gravity struck.

Linda plunged right. Snow exploded through her window. She ricocheted left. Her side door broke in. Snow blasted Brian against his partner, burying them both. Then *Linda* fell, completely vertical, racing straight down, pulling her sled after them.

Linda crashed against the edge of an ice wall, wedged. Her windshield broke out. The snow that had encased Brian and his partner spewed into the black void below. They hung up on *Linda*'s dashboard, waiting for the dynamite sled.

It never fell.

They found the throttle under what snow remained in *Linda*'s cab and killed her engine before its fumes killed them. One hundred gallons of diesel from *Linda*'s tank had spilled over everything. Brian killed the pilot flame on the cab heater, refusing to burn to death in the icy crevasse.

Neither Brian nor his partner spoke after that. Moments became minutes. Brian checked to see if he was all there and working right. He looked straight up through the broken rear window. A promise of light filtered through a ragged aperture at the surface. The dynamite sled's front skis dangled in space, held back by a heavy chain. Its deck had rammed across the collapsed snow bridge into the opposite wall of the crevasse.

The dark fissure clouded with their frosty breath. All was silent but for the "tink" of metal on metal shrinking in the intense cold. A scratching sound prompted Brian to dig for their radio. Its red light came on when he pressed transmit. They still had battery. Brian looked at his watch for the first time: 7:45 p.m. He couldn't make out the reply, but he recognized the mechanic's voice.

Russ Magsig had seen *Linda* disappear. He stopped *Pam*. One step at a time, the bearded mechanic in grease-stained overalls plunged a slender eight-foot metal rod into the snow in front of him. A well-dressed mountaineer probed from the opposite direction. Both converged on the twenty-ton sled bridged across the gaping black hole. A half-hour later, Russ reached it first. He lay on his belly, looking into the hole, and shouted.

Brian spotted Russ's silhouette against the vague light. He considered climbing up the dangling chains with the mountaineer's rope around him, but his partner's legs and hip ached. Brian stayed with his partner. The mountaineer had already called for a rescue team. No one else would approach the crevasse until it arrived. Insidious, -55 degree cold penetrated them.

Brian's partner shifted his weight, kicked at some snow and hit something. They found the military thermos they'd filled with coffee before they left Williams Field. The coffee was still hot.

The first of three helicopters flew over. Brian never looked up. He looked at his watch the second time: 9:30. A chunk of snow hit *Linda*: 10:00. Another Kiwi mountaineer hollered that she was coming down. Her rope swung six feet to the side of *Linda*'s cab, dangling into the void. She kicked over the edge and rappelled sixty-six feet down to them. In the closed space she smelled the stink of machines, fuel, and human bodies.

They hauled Brian's partner out first. Then Brian roped up and swung over the abyss. He reached the surface at 10:25 p.m., startled by the clear blue sky and bright sunshine.

They'd been in the crevasse for three hours and ten minutes, cold soaked. Brian warmed a bit during the forty-minute flight to McMurdo. When he got there his core temperature was up to 95 degrees. The doctor thought the coffee had saved them.

Linda stayed in the crevasse. The place where she fell was called the Shear Zone.

|2| Denver

Early Sunday morning in the spring of 2002, I left my mining town home, my wife, and four-year-old son, and drove over Red Mountain Pass for Denver. I'd driven the Pass countless times over the past thirty years—it was one of only two paved roads leading out of the county. Denver, the city, held the corporate offices for the Antarctic Program's principal support contractor. There was a job for me if I wanted it. But I was thinking about bad ground and bad ideas growing in the dark.

A momentary mental picture of Brian in the crevasse floated over the steering wheel of my pickup truck. I'd met Brian earlier in the week, halfway and a long drive for both of us, at the True Grit Café in Ridgway. He said he'd never heard of the Shear Zone until he became a part of it. We spent a couple hours going over *Linda*'s fall and the daisy chain of events leading to that.

Now the program wanted to try again, this time going all the way to South Pole and back. It'd asked me to lead that job, and that meant crossing the Shear Zone. While Brian dredged up twelve-year-old memories of *Linda* over burgers, I asked myself what had changed. Brian's story frightened me. It was a complex mistake—the kind that lurked in institutional systems. A popular hubris gave an idea momentum, but no one could imagine the unintended consequences of the idea. I could never get a handle on why mistakes like that happened because nobody wanted them. But I recognized their shadows, and tried to avoid them. When Brian and I parted, our hands clasped, and standing eye to eye, he told me this: "Never turn your back on anything—or anyone—in that place."

The Pass's snaky twists and turns took me by mines I'd worked in off and on for three decades, and many more mines I'd not. Those holes in the mountainsides turned my thoughts to our third year on the South Pole tunnel project, two years ago. Not a miner among my crew but me, yet we made two spectacular intersections that year. Two tunnels connecting face-to-face at three inches off centerline would've made me happy. I'd never heard stories about hole-throughs like ours: perfect. The crew listened. They learned. When the tunneling machine broke down, we went at the face with chainsaws, picks and shovels.

We stood together at the end of that season by the skiway while they waited for their flight north. When the LC-130 bore them off to McMurdo, sobs of relief, sobs of thanksgiving overcame me; not one of them had been hurt. They were going home intact, happy . . . and proud. I remembered this, driving across Colorado, seven hours on the road. Not one of them hurt.

Hurt. Through the farm country of Montrose I remembered floating on a litter years before, a crew of raven-haired miners lugging me through a maze of tunnels in New Mexico, beams from their cap lamps bouncing through the darkness like animated spirits. A slab of rock had fallen off the tunnel face just as I finished centering the start of my partner's drill hole while he ran the 125-pound pneumatic drill at the other end of his six-foot-long drill bit. Stepping back to take up my own drill, I found myself lying across his, dazed, hit harder than I'd ever been. I lay there, knowing I was hurt but not yet in pain. My partner grabbed me by the shoulders and dragged me back from the tunnel face. He left me lying in a cold puddle of muddy drill water, and then went for help. Alone then, eyes closed, I felt the intense pain in my back.

Riding up the thousand-foot vertical shaft on the metal floor of the cage, lying in the back of that ambulance through the starlit wintery night to the hospital in Taos, I thought, *What've I done? A newborn son in Colorado. A young wife who cares lovingly for him. I have to shelter them. I have to feed them . . . I have to work. Am I a broken burden to my family now?* I remembered all that, driving to Denver. That was bad ground at that mine. But from the distance of an engineer's office, it all worked out on paper.

Brian got into bad ground. If you draw a line on a map from here to there, do you know what's under that line? They sent *Linda* out. Had anything changed? I'd changed. That cave-in shrunk my backbone an inch. Best I could do now was six-foot-three. My truck's mirror showed me gray hair and gray beard where dark brown used to be.

I topped 11,312 feet at Monarch Pass, hunting more pavement. *The terrain I'll do well with.* I'd made my living for years as a professional geologist. I didn't care for the academic stuff, but give me a project and I was a happy man. *The organization I'll have trouble with.* I've always worked better with the man standing beside me than with the idea of a company. Companies seemed like fictions to me that men personified with phrases like "The Company wants" or "They won't like," as if companies were flesh-and-blood that you could shake hands with.

I'd long ago bought into the idea of a transcontinental traverse, a safe route over the surface of Antarctica for caravans of tractor trains hauling supplies to South Pole. But for me this mission wasn't about supporting the juggernaut running the program, nor its superstructure. A mission accomplished did that. This mission was about supporting the people on the ground, people who risked their lives.

I had negotiated a week's worth of work in Denver, without commitment to accept the overall job, in order to consider the proposition and decide for myself. Crossing the high plains of South Park, watching for antelope in the distance, I found my resolve: *I will not lead, or be a party to, any plan that puts one person's life at risk.*

Monday morning I found my boss-to-be. An affable fellow with white-gray hair, he'd hired me for my first job on the Ice nine years before this, but he'd stepped out of the program the next year to deal with a death in his family. Now he was back. I was glad to see him. He showed me to a cubicle desk, dead center in a sea of cubicles. It came equipped with a phone, a computer, an ergonomic chair, and two sets of drawers. The cubicle's four-foot-high walls supported an empty bookshelf. The desktop was bare. There was no drafting table, nor wall space for maps.

"This will be yours. It's a manager's desk," he said.

A skinny, pony-tailed fellow stepped up with an armfull of reports and plunked them down on the manager's desk. "I knew you were coming. I took the liberty of collecting these for your review. Welcome aboard," he said cheerfully. "I'm here to help." The fellow would be my part-time support man.

"Thank you," I returned. I recognized him from my first year on the Ice, too, when he worked for the field support group. He was energetic and brimmed with enthusiasm. But I was cautious about the whole business. "I'm only here for a week. Perhaps longer, depending on what's in this stuff."

Brian had never heard of the Shear Zone before setting out in *Linda*. The mountaineer told him nothing about the route. He was never issued a map and compass like he always had been in Vietnam. His boss simply asked if he wanted to take a bulldozer across the Ross Ice Shelf. His partner, with seven years on the Ice, thought they might be out six days. All they had to do was drive out past Minna Bluff and turn south. Brian told me that when he and his partner went for their briefing, all they got was "what to do with human waste." I said, "You've got to be kidding?"

"No, really, John. The guy said 'You won't need to haul back your waste,'" and Brian laughed, though he barely cracked a smile.

That was funny. But a familiar shadow lurked in Brian's story: the assumption that everyone knew what they were getting into. What Brian knew in advance was a measure of what the system knew before allowing them to come into harm's way. But Brian's brain worked differently from mine. Faced with an unfamiliar problem, Brian gave orders. Facing the same problem, I asked: how did things come to be this way?

I looked at the reports, anxious to review them here, on the basement level of the office building. But my boss spoke up. "Before you get started, you need to go to human resources and sign some papers." He led me over pathways and up stairs to the third and highest floor of the building. "They're in here."

I found my desk an hour later and picked the thickest report from the stack. *The McMurdo to South Pole Traverse Development Project—Final Report* was the legacy of a predecessor project from the mid-1990s, five years after *Linda*. I'd only heard rumors about why that project ended. The U.S. Navy was phasing out of the Support Force Antarctica business. The New York Air National Guard (NYANG) was phasing in. The Guard promised higher cargo delivery to South Pole than the U.S. Navy had provided.

Resupplying South Pole, anticipating massive material requirements for building a new station there, provided the pretext for developing a surface traverse. But the NYANG's—I loved that acronym—promise of increased cargo delivery ruled against spending for traverse development. A divided camp at

NSF saw one group sided with the established airlift, expensive but proven. The other sided with surface traverse, at least as an auxiliary capability. Airplanes won out, and the South Pole Investigative Traverse—SPIT—foundered.

The fat binder held dividers, map pockets, and pages of text. It collected "deliverable" reports provided by institutions of higher learning in support of the overarching project. A loose-leaf introductory letter fell from the front of the binder as my hands grappled with the weight of the assembly.

The SPIT project manager wrote that letter. I knew John Evans—not well at the time, but I respected him from a distance. My eyes lingered on his last sentence: "I have tried to summarize the project from its conception to its demise on the *shoals of intractable funding* [emphasis mine] and timing difficulties." If Evans was still working in the program, I needed to find him. Maybe he was in this office.

Evans's report would take some time to work through. I set it aside, and turned to another collection of reports. These dealt with ground penetrating radar (GPR) and detecting hidden crevasses. Cold Regions Research and Engineering Laboratory (CRREL) authors were names I'd heard on the Ice but no one I really knew. The reports indicated a technical capability for locating hidden crevasses did exist, but how to adapt that to a moving traverse on ice shelves and glaciers, which were themselves moving, was not clear.

One of the CRREL authors wrote, "the ground penetrating radar never misled us." That report covered some testing in the Shear Zone. Its engineered language applied to what they saw, not to what they might have missed without knowing, and not to anyplace where they did not look. Though radar offered a promise of Superman-like x-ray vision, I'd have to see it for myself.

Did we need a CRREL expert with us all the time? Could we train our own specialists—a mechanic, or a mountaineer, or an equipment operator?

I met my boss again that afternoon. "Were you around when *Linda* went in?"

"I remember it well," he answered.

"Did you go out there?"

"No. I was in town when it happened. " He described the incident with phrases like "poor planning," "should never have happened," and "ill-prepared."

We turned the discussion to ground penetrating radar. He asked if it really worked.

"These reports say it should. But they don't deal with traversing, or with building a road across the Shear Zone. There is this." I showed him: "'*never misled us.*'"

His eyes opened wide at reading the claim. "What do you think?"

"Those guys never had to look somebody in the eyes and tell them 'You go out there with that D8.' It's a technical report. '*Never misled us*' can mislead you into thinking the radar will never mislead *you*."

"What do you want to do?"

The boss's cubicle was one in a cluster of four. Over their partitions, cubicles vanished to the horizon; an office, not a sea of white. We'd try the radar, but I needed to know more about it. The whole project depended on reliably detecting hidden crevasses. We'd not go where somebody said there were no crevasses just on their say.

"If it works," I said, "we should go over every step of the thousand miles with it before we ever bring a tractor onto the same ground."

"I'd favor every inch."

We shook on that. If the radar worked, I promised to radar every inch of the way between McMurdo and South Pole before a traverse fleet crossed that same inch. If the radar didn't work, we wouldn't go.

"And I will support that," my boss declared. We had a pact.

I revisited Evans's tome and the rest of the stack throughout the week.

A paper dated 2000 contained a colorful map of the proposed route. It plotted a straight line from the Shear Zone across the Ross Ice Shelf to a specific pass over the Transantarctic Mountains. Curiously, the line passed directly over a well-known crevasse zone isolated in the middle of the Shelf: the Crary Ice Rise. The line then followed a zigzag path over the mountains, ultimately connecting to another straight-line reach over the high Polar Plateau to the Pole. The map looked like a show-and-tell exhibit rather than a carefully rendered navigational tool.

But straight lines suggested uniform terrain. They implied ground without difficulty or hazard or variation. "Straight" also meant nobody had really looked at it. I wanted more information about the Crary Ice Rise.

A CRREL paper dated 2001 gave a list of coordinates fixing the turning points on the colorful map. The list included eighteen points labeled "L" for a route segment on the Leverett Glacier. The SPIT work targeted the Leverett as the leading candidate for passage over the mountains. I didn't know much about that glacier yet. Why did they select any of those points?

I'd often worked with hundred-year-old field notes of mining claim surveys recorded by U.S. Deputy Mineral Surveyors, filed then with the General Land Office, and archived today by the Bureau of Land Management. The notes invariably led me to rediscover original claim corners, perhaps a blaze on a spruce tree, then twelve-inches in diameter, bearing letters and numbers carved just so according to their instructions. Were the CRREL notes as reliable? Lives could depend on it.

One report in Evans's tome outlined the basis for choosing the Leverett. A sieve-like process screened twenty or so candidate glaciers, rating them from "excellent" to "forget-about-it." The sieve caught the Leverett on top, the only one to win a "good" rating. All the other candidates fell through. The next highest was rated "poor." That was the Skelton Glacier, the one Hillary used in 1957.

The SPIT team landed on both the Leverett and the Skelton in 1995. After scooting over their surfaces on snowmobiles, their verdict lay squarely with the Leverett.

Getting to the Leverett was another matter. There was the Shear Zone, only a few miles out of McMurdo. The SPIT team had been there, too. And they had radar.

The proposed route covered more than a thousand miles one way. Evans's team examined only 10 percent of it. They focused on "problematic" spots. Problematic meant what one *perceived* as a problem. If one did not perceive a problem that did not mean no problem was there. Nevertheless, I saw clearly where Evans left off and where I might take up his trail. I could accept or disagree with any of the proposed route.

The other 90 percent had not been traveled by anyone, ever. But many others' tracks had crossed the proposed route: Shackleton's, Scott's, and Roald Amundsen's. What did they have to say about the land around those intersections?

Albert Crary, the American glaciologist, circumnavigated the Ross Ice Shelf in the late 1950s. Sir Edmund Hillary made his run up the Skelton to

Pole the year before. Our route would cut across the middle of the Shelf, ground neither of them had traveled.

I located both Hillary's book recounting his 1957 tractor traverse to Pole, *No Latitude for Error*, and Crary's technical report *Glaciological Studies of the Ross Ice Shelf, 1957–1960.*

Hillary described encounters with crevasses radiating off Minna Bluff and White Island, lands visible from McMurdo. Apparently he thought the crevasses formed where the Shelf ice impinged on those two points of land. When he set off in his Massey Ferguson from Scott Base, he swung deliberately wide of the landmarks to avoid those crevasses. He succeeded in reaching the Ross Ice Shelf after a tense, though uneventful, passage.

Crary's work there showed a belt of crevasses in contrast to a radiating pattern. The belt ran seventy-five miles long from the point of Minna Bluff to the tip of Cape Crozier, the easternmost point of Ross Island. Yet even Crary had crossed the belt a couple times in a Tucker Sno-Cat, and he likewise reported no incident.

How could both those men cross a place full of crevasses without incident? *Linda* had followed an "established route," Brian said—Hillary's route. Crary's information had been bought by American taxpayers and published. It was available and I was looking at it. Had *Linda*'s planners ignored it? What good was institutional knowledge if nobody paid attention to it?

Crary drew several maps projecting ice shelf characteristics into the central regions he had never traveled—projections of ice thickness, elevations, snow pack, and others. The one that caught my eye showed a region of soft snow right where the line on the colorful show-and-tell map went. *What's that like . . . under that line? How will heavy tractors handle soft snow?*

I set Crary's work aside. The more I looked into it, the more I realized how much I didn't know. That intimidated me, for *Linda* was never far from my mind.

Turning back to *Linda* herself, I asked around the office; who was there then, who remembered what? The McMurdo station manager at the time advised the operations director against going at all. The ops director dismissed his warnings, bowing instead to the NSF representative's interest to proceed. The

NSF rep at the time occupied the "big chair" in McMurdo. He was the godlike boss of all. I never learned what was on his mind. But the ops director's acquiescence told of the contractor's need to please the client. *That's dangerous.*

After *Linda*, the ops director remarked to the station manager, "You never said 'I told you so.'" The manager replied, "I told you the first time."

Had there been too much project inertia? Who actually said "go"?

John Evans occupied another cubicle on the basement floor we shared. His desk lay over the horizon from mine.

"Yes?" he said, cheerfully, when I approached his desk. John was a clean-shaven, bright-blue-eyed, and fair-haired man perhaps ten years my senior. A rugged mountaineer, he'd made the first ascent of Mount Vinson, the highest mountain in Antarctica.

"Ah yes," he said. "I remember you. How can I help you?"

"I'd like to talk to you about the South Pole Traverse project."

We decided to talk outside, away from the nearby cubicles and folks we might disturb. In the parking lot, we enjoyed deep breaths of fresh air. The Rocky Mountain's Front Range lay snow-covered on our western horizon. It looked strikingly similar to the Royal Society Range of the Transantarctic Mountains, across the Sound from McMurdo Station.

I began, "John, I reckon you know the NSF is starting the South Pole Traverse business back up. The job of running that project is not awarded yet. That's why I'm here this week . . . to scope it out. I've spent the week reading through your legacy reports. Great stuff."

"Well, I thank you for that—"

"I mean it. So much so that I'm prompted to ask why you don't go for that job? Here's a chance to complete it, maybe. You're a natural. And if you are going for it, I'd like to work for you to make it happen."

"Oh. Well thank you again. That's very kind of you. But no . . . I'm quite happy with what I'm doing now." John organized and landed field parties by boat in and around the Antarctic Peninsula, and the many islands in the region.

"Then I have to ask . . . is there anything at all about this project, something you learned from the SPIT work, something about the organization that warns you off the traverse project? Anything you might care to share with me?"

"Nothing except the usual. Politics and personalities. It's a grand project. It can and should be done. But I can think of nothing to warn *you* off. If NSF is going to take the next step . . . make certain the money is there. "

"Shoals of Intractable Funding?" I offered.

"Precisely," he laughed. "And if you take the job, I wish you the best of luck. Feel free to talk to me at any time. I'll be happy to help you."

We walked back into the office where I made my way through the geometric maze to my desk. I dialed a number in Washington, D.C. There was the matter of my original concern. It was a question of *time*.

"Dave Bresnahan, this is John Wright. I'm calling from the Denver office. And I'd like to talk about the traverse project. Is this a good time?"

"I've been expecting your call." Dave was the operations and logistics officer for the U.S. Antarctic Program. He was NSF's sponsor for the project.

"Dave, I've been here a week going over reports and gauging the support I might get. I'm happy to find high quality in Evans's legacy documents—"

"You should see the smile on my face to hear you say that, John."

Dave might have sat in a cubicle like mine, in some endlessly bigger government office, but he sounded comfortable. Perhaps he sat at a deluxe executive desk in its own room. With a door. When the SPIT project lost its funding, Dave had instructed Evans to leave a record that the next person could start right in on. "Very happy indeed to hear your opinion. We had no idea how long it'd be, or even if we'd start up again. And if there's ever another hiatus in the project, I'll want you to leave the same kind of trail."

"If I take the job, I will. But we need a reckoning about that. This is not a three-year job. I read the draft proposals while I was at Pole. And I wrote back that it was a five-year job at a sane pace, a four-year job with luck. Now that I'm in the office, I find the project is slated for three years. We don't know the terrain, and we do not know what kind of tractors or sleds will work on it. Three years assumes we know everything at the outset, and that ain't so."

Dave's voice became less familiar, less friendly. "We're going to fund the project incrementally. We'll take stock of lessons learned each season and fund the next step. And we'll hope to get the concept proved in three years."

Dave had advanced the cause in little steps for more than one decade. And he was passionate about the project. But three years was not entirely a matter of reckless bravado; it was a matter of what he could sell. A longer project would not have sold in the upper echelons at NSF. The contractor wrote what Dave told them to. As for me, the nature of my employment through the support contractor would not be full time, rather individual contract employment from one six-month period to the next. The incremental project funding Dave described offered no promise for the project duration.

"Three years is too fast," I declared.

"You let me worry about that," he said. "You are the right man for the job. Call any time, with any concern you may have. And keep me informed."

"If I take the job, I will." We hung up.

Even with the promise of support from NSF's sponsor, pay-go was vulnerable to a three-year pass-fail. On the flip side, the support contractor's cost-plus contract held no incentive for project success, only for its duration and the total dollars spent on it. Where were my allies? I'd just hung up the phone with one.

The footpath winding around the Denver office park, where the contractor's huge building was only one of many, followed a drainage stream that babbled over artfully placed rocks in a manicured streambed. The sun overhead warmed the crisp, spring air. I strolled alone.

A years-old conversation with a mechanic in the McMurdo shop came to mind. My traverse partner and I had managed a field fix on our fifteen-ton Delta truck on the frozen waters of McMurdo Sound. With radio support from the shop, we completed our delivery to Marble Point, and we drove our vehicles back to town.

There I met the mechanic foreman in the eight-bay cinderblock "Heavy Shop." Folks spoke of him with awe, for he'd been in the program a long time and had worked at remote outposts on the continent. He looked like their stories painted him: a shaggy-bearded, grease-stained Harley-Davidson biker, a half a dozen years older than me. He'd chew me out, so I approached him apologizing for our fix out on the sea ice. I'd blown a hydraulic steering hose.

He treated me kindly instead. "Yeah," he grinned. "But you brought it *back*! That means one of us didn't have to go out and get it!"

"Well, I . . . I appreciate that. I like this traverse business." That caught a twinkle in his eye. Emboldened, I asked him casually, "What do you think of a traverse to South Pole? Think it can be done?"

"I ain't going unless I can take a shower," he said gruffly, more like the tone I expected in the first place.

"What are you talking about, shower?"

"I've been traversing with those French at Dumont D'Urville. We dug up an airplane out there. Man, they *never* took showers! You *got* to have a shower, or you can't live with yourself!" He was speaking of places and times in Antarctica I'd never heard of.

"Showers, huh?" I walked away. On the local traverses, we had showers at both ends of the line: at Marble Point and at McMurdo.

That conversation was six years old. Only last week Brian had explained this same mechanic was the one who followed *Linda* in *Pam*, the one who probed his way to the edge of the crevasse and first looked down.

The program later razed the mechanic's home at Williams Field, ten miles out on the Ice Shelf from McMurdo. I did the blasting on that job. Not liking life in McMurdo the next year, the mechanic found work on an island in the South Pacific. I pictured him in baggy shorts and a t-shirt, standing idly on a rusty World War II dock, staring deeply into the water, working out some intricate mechanic's dilemma.

"Never turn your back on anything—or anyone—in that place," Brian had told me. Yet even with a reasonable promise of support, most of the job was up to me and the sweeping scope of it all was intimidating. But as I walked along the footpath I began to understand the job as a series of sequential critical steps that could only be taken one step at a time. Each step headed toward the goal, but each step may or may not succeed and so the ending was uncertain. Now, though, seen in increments, the job became more comprehendible. I'd take the job and see if we could even win the first step: crossing the Shear Zone. The rest of it could wait.

My walk was over.

"Anybody know how I can get in touch with Russ Magsig?" I asked around the office.

Russ did not keep a computer, did not have an e-mail address, and rarely answered his phone. Nobody really knew if he had a phone. But he was the one man I knew who had been in the Shear Zone, and who might be willing to go back.

Sooner or later a phone number appeared on my desk. I called it. "Hello, Russ? This is John Wright . . . I doubt if you remember me—"

"Yes," said his familiar voice. "You used to do the blasting and the Marble Point runs. What's up?"

"Russ, I promise there will be showers . . ."

|3| Frontier Attitude

If we hurt one person . . . if we killed one person . . . if we had anything like another *Linda* . . . there would be no hiatus for this project. We were the South Pole Traverse *Proof-of-Concept* Project (emphasis mine). We asked, was the traverse even feasible? Could we pioneer a route to South Pole and run it safely? Who was "we"?

NSF had recently hired a defense contractor to run the support job for its U.S. Antarctic Program. At NSF's urging, the new contractor hired me to pull off the traverse project. The traverse was a dangerous undertaking. How would the new contractor help me do it safely? I got an inkling in the tunnel.

Since the millennial year of 2000, everybody who got off the plane at South Pole wanted to see the tunnel. Neutrino hunter Bob Stokstad and his crew of astronomers, who'd spent a summer at Pole looking for those sub-atomic particles from outer space, saw to that.

Our crews exchanged tours one Sunday: Bob's telescope for our tunnel. Bob rotated back to McMurdo, debriefed his science project, and spread the word that the tunnel was the best tour going at South Pole. When U.S. representatives and distinguished visitors stepped off the LC-130 Hercules at Pole, they all wanted to see the tunnel. Never mind the new station going up on stilts, standing boldly against the skyline. The tunnel below them, that thing they could not see, was what they wanted to see the most. The chief operating officer (COO) for the new support contractor was no different. Station manager Katy Jensen told me so.

Katy was sharp. At thirty-three, the new contractor identified her as a "star" for future career interest. And she was well liked by everyone at South Pole. With her swimmer's broad shoulders, and long, straight dark hair, she was attractive. Folks vied to win smiles from Katy. She freely gave them. Her laugh had the quality of a baritone bell, clear, from somewhere deep inside her, a sound that turned your head. She'd accompany the COO.

I looked forward to showing off the nearly completed tunnel. This was the last year of the four-year tunnel project, and the second year for the new contractor: 2001–2002. The COO was young, clean-cut, and energetic, keenly interested in everything it took to make the Antarctic program work. He'd worked a shift with the shovel gang in McMurdo. You could see gears whizzing behind his bright blue eyes when he engaged you.

I had to check on the night shift anyway. "Tell him it's cold. You know, parka, gloves, bunny-boots."

The main tunnel was long enough to be impressive. We walked on and on in the darkness, dimly lit by my wandering cap-lamp and a string of light bulbs lining the left side of the tunnel. For the sameness of it all in the numbing cold, it seemed like we got nowhere. But we stopped at the perfect hole-through.

"Look behind us as far as you can see." My cap-lamp beam swept sideways over the COO's head. "Now turn and look the way we're headed." Either direction, points of light receded like an infinity of opposing mirrors.

"Think of starting your tunnel way out there, beyond the last light you can see. Think of another one starting behind you. Now imagine the two tunnels approaching each other in the dark. They have to meet squarely, face-to-face . . ." My mittened fists demonstrated, meeting knuckle-to-knuckle. ". . . on line and on grade. If they don't meet like that, well, imagine the consequences: you've driven your tunnels too far, past where you were supposed to meet. You haven't found the other tunnel. So where do you look for it? Do you look up? Down? Sideways?"

The tunnel would carry sewer and water pipes connecting the unique water wells bored into South Pole's ice. The pipes had better align. Katy smiled. She knew what was coming next.

My hand and cap-lamp pointed above our heads, lighting a two-foot-long block of unmined snow. That was our hole-through monument. My mitten grazed the tunnel walls, pointing down to the floor. "And this is where the two tunnels met."

I looked at him sideways like a miner, keeping my light out of his eyes. "You won't find more than one-eighth of an inch off line. You won't find that much on the bottom grade."

"How do you do that?" he asked, properly awed.

"Miners know how to do that," I said proudly. "The cost of failure is too high." That knowledge had been passed on from one miner to the next since humans came out of the Stone Age and dug in the ground for metal. In some places we'd used techniques as old as Babylonian times.

The COO soaked in the constant -55 degree Celsius tunnel temperature. "Shall we go to the dog-house?" I suggested to Katy.

"Lead on, mister." She smiled.

In a few hundred feet we reached the eight-by-eight-foot plywood shelter recessed into the right side of the tunnel. I slid its door shut behind us, welcoming the 20 degree warmer air inside. Our breath filled the closed room with fog. Diffuse yellow light from a lone bulb reflected off the walls and created an illusion of cozy fireglow.

The COO and Katy sat on a bench along one wall. I took a folding metal chair and sat facing them. Each of us leaned over the electric space heater in the middle of the floor. We'd stay inside warming our faces and hands until I gauged the COO's condition. We might turn around and go out, or continue deeper into the tunnel. For now he looked okay, and he wanted to talk.

"I remember some guy you had on your crew last year. A hillbilly-looking fellow, sort of skinny, wild-eyed . . ." he began. I knew exactly whom he was talking about, and I remembered the fellow fondly. But I'd not heard a question.

"He said you were the best boss he'd ever had. He went out of his way to tell me that . . . after I asked him about you." Nobody that year had any mining experience. I gave the guy a chance and he did well.

"How come he's not back this year?"

Clever. If I was such a good boss, why didn't he come back? He wanted to. And I'd tried to get him. "I couldn't get him off work-release. I wrote to the judge in Idaho and everything. Nothing doing."

Katy's laugh rang through the dog-house. But I didn't take my eyes off the COO.

He probed a new line: "I understand you have an excellent safety record?"

"You mean nobody hurt? Nobody killed? Yeah."

"How do you do it?" he asked.

"Mostly luck I don't have a lot to do with." I bought time, considering another answer. I had no illusions. I'd been lucky.

The new contractor invested a lot of words at our multiple orientations on work-place safety. This very COO spoke to eighty souls waiting to catch a military transport in New Zealand for our flight to McMurdo. He pointed to colorful slides of charts and statistics. He described trends in Total Recordable Incident Rates. He lectured on the new company's drive to reduce the total number of incidents. "Of course we don't want any of you to get hurt," he said about no one in particular. I saw an MIT grad.

"It can't be all luck. What're you doing that's different?" The COO stayed on me.

I stole a glance at Katy, hoping for help. Both our fathers had served on submarines in the Pacific in WWII, and that became something she and I discussed often. I told her once that driving two tunnels to meet face to face in the dark might be like steering a submarine blindly through a deep ocean. I'd mentioned the same point to Dad. He said: "I wouldn't know, Son . . . I've never driven a tunnel."

A few years back I went with my father to the fiftieth anniversary of the commissioning of his submarine. Many of the crew were at the reunion. Their skipper spoke. One by one afterward the teary-eyed, gray-headed veterans quietly thanked him. I asked my father about that. This is what he said then: "One out of every four men who served on a submarine in WWII died of it. These men are thanking the skipper for bringing them home safely. They are thanking him for the rest of their lives . . . lives they have gone on to lead, and the families they have gone on to raise."

I never forgot those old men gathered in that Fort Worth banquet room, grateful for those years—years that I still had in front of me. I had told that story to Katy, too. As I read her now, with the COO, she was saying, "Go ahead."

"Okay. First of all, I'm a professional miner, and I'm good at it." I let that sink in. "If I want it to be safe, I've got to make it that way."

But the COO wanted policies and procedures, something in writing that my crew could read and sign off on. He would not let up.

I did have the *Federal Metal-Nonmetal Mine Safety Code of Regulations*, published by the Mine Safety and Health Administration (MSHA). And I'd consulted with Colorado state mine inspectors on ventilation issues for this very tunnel. My crew knew how I felt about safety. In our safety meetings, meetings required by both Federal Regs and by the new company's own policies, I told them that safety is a deeply personal and shared responsibility.

"Statistics are fine for suits in offices," I looked right into the COO's eyes. "They have no place underground. Here, you look after your partner, and your partner looks after you."

Katy vanished momentarily in the growing tension. Better to laugh.

"But I do have my own rules for tunneling at South Pole, and I did write them down. They're posted on the door to the top-lander shack on surface." I struck a theatrical pose: "Wright's Four Rules for tunneling at the South Pole!"

With a laugh, Katy rematerialized. The COO wanted an explanation.

"First rule: nobody gets cold. Simple."

It lacked the legal ring of a policy statement, and the COO looked puzzled. He had already felt the cold. That's why we were in the warming shack.

"When you get cold, you get preoccupied with your own discomfort. That takes your mind off your work. If your mind comes off your work, you're going to make a mistake. If you make a mistake, you're going to hurt yourself, and you're likely to hurt somebody else. If you try and work through the cold, you'll get stupid-cold. So if you get cold, stop work immediately. Tell your partners you are cold, and take immediate steps to restore warmth. There are a few places in the tunnel where you can do that. There is this shack here. We have a portable warm house in the other tunnel. There is the top-lander shack above us. And there is the heated cab of the tunneling machine itself. Nobody gets cold. Period."

He asked about my other rules. I rattled them off. Anything other than clean, white snow in the tunnel face, stop and investigate. Any tunnel footage not driven on line and grade is not worth driving. No writing on the tunnel walls. "That's it. The rest is MSHA and Colorado stuff."

This cross-examination wearied me. Katy seemed entertained. But the white snow rule puzzled him again. I straightened my legs. My metal chair rang across the floor.

Our tunnel drove through snow accumulated since 1956 when the United States first occupied Pole. Back then some U.S. Navy Seabee might have dropped a chain and the snow drifted over it. That chain could now be thirty feet below surface, as was our tunnel in places. Or deeper. What might happen if we tunneled into that chain with the tunnel boring machine? Or worse, with electric chainsaws when we were going at it by hand?

"We found a piece of rope and a canvas trenching-tool cover. We found a parachute in the access trench. Last year, we tunneled through hundreds of nuts and bolts somebody spilled. No damage or injury. But the rule proved itself when we tunneled into pink snow."

A tentative smile drew across his face.

". . . A gasoline spill. I don't know how old it was, or where the top of it was. But it stunk up the tunnel. I shut everything down until we could prove the tunnel air was breathable, and the stuff was not volatile. Gasoline and underground do not mix."

My other rules had deeper meanings, too. But he didn't want to hear about them. "You've got a great safety record. I want to know what makes you tick."

Bingo! Now he wanted to know about me, not just what I did. I already trusted Katy, but the COO's motives were unclear. I raised my eyebrows. "That's personal. Are we going to keep it that way?"

"Yes."

So I trusted him, and I leaned forward in my chair once again.

"Do you have a family back home in Colorado . . . a wife and kids?" I asked, friendly enough.

"No. My family, parents and brother and sisters, all live back east." He answered a question of mine for a change.

"Where back east?"

"Boston."

He *was* MIT . . . even though Boston and every other place in the world was north of this particular dog-house.

"Here's what I know about you now: You don't have any kids. You're not married. But your parents and siblings are alive. They care about you, and you care about them. You ever seen or handled a mangled body . . . a dead or a live body?"

"No."

It *was* just statistics in New Zealand.

"Who gets hurt when you get injured in this tunnel?"

Silence.

"Do you think it's just the guy you carry out?" I asked, then looked over at Katy.

"If Katy falls down the manway, you think it's just her? You'd be carrying out a lot of people. You'd be carrying out her husband. I don't even know him. And you don't know him 'cause he doesn't work for you."

An elegant summary eluded me in that frosty plywood dog-house.

"If it was you we were carrying out, we'd be carrying out your parents, your brothers and sisters. Your whole extended family. Your neighbors. The ones who love you."

I'd worked at mines where folks got seriously hurt, sometimes once a month. Sometimes they got killed. Somebody always stood outside the portal holding a hat for the widow, and we'd drop money in it. But you could never undo what happened. It was devastating to those people. I hated that. Safety was not a statistic for me.

"I know a little bit about each of my crew. I make that my business. Dave Watson, over in that other tunnel right now, has a son, same name as my son. When I look at Dave, I see both him and his son. If I hurt Dave in any way, I have hurt his family. Any questions?"

"No." He'd found whatever he was angling for.

I looked down at my feet, finished. It got quiet. Only the electric heater's hum, vibrating against the dog-house floor, remained. I did not like recalling the terrible damage wrought upon people and families I was beginning to remember.

Our breathing had built up frost on the plywood walls of the dog-house. Ice crystals formed half-inch-long whiskers over our jackets, hair, and faces. My heated performance stunned Katy. The COO, I judged, had rested enough. Now he needed to get his warm blood moving.

My chair scooted back across the frosty floor when I stood up. "There's a mighty fine tunnel to finish showing you. A beautiful piece of work. Down yonder, another thousand feet, is the end of it. There's a fifty-foot ladder where we can climb out through the escape raise. Let's see where we come up?" I smiled.

The cold blast of tunnel air assaulted our warm faces when I slid the plywood door open.

✧ ✧ ✧

With the tunnel job finished at Pole in February 2002, I found more work in McMurdo that season driving a truck at "Ship Off-Load," an exciting annual event for USAP workers on the Ice. Open water to see for a change, and all that went with it: waves and ripples instead of ice and cracks, and boats bigger than any single structure in McMurdo.

First came the icebreakers opening a channel in the sea ice. If the wind blew the ice chunks north, open water emerged in the channel and brought whales. Then came the U.S. Merchant Marine tanker delivering several million gallons of fuel. Finally, in February, the container ship tied up, loaded high over her decks with a rainbow spectrum of shipping containers.

For a week every worker on station bustled around the container ship. McMurdo was full of noise: air brakes exhaling, engines straining, transmissions whining, and back-up alarms beeping. Ship's cranes swung containers down onto trucks. Trucks drove the snaky roads around town and into forgotten crannies. Forklifts of all sizes unloaded the trucks. Ground-pounding pedestrians checked off cargo as stuff came out of containers. A year's supply of food, goods, and construction material came off that ship. Then three or four days into the cycle, everybody changed direction. Equipment slated for retrograding, and the accumulated waste of a year or more headed back from other nooks and crannies down to the ship, bound for the landfills and scrap yards of the United States. We kept little waste in Antarctica.

Often during the cycle, a ship's crane might stall, or a ship's hatch must be opened to the 'tween-decks. The delay would bring the flow of trucks on the pier to a standstill for an hour or more. Then truck drivers, equipment operators, cargo handlers and dockhands freely mingled in the shadow of the big ship playing catch, joking, and laughing. A joyful sense of the end of season filled the atmosphere. Many of us would go home soon.

During such a lull at another offload several years before, the pier supervisor asked if I would bring my bagpipes down to the pier and play a tune. Happy to oblige him then, bagpipes became a nine-year offload tradition. I kept the pipes in my truck after that, but I always waited for an invitation to play.

That's how it was the year I finished the tunnel job at Pole. I drove my truck down to the pier. The Kiwi pier boss hailed me. "Hey mate! You bring your pipes this year?"

"I did," I answered, smiling.

"Well, play us a tune!"

I broke out the pipes, climbed atop the empty flatbed deck of a waiting truck and started to play. The "Free Man's Whistle," a high-lonesome wail from out of nowhere, first turned heads. Leading into the rousing "Scotland the Brave" brought shouts of joy from the dock hands. Many at the pier looked forward to the return of the pipes.

As in past years, the truck on whose deck I stood started rolling forward slowly. We circled the pier starting our own makeshift parade, breaking the boredom of idle minutes that had grown to an hour. The pier boss suggested, "Shall we give them a tune in town?"

"Fine by me," I shrugged.

The truck drove slowly off the pier, and climbed the high road into town. We crept past the galley where half the town crew was already at lunch. I got winded then, so I signaled the driver I was ready to quit. He stopped the truck. I jumped off the deck to the ground.

While I was stowing the pipes in their case, an angry voice sounded behind me.

"That was a *dumb-ass* thing to do! You are flaunting the very *culture* I am trying to change!"

I turned to face a complete stranger, a middle-aged fellow whose pale, clean-shaven countenance exhibited his displeasure. *Culture?*

"Who are you?" I asked.

"I am the director of safety, and you are making a mockery of the *safety culture* I am trying to create in this program."

The man had just announced his importance. So I responded: "Okay. I copy you don't like bagpipes on trucks. I promise: no more bagpipes on trucks."

Then I turned my back, climbed into the cab, and told the driver, "Take off before he gets a good look at you, too."

Culture, in the sense the man had just used, was new to me then. I'd always thought of it in anthropological terms, or as describing high-class art. Now it was a borrowed word that had crept into boardrooms and become corporate jargon. Like *paradigm change,* not quite what Thomas Kuhn meant in *The Structure of Scientific Revolutions.* You had to know the jargon to get the message. But I had to laugh at myself. At first I'd thought he didn't like Celtic music.

The contractor fired me that day for "violating the corporate safety culture." It hired me back the same day when I explained the fellow's authoritative anger was probably more aroused when, in the face of abusive language, I turned my back on him and refused to engage in conversation. Funny how organizational culture worked.

Back at the pier to finish the offload, I found the crew had all heard about the incident. "What happened?"

"Ah, nothing. No more bagpipes on trucks is all." I shrugged.

The corporate safety culture was founded in statistics. But I had my own notion of what safety meant: does someone get hurt?

The number of times someone gets hurt is the safety *metric*. A favorable metric benefits the contractor: monetary reward, perhaps greater productivity, maybe a prize. When a COO, or a safety director, proclaims his intention to reduce the Total Recordable Incident Rate (TRIR) to a more acceptable number, I listen for clues. Is there a compassionate interest in a real human being?

Two months following the ship offload incident I accepted the job to head up the traverse project. I found myself in a large meeting room in the contractor's Denver office. A dozen of us, including my boss, gathered to hear about "A New Culture of Safety."

The safety director stood at the front of the room before a screen displaying his PowerPoint slide show. He showed charts and numbers depicting Total Recordable Incidents reported by the previous contractor. He broke them down by category and type, explaining what was *recordable* and what was *not recordable*. And he explained how the Incident Rate was calculated.

"Now this is the existing culture of safety," the safety director said, "and this is how I want to change that culture . . ." He turned to face a new slide on the screen.

"Of course we don't want anyone to get hurt," he interjected, looking back over his shoulder. The new image bore simple black text across a plain white background: "NO MORE FRONTIER ATTITUDE."

"I don't want to see any more frontier attitude in this program," he read from the screen. "That's gone. A thing of the past."

I was supposed to explore for a route from McMurdo to South Pole. Lewis and Clark were supposed to find a route linking the Missouri River to the Pacific coast, through their own frontier. Our mission was not as grandiose as theirs. We'd be well supported by any comparison. And we, as a country, weren't trying to colonize the place, nor prepare the way for civilization's march. But we *were* tackling a continent. "Frontier" meant remote, unexplored, dangerous, and wonderful. The dot at the bottom of my grandfather's 1918 Rand McNally globe is surrounded by a watery Antarctic Ocean, enclosed by an archipelago of islands, all labeled *unexplored*. That wasn't that long ago.

Yet in this room paneled with acoustical walls and lit by filtered fluorescent lights, "frontier attitude" meant something undesirable.

I raised my hand: "Would you explain what you mean by 'frontier attitude,' please?" He remembered the bagpipes, though his expression remained blank.

"'Frontier attitude' is responsible for the culture of safety that exists in the Antarctic program, the culture that has produced the high TRIR." He fished for words. "I don't want to see any *cowboys* in the program."

When he spoke the word "cowboys" his shoulders rose to his ears, his palms turned out towards me. He gave a couple of quick nods to co-opt my understanding.

I knew what he meant. He implied a reckless character. But a lot of displaced cowboys and cowgirls came to the Antarctic program. They were among the most versatile, resourceful people down there. They could make a bad situation into a better one working with almost nothing. I needed cowboys on my crew. But I decided to shut up. The impression I was forming disturbed me: Did these guys just not get it? Were they that much out of touch with the nature of our work, with the nature of that place? *How far out of step with them am I?*

When the meeting broke up, my boss caught me deep in thought in the long hallway separating the massed cubicles from the meeting room. "There's something you should know," he said, softly. "When your name was discussed for the traverse project manager, the COO spoke strongly against you. He said, 'I have heard his safety philosophy directly from his own mouth. He is opposed to our corporate philosophy. I don't think we want him for the job.'"

I cursed, silently.

"What did you think of the meeting?" my boss changed the subject.

I looked around to see who else was in the hallway. "I think the safety director just told me Antarctica is not a frontier."

|4| French Connections

Getting started, the hardest part of any job, became easier with a generous boost from Patrice Godon and the French Antarctic Program. I might've met Patrice a year earlier, but something got in the way.

I was off contract following the third year of the tunnel project and at home when an unexpected e-mail from Steve Dunbar landed. When I heard from Steve, and that was rare, I paid attention.

"Do you think any of these scenarios will work for you?" he asked.

Steve managed USAP Field Science Support these days. His note came at the head of a long e-mail string originated by unfamiliar names. It mentioned timetables and places foreign to me, and had circulated between high levels of the USAP and the French Antarctic Program. I scrolled down until my eyes lit upon my name.

Sent: Monday, September 10, 2001
To: Stephen Dunbar
Subject: FW: Participation of NSF personnel to Dumont d'Urville/Dome C
Steve-I assume John knows he's going?
BRIAN STONE
Research Support Manager
National Science Foundation
Office of Polar Programs

Do I know I am going where? Dumont d'Urville and Dome C? I'd overhead those names from passing conversations going the other way in a McMurdo hallway since 1993 when I first started in the program. Russ once said something about digging out a buried airplane there. But Brian Stone was asking the question. He'd worked logistics for the support contractor before his comet-like rise took him to NSF's Office of Polar Programs. I paid attention when Brian Stone spoke, too.

Below Brian's note to Steve, I found my name again. This time Erick Chiang addressed Dave Bresnahan. I knew *of* Erick Chiang, but I could think of no reason he would know me.

David—FYI and planning for John Wright. I have forwarded the message to Mario to make sure that he is aware of the plan. Let me know which option is preferable.

I think we will have to get John to and from TNB.—**Erick**

The aspen leaves on our mountainsides were turning autumn gold and red. Though the sun warmed our south facing valley, inside we wore sweaters. Soon I'd leave my family for winter's work. This morning my wife joined me at the computer.

At the bottom of the e-mail string was a lengthy note from Patrice Godon, head of the Technical Department, French Polar Institute, to Erick Chiang, NSF Office of Polar Programs. Godon recognized an agreement in which the USAP would provide an observer-participant for the French traverses. He offered three scheduling options for the then coming austral summer, November through February, to accommodate that observer-participant.

"Apparently I'm being considered for that observer-participant role. That's exciting," I told my wife.

"And you *love* traversing, honey. What does an observer-participant do?" She met the prospect enthusiastically.

This was the first I'd heard anything about imminent plans for the USAP traverse development. Brooks Montgomery, a USAP mountaineer, had joined a French-Italian traverse in 1995 that ran between those same two places. He'd retrieved a payload package from a downed research balloon that dropped near the French route. His trip log described their daily routine, progress, their equipment to some extent, and a bit about the terrain. He told of long stretches of rough ground, rough enough that he didn't want to go again.

"And you want to do it?" my wife asked.

"Well, yeah. I've never been to those places."

"But you're going down to finish the tunnel. Can you do both?"

Poised to complete the tunnel job that year, I found myself torn between tunneling and traversing. We studied Godon's schedules. After a couple days soul searching, I wrote back to Steve:

I have read your sending and agree that Patrice Godon's Option 3 would be optimal for an observer to get the most return in helpful information for the USAP.

As to Brian's question: No, I did not know I was going anywhere. On August 02, I accepted the contract to complete the SPole Tunnel project. The SPole Tunnel Project—starting in November—will be in full swing during the December to early February dates put forth in the three options. "Full swing" historically has not meant smooth operations, rather a succession of crises. My concerns for the well-being of the crew, as well as for the successful completion of the project, are heightened. And I take my responsibility for the crew's safety personally.

Therefore, I do not project my availability to participate on the French traverses. This is a difficult pill to swallow for it is my heart's desire to participate in a meaningful way in building the USAP's surface traverse capability.—**John**

That same day, Steve returned a thoughtful consolation:

I understand the position you are in quite well. It is often ironic that the reason one is offered these opportunities is because one is responsible, and that responsibility often precludes one's participation in the opportunity.

Brian Stone was sorry to hear that you are unavailable. He wanted me to pass along the consensus at NSF that you are our best resource for traverse issues and that they will keep you in mind as other opportunities arise.—**Steve**

I never got to go on the French traverse, but I did get to go to France.

✧ ✧ ✧

Like traverses of other nations, the French link a coastal facility to an inland station. In this case, their link runs between Cape Prud'homme/Dumont D'Urville to Dome C, six hundred miles inland on the Polar Plateau. The United States hoped to establish a similar link across the one thousand miles between McMurdo and South Pole Station.

The USAP had no solutions at the start and little time in its three-year schedule to cycle trial with error. We had to specify and purchase the traverse fleet for use in the third year before we ever took to the field in the first. French solutions became our starting point.

In June 2002, five of us converged on Brest, France. "Us" included Dave Bresnahan of NSF, George Blaisdell and Jason Weale—both engineers with the U.S. Army Corps of Engineers Cold Regions Research and Engineering Laboratory—and Ralph Horak and me, both contract employees for the support contractor. Ahead of us lay two days of conferences with Patrice Godon, leader of the French traverse.

Besides me, Dave was the only one who wore a beard. His was salt and pepper. Mine was considerably whiter. Both were neatly trimmed. Dave was a stern looking character with bushy eyebrows and piercing blue eyes. He stood as tall as me, often intimidating folks at their first encounter. I never found him intimidating.

Ralph, a Yankee from New Hampshire, was my old traverse buddy. He was a portly fellow, and dry-witted. We took turns playing the straight man off one another, and that always made me smile. When I started the tunnel job at Pole, I turned the sea ice traverse business over to Ralph. We'd spent one memorable day stuck out on the sea ice. A sharp piece of it flattened a six-foot balloon tire on our fifteen-ton Delta truck. While we snoozed in the cab, waiting hours for a helicopter to fly us a spare, I broke the silence:

"Ralph, all my adult my life I've had but one birthday wish. And that is to be left completely alone on that day, to see no human being, and to spend the day contemplating the meaning of life and my place in it."

"That so?" Ralph yawned.

"That is so. Ralph, today is my birthday. And this is the closest I have ever come to realizing my wish. Here, on the frozen surface of McMurdo Sound, miles from anybody, I am stuck in this cab with *you!*"

"Better luck next year." Ralph chuckled. He didn't offer to get out of the cab.

Ralph and another traverse buddy, Steve Carr from Port Townsend, Washington, would join the French traverses in the coming season as observer-participants. Together, they'd report their lessons learned to all of us. Meanwhile, I'd be occupied with crossing the Shear Zone.

Patrice Godon met our group at the Brest airport and drove us across town to the offices of the French Polar Institute. Here was a long, modern two-story building with plenty of windows, perched atop a low hill surrounded by lush, green foliage. Maritime scents filled the air.

Patrice was an athletic man of middle age, clean-shaven, poker-faced, and ruggedly handsome. He ushered us into a second floor conference room where we seated ourselves around a long table. Scale models of sleds and other devices decorated the table top.

Patrice spoke English well from an agenda he'd already prepared. He included a summary proposal to deliver fuel to South Pole Station. His dogleg traverse, beginning at Dumont d'Urville and running by Dome C, took Ralph and me by surprise. Supplying Pole was our mission.

Dave later explained that Erick Chiang had asked Patrice to prepare a study of the option. It was not entirely a cold pitch. But as Dave pointed out, Dumont D'Urville and Cape Prudhomme didn't have the infrastructure to support such an operation.

"Then I trust he got paid for his study," I remarked. "They'd have to drag all that fuel uphill right away, and then go another several hundred miles past Dome C. It'd be longer than the USAP route. That's a lot more fuel burned and a lot less fuel delivered for the effort."

"I know, I know," Dave shrugged.

We enjoyed a catered lunch with Bordeaux wine in the same conference room we'd occupied all morning. After lunch, Patrice described terrain problems they faced on their route and the novel solutions they applied to them. To deal with rough or undulating surfaces, they installed shock absorbing systems on their sleds, and they replaced traditional steel hinges with elastomeric bushings.

The French ran two-thirds of their traverse on the Polar plateau. That's where Brooks told of rough ground over sastrugi—long, wind-sculpted forms in dense, hard snow. Brooks reported they ran a dozing blade ahead of their fleet. They still did according to Patrice. The blade rough-leveled the snow, pushing it into a berm on the downwind side of their road.

The berm became a snowdrift catcher. Every time they pushed new drift snow against the old berm, their freshly plowed road crept gradually upwind. That meant their heavy tractors following the blade always tracked on virgin snow.

The USAP had not traversed heavy sastrugi in years. We really didn't know how. Would we need a forerunner blade, too? Around McMurdo, we dealt with sea-level snow on the ice shelves. We learned to get on top and stay on top of the snow. We dragged grooming equipment behind us. Slowly we built a stronger, compacted road under us.

The years-old berm on the French road became their trail marker. But in flat light the berm was impossible to see. So the French installed forward-looking stadium lights, little suns atop their tractors, to illuminate it. When an operator wore special goggles fitted with yellow lenses, the berm appeared through the white-out. Our project had no proven route in front of it, hence no berm. For the time being we'd use flags on bamboo poles to mark our way.

"Patrice, how much does the ice under your road move?" I asked, awkwardly trying to overcome our language barrier.

Patrice looked at me questioningly, then over to George for help. He'd known George for several years.

George stepped up. A broad-shouldered, lean, athletic fellow himself, his tow-headed crew-cut and aquiline aspect suggested a scrapper. But his musical diction put one at ease. "John is asking about glacier and ice movement along your route, Patrice. Do you know how much your road moves as a result of the movement of the ice on which it is built?"

Patrice showed us a map of a former route from Dumont D'Urville to Dome C. Overlying the old route was the trace of their current one, which showed they had blazed some short cuts. I made a mental note: "meaning lost in translation."

"How about crevasses along your route, Patrice?" I asked on a slightly different tack. Ice movement often caused crevassing.

"We have a few at the start of the climb out of Dumont d'Urville, but that's all. Nowhere else," Patrice allowed.

"And how do you know they are there, and nowhere else?"

"Because we see them with our eyes," Patrice answered, nonplussed.

Again I let it go, wondering what manner of glaciological study might have been applied to selecting their route. They had established it long before ground penetrating radar was available.

Our discussion turned to their sled fleet: cargo sleds; fuel tank sleds; and berthing, galley, and energy-production sleds. The USAP had none of these things. Every one of them would have to be designed, specified, shopped, built, and delivered. We discussed which sleds worked for the French and which needed improvement. Patrice gave us construction drawings for their sled fleet.

The second day covered operations. Patrice emphasized the importance of personal comforts and cleanliness for the crew. Ralph and I raised eyebrows to one another in agreement. Our traverses around McMurdo had been sixty-mile day trips to well-provisioned outposts. Neither of us could imagine what day-after-day might be like on a long traverse. We didn't want to spend the end of each day setting up tents and camping on the snow.

Patrice gave me a crew roster and duty list. "You carry a physician, a full medical doctor . . . is that your standard practice, or is this one who just happened to be available?" I asked.

"Yes . . . we always bring a physician."

"And what does he do when he is not doctoring?"

With a shrug of his shoulders, arms outspread and palms upturned, he answered with a heavy accent, "We train him to drive a tractor, and he drives a tractor."

I smiled. That would be difficult for human resources. But should we have a doctor, too? With all our aircraft available in the summer, and our extraordinary search-and-rescue capability, could we make do with a paramedic instead?

"And you have no designated cook?" I looked at him questioningly.

Patrice's face became animated for the first time. "Ah! Never again will I hire a cook! They are temperamental! All they do is throw flour around the kitchen!"

Frenchmen were famously finicky about food, yet Patrice adamantly refused to have a cook. A Tasmanian caterer prepared their frozen meals in bulk. They pulled the day's meals from cold storage every morning, thawed them inside their galley module, then heated them at meal times. TV dinners would not be particularly welcome with our crew, so I asked Patrice for a sample menu.

"Pretty good," I looked up from the menu to Dave. "Fascinating . . . no cook . . . that opens up a whole bunk space. Maybe a second heavy mechanic? Maybe a surveyor. Maybe a mountaineer?"

The first evening in Brest, we five Americans found ourselves strolling its pleasant streets, checking out restaurants for exciting menus.

George and Jason paired together for a while. Jason, a sharp young engineer newly on board at CRREL, was also new to me. George had Jason in mind as CRREL's technical contact in support of our project. The scope of CRREL's opportunity occupied their discussion. Jason had never been to the Ice. For that matter, neither George nor Jason, nor even Dave had ever traversed.

Dave strolled apart, deep in thought. I commented to Ralph: "You know . . . Patrice has been there. We're hearing from a guy who's fought his way down the trail."

Ralph and I had been on some tough traverses. We shared an admiration for Patrice because we recognized his struggle. Ralph added, "When things are going good, it's all good. When it hits the fan, it really hits it. I wonder if these other guys understand that you're on twenty-four hours a day? That saps you. You know it."

I did know it. And I'd been meaning to talk that up with Dave. He strolled ahead of us across a broad plaza decked with granite-gray flagstones, bronze statuary, and brass handrails leading up stone stairsteps. High summer at Brest's northern latitude brought full sunshine at this late hour. I caught up from behind, leaving Ralph so Dave didn't feel we were ganging up.

"Dave, you and George worked up the feasibility study that launched the current project. Do you remember the section that dealt with shift cycles and hours of work?"

They'd concluded that the best shift cycle ran twelve hours on and twelve hours off. Better than twenty-four hours around the clock, hot-bunking multiple crews. Better than two shorter shifts back-to-back. The standard work contract on the Ice called for six nine-hour days per week. We'd have to pay extra for daily twelves. I wouldn't depend on the goodness of dedicated hearts to give it up. And I needed good people, especially when we were getting started.

"What are you thinking?" Dave reserved judgment.

"I don't know yet how to manage this with the support contractor, but I do know that if we don't pay for the extra time, then all I'm going to give *you* is six nines on the trail."

Dave asked about weekends and holidays. I'd stay silent on those and make them field calls. We'd all want to make hay when the sun was shining, but if weather or breakdown stopped us, I'd call break.

"What do you need from me?" he asked, pausing momentarily, his eyebrows knitting.

"Your support for winning appropriate pay for twelve-hour shifts. I don't know how *pinche* NSF would be about that." I spoke the latter with an accent of Mexico.

"NSF won't be that way if your request is reasonable. See what you come up with out of your own offices and make a proposal. I'll support you."

The pay hike didn't come that first year crossing the Shear Zone, so we put in nines. The hike came the next year, and we launched our fleet with twelves.

Our berthing and energy production sleds came straight from French plans. We modified their fuel tank sled with a longer but smaller diameter cylinder. For the same three thousand gallon capacity, we both lowered the sled's center of gravity and improved its stability. The French elastomeric bushings, which were actually bridge support components that accommodated structural squirm, found their way into our fleet in abundance.

I never saw Patrice again, but over the years we corresponded frequently. We exchanged my route notes and operations reports for his annual traverse summaries. My heart broke when Patrice suffered a mishap on the trail. I cheered when they commissioned Concordia Station at Dome C. Patrice's traverse delivered all that material.

On our own trail, I often wondered, "How would the French handle this particular problem?" Sometimes I found an answer.

PART II.
CREVASSES, SWAMPS, AND DISAPPOINTMENT

|5| Crossing the Shear Zone—Year One

October 31, 2002. Five souls stood on the snow beside a ten-foot-tall wooden post. Two upright fifty-five gallon drums flanked the post. Carved deeply into its top were the letters G, A, and W.

"GAW" stood for Grid A West, a theoretical relic of the SPIT work. Three miles east of GAW stood another post with two more black drums next to it. That was HFS. Home Free South. Two weeks before, a helicopter flew us out from McMurdo to plant these posts. The helicopter jumped us safely over the ground between them.

Between GAW and HFS lay the McMurdo Shear Zone: badlands of hidden crevasses wide enough to swallow a bulldozer. *Linda* went down in one of them twelve years before.

The ground toward HFS looked identical to the ground we'd crossed getting to GAW: a featureless plain of white, flat as a pancake. From the helicopter, we saw no gaping fissures in its unbroken surface. The crevasses, if they were there, were bridged over with snow.

We'd flagged a twenty-three-mile route from McMurdo's Williams Field skiway to GAW. That was easy. Our radar never saw a crevasse. We staged our gear over the route many times. We radared a safe perimeter just short of GAW, flagged it off, and built our tent camp within it.

In the still, cold air of a day when the sun simply would not set, we stood on the snow looking east at our job. Build a road across this place. Build it twenty feet wide. Make it safe for tractors and sleds. Search all ground in front with ground penetrating radar. If it detected a void lurking under a bridge, stop. Blow up the bridge. Bulldoze snow into the slot. Fill it. Pack it. Drive over it. Look for the next crevasse. Search and destroy.

There were four others besides me. Richard "Stretch" Vaitonis, a tall Wisconsin corn farmer, would run the new D8R bulldozer. Shaun Norman, a world-class mountaineer from New Zealand, and American mountaineer Eric Barnes knew alpine crevasses well. Russ Magsig, the mechanic, was the only one among us who had seen the Shear Zone.

CRREL radar experts were scheduled to join us, but the program's ponderous deployment process delayed their arrival. We'd trained with them in New Hampshire months earlier. Everything in New England then was green. Working in leafy woods, we practiced finding bedrock cracks in abandoned quarries. We studied printed radar images of hidden crevasses.

At McMurdo early in October, we cobbled a vehicle-mounted radar platform to a PistenBully. This was a light, ten-thousand-pound snow crawler borrowed from the science fleet. Painted red and black, it looked like a lady bug on tracks. Its cab sat two. Behind the cab, a passenger box could hold four. A twenty-foot-long radio tower from McMurdo's scrap yards became a prod we pushed in front of the PistenBully. The radar antenna fit to the front of the prod, cushioned off the ground by an inflated inner tube. A cable ran back from the antenna into the cab. It connected to the smart part of the radar device where a computer screen displayed what the antenna saw.

In tests over known crevasses near McMurdo, one of us drove the PistenBully while another monitored the radar. At seven miles per hour we could detect a crevasse under the antenna and stop the vehicle before it overran the crevasse edge.

Five days earlier, the McMurdo surveyor came to our Shear Zone camp and planted a line of red flags on bamboo poles. The flags pointed past GAW toward HFS over the horizon. We couldn't see HFS, even with binoculars. High ground, perhaps a snowdrift or an ice rise, hid our target. But the surveyor's back sights showed us which way to go.

There were no more preparations to make. I focused on the enormous whiteness ahead and held back loving visions of my wife, son, and growing family. This was how I made our living for now. *There is no other job. This is the job.*

We crossed the imaginary line at GAW and entered the Shear Zone for the first time. We went hunting for crevasses.

One thinks of ice as a solid substance, not as a dynamic piece of real estate. But with masses of ice hundreds of feet thick, the ice at its base turns plastic under the sheer weight of the ice above it. The mass flows like a viscous fluid seeking its own level, impelled by gravity. Ice near the top of the mass does not flow like plastic. It remains brittle, breaking into cracks called "crevasses."

A belt of such crevasses stretches seventy-five miles from the tip of Minna Bluff to the tip of Cape Crozier. The belt forms where two floating masses of glacial ice come in contact. These masses are so large they go by the name "ice shelves": the McMurdo Ice Shelf, the size of a small county, and the Ross Ice Shelf, as big as France. Both are covered by deep snow.

The ice shelves meet twenty-three miles east of McMurdo. Where they meet, they flow at different speeds and in slightly different directions. As one shelf drags against the other, the ice along their contact shears into crevasses. That is the Shear Zone. And as the two ice shelves flow implacably north, out to sea, new crevasses constantly form in the zone and old ones close.

The first 640 miles of our route to South Pole led over the Ross Ice Shelf. To get onto the Shelf from McMurdo we had to cross the Shear Zone. If we could cross it, we'd have done plenty this first year.

The PistenBully crept past GAW. Eric Barnes sat shotgun operating the radar while I drove. Three hundred feet forward . . . nothing. Another three hundred feet . . . still nothing. Another, and another. Nothing. I stopped.

"Are you sure?" I asked.

"Nothing but flat lines," Eric confirmed. "Horizontal stratigraphy."

At thirty-ish, Eric was the youngest of us, cheerful and astute. He wore a goatee but kept a clean-shaved head. Evident even under his fleece jacket, knotted arm muscles signaled the rugged climber he was. We steadied our nerves, and tried again.

Three hundred feet more. Nothing. Three hundred feet more. Nothing. Three hundred feet more. Nothing.

"This is getting ridiculous."

"STOP! We got one!"

We stopped exactly as we'd practiced. The radar screen showed a slender, vertical black image reaching from the bottom of the screen to nearly the top. Our first crevasse hid under the snow, somewhere between the end of the boom and the front of our vehicle.

"We have one here," I radioed back to the others waiting at GAW. "Come forward with the ropes and probes. Follow our tracks."

Two snowmobiles pulled up behind us. Shaun and Eric roped up like a well-practiced team, tying off to our PistenBully. They probed along the length of the boom, poking their slender metal poles into the snow, looking for a void beneath them. The rest of us watched.

Shaun shrugged. He was another compactly built mountaineer and, at sixty-ish, the oldest of our group. His weathered face sported a stubble of whiskers, and he too kept his topknot close cropped. Crevasses were nothing new to Shaun. "Could you have been wrong?" he asked.

We could've been. We were not yet experts with the radar.

Shaun walked back toward the three of us waiting behind the PistenBully. Just in front of the vehicle he tripped and fell forward. "There it is," he said.

Shaun's boots had poked through a thin snow bridge. We looked into the hole and found a vertical crack, six inches wide. We exposed more of the thin crack with shovels, then a long tape measure plumbed it to seventy feet. With the radar we traced its long course, and marked it with a line of black flags.

"This thing's just a minnow," I laughed. "We might as well throw it back in."

We named it "Baby," and that was good enough for now. Then we headed back to in McMurdo to get our PistenBully into the shop, showers for ourselves, and a home-cooked meal. Sunday we'd have another go at it.

But they wouldn't all be like Baby. And we didn't know where they were. If we had some way of looking through all that snow, from up in the air. . . . If we could map the whole field of crevasses laid out all at once. . . .

A wretched blow of foul, horizontal weather pinned us down for two days after we returned to camp. When it blew itself out, a clear line of seven green flags, spaced every three hundred feet, led out from GAW and stopped at the black flags marking Baby. We were safe to that point. Beyond the black flags lay the white sameness.

Tiptoeing into it, one hundred feet past Baby, the radar found the second crevasse. It lay just south of our road. This time we brought up the drilling and blasting supplies.

Shaun and Eric rigged ropes and belays. I dragged a pair of wood planks over what we thought was the bridge. If I fell through, the ropes might save me. But I tested the boards, and the snow bridge did not collapse.

I brought the Jiffy drill back over the boards. Its power head was a two-stroke gasoline engine weighing twenty pounds. It took both hands to run it. The drill chucked five-inch-diameter steel auger bits, each one three feet long and five pounds. I drilled one bit section down, added another, and then drilled down some more.

At twelve feet deep, my hole had found no void. I lifted the whole string a couple of feet, and then slammed it all back down. It landed on firm bottom. Drilling farther, at fourteen feet the hole broke through, I lurched forward, and fell off of the timbers.

"There she is." I regained my footing and withdrew the drill string.

Four more holes made the five-spot pattern. The first hole made the middle spot, like on a dice, and one more in each corner, five feet to a side. Russ volunteered to drill them, but I needed to see how it went. The whole business was awkward. Ropes in the way. Balancing on the boards.

After drilling, it was time for blasting. I talked through the next moves while all of us squatted on the snow. "We drilled five-inch holes because we brought out three-inch dynamite. Next time we'll use the inch-and-a-quarter dynamite and drill two-inch holes with the little power head. Now, this is this end of the stick; this is the other end. The ends are different. This is how you punch holes in the stick, and this is how you lace it with detonating cord . . ."

Each one helped assemble the charges, then I carried them back over the boards and lowered them into the holes. We pulled back all our gear to the firing line. I walked one end of the wire from a blasting reel back to the loaded holes. The electric blasting cap I carried was no bigger than a short nub of pencil, and it had two thin wires wrapped around it.

"Nothing with these explosives is particularly dangerous until I connect this blasting cap with those charges. Each of you will be handling dynamite and detonating cord. Nobody but me handles the blasting cap."

After fixing the cap to the detonating cord and connecting the wires, I smiled: "Now let's see how this will work."

Back at the reel, the other end of the blasting wire connected to two brass lugs on a wooden box. The box had a T-shaped handle. Lifting the handle pulled up a toothed metal rod through the box. I explained to Shaun, while demonstrating: "Stand like this, grab the handle like so, and when you hear me say 'Fire in the hole,' push the handle down. Hard. Don't be shy about it."

Taking one more look around the place, I started the count: "Blasting in five . . . four . . . three . . . two . . . one . . . *Fire in the hole!*"

Ka-whammmmm! Bits of snow and ice filled the air, though they didn't amount to near the volume we had just drilled and shot.

Shaun roped up after the smoke cleared on surface, and Eric belayed him to the edge of the hole. "The crater's about eight feet in diameter," Shaun announced over his shoulder. Peering over the edge once more, he turned back to us, wide-eyed. "Now that's a hummer! And it's all black down there, full of smoke."

We'd let it air out and have a look into it tomorrow.

GAW was just a post in the snow the week before. Now we relaxed there in our Shear Zone camp. A carpenter crew had come out from McMurdo and erected a Jamesway tent for us. An olive drab, canvas-covered relic of the Korean War, it would be our shelter for the season. Its insulated skin stretched over wooden arches in the style of a Quonset hut. Ours measured sixteen feet wide by forty-eight feet long. Wooden boxes that contained the tent pieces for transport now formed its plywood floor. Exposed ribs inside the tent caricatured the inner belly of Jonah's whale.

The carpenters built in conveniences for which we'd have never thought to ask. A partition inside the tent separated sixteen feet of sleeping space from thirty-two feet of common space. Two dormers in the common room, one on each side, were both fitted with windows. A long, narrow plywood table hung from the arches along one wall. It served as our radio station and catchall working surface. A propane cooking stove fit neatly into one of the dormers. Farther down that wall a fuel-oil heater not only heated the room but also melted snow for drinking and cooking water. At both ends of the tent, vestibules gave us space to sweep snow off our boots and clothing.

Having several metal folding chairs, tables, and cots, we arranged our inside space to suit us and wound up with a cozy home. The mountaineers, preferring comforts peculiar to their trade, set up their own small field tents apart from the Jamesway.

We kept our frozen food outside, upwind, in large cardboard boxes covered with shoveled snow. Downwind and off to one side, we located our bucket-equipped privy. Downwind and to the other side, we stationed our bulldozer and camp generator in the lee of the huge steel fuel tank Stretch had skidded out from McMurdo.

Our camp lay within very high frequency (VHF) radio range of town. Daily we reported our well-being to Mac-Ops, the radio communication center. In case our VHF radios failed, we set up a ultra high frequency (UHF) unit, running its long-wire antennas outside, suspended to the tops of bamboo poles. Sometime later, radio technicians would set us up with a radiophone and e-mail links to McMurdo and the world.

This was our home for now. At season's end, it all would vanish, boxed up and carted back to McMurdo. For the time being, we were warm and comfortable in camp, thinking about the "Hummer."

Shaun and Erick rappelled into Hummer's hole while I lay on my belly, peering over the edge. We were all tied off to the PistenBully, its brakes locked and parked a safe distance from the crater.

"This one measures fourteen feet across at the base of the bridge," Shaun called up.

"What does the underside of the bridge look like?" I hollered.

"It's arched, and smooth for as far as I can see. Blocky around the shot hole, but I'm not worried. "

Dangling from the slender rope, Shaun spread his arms to show the direction the fissure took. It ran back toward our road, though our radar had not traced it that far.

"I want to go to the bottom now. This crack pinches to nothing, but there's a big pile of snow right below me. Must be the stuff we shot."

A person could get wedged tight at the bottom, but Shaun stood safely on the snow pile. I lowered the zero end of our measuring tape. It was three hundred feet long, if we needed all of it.

"I got it. Take your mark."

"Seventy-nine feet," I hollered loud enough for the others to hear.

Shaun stood on a fifteen-foot-high pile of snow. That made the overall depth ninety-four feet. From the top of the pile he looked back through the shadowy gloom toward the road. The crevasse ended in that direction like a ship's prow, eighty feet from where he stood. Shaun described the crevasse walls below the bridge: nearly solid ice, frosty, and bluish.

"It's actually quite lovely down here. It is cold. And quiet." He took pictures for us before he came out.

We were going to school. If big crevasses could hide right next to us and pinch to nothing a few feet away, how would we know that without going over every square inch of ground? We needed some kind of map to make sense of the place, but those maps didn't exist. We'd have to make our own.

Over the next weeks, like blindfolded men probing a chessboard, we groped forward with the radar. Black flags became our pawns. The PistenBully ran down our centerline a tenth of a mile at a time. If we found a crevasse, we stopped and planted a black flag. If we found nothing, we marked the end of that run with a black flag. Then we backed straight in our own tracks, retreating to our starting point, and started another search parallel to our first line. Maybe we found something on this new line, maybe we didn't. But when we'd searched out a hundred-foot width on both sides of our centerline, the white field before us took a shape we could now see: pickets of black flags marked either a "found" crevasse, or the limits of clear forward progress.

We parlayed in camp over the meaning of the radar images, our chessboard maps, and how we could do things better. We assigned numbers to the crevasses. Baby became Crevasse 1. Crevasses 2 and 3 lay to the south, and as far as we could tell, neither crossed our road. Beyond those, the radar showed us mysterious black blobs. They didn't look like crevasse images we'd seen in New Hampshire. But black images meant whatever caused them did not reflect radar back to us, like a void would not. Since real voids were black and shadowy, any black image on the radar conjured that same sort of demon. Some black blobs looked like amorphous amoebas. Many looked like eyes staring back at us.

We didn't know what the black blobs were. But we did have tools to look into them: our little drill and a twenty-one-foot string of auger bits to go with it.

While two of us mapped ahead with the PistenBully, others drilled black blob targets in the middle of our road. We found no voids down where the blobs lived. Shrugging, we marked those spots with black flags, called them "questionable areas," and moved on.

At the site of Crevasse 4, just beyond the black blobs, our radar identified a distinct crevasse image striking across our path.

Again, we brought up the explosives and drills. Stretch and Russ drilled the pattern through the snow bridge. Shaun and Eric belayed them. I sat off to the side, preparing the charges, watching the two men drilling. Their first holed through at nine feet. The two-inch holes and little sticks would work fine.

Everybody helped finish making up the charges and loading the holes. The shot came under a beautiful blue sky, near the end of our day. When the smoke cleared away, Shaun peeked over the crater's edge.

"Not so big . . ."

By next morning the air inside Crevasse 4 had cleared, and Shaun and Eric explored it.

This one was only four feet wide. It measured 102 feet deep, and bottomed to a pinch once again. When they came out of the hole, Shaun approached me. "This is a pretty one. What do you say to us taking the others down?"

"I'd say that is a good idea. Ask if they want to first. I'd like to go."

The blueness inside the crevasse was dazzling. The graceful sweeps and curves of the crevasse walls seemed feminine; its space both quiet and close. It seemed anything but treacherous. Seductive perhaps.

And cold enough that an hour shuttling up and down the ropes ran us out of the hole. We had work to do, and we were much warmer on top. The skies had grown overcast, flattening our light. A light wind brought ground snows swirling around our ankles.

We needed a slot here, one that measured as long as our road was wide. I'd open the slot by breaking the bridge toward the access hole that we'd just climbed out of, and I laid out the drill pattern to do that. "Russ and Stretch, you guys will drill."

With no particular reaction, they nodded in assent.

"Use the big auger. You won't have to drill as many holes. Pound for pound, the big stick weighs ten times the little stick and packs that much more wallop."

They smiled at that.

The two men tied off to a pair of snowmobiles parked to the side, and stepped onto the boards. Drilling proved as awkward for them as it had been for me working alone. The knowing glances they stole to each other indicated that they agreed: "This is work!"

Gazing eastward toward HFS, I thought the same thing. Evans's legacy suggested we might find thirty to forty hidden crevasses. They'd strike across our line, angling right at forty-five degrees. The typical crevasse should be ten feet wide and ninety feet deep. Its length and bridge thickness would vary. And if those predictions were right, we had a lot of drilling, and a lot of work, ahead of us.

Shaun and Eric manned the PistenBully looking for crevasse-free ground behind us. We needed a safe place to gather snow, and a safe path to push it up to the crevasse edge. I wanted to bring the bulldozer into the field and fill Crevasse 4.

Russ and Stretch retired from the bridge, bringing the drill with them. Fatigued, they sank onto the snow and helped me finish making charges.

"There's got to be a better way," Russ said.

"Know one?" I asked but got no answer. Then, grinning, "Well, I hate to blow all your good work to smithereens. . ."

Stretch chimed in, "I don't mind that one bit. That'd be a good thing to do with those holes."

"Very well then. You fire the shot." I smiled again.

The mountaineers had nearly found us a snow farm when they brought the PistenBully to our firing line. I gave the countdown. Stretch rammed the handle back down in the blasting box. *Ka-whammmmmmmmm!*

A long curtain of smoke and snow flew into the air. The light breeze pulled the smoky drapery aside. Airborne snow bombs arced gracefully down around us.

The last bulldozer that went into the Shear Zone did not return. Twelve years later I was about to order another one into the field that took Brian and *Linda* down. I wished it were an easier decision, but I couldn't shake the weight of it. Stretch's bulldozer warmed up while we ate lunch. Its eighteen-foot-wide, seven-foot-tall "U-blade" readied itself for real work.

"I'm going to take a snowmobile out, and then I'm going to stand right by that black flag. The one over that big blob we don't know what it is. I'm going to watch," I explained in our Jamesway. "When you bring out the D8, Stretch, and you come up to pass me, watch me. If I wave you off, throw it in reverse and back the hell out of there."

Stretch nodded. If we got it to Crevasse 4, we'd learn what the crevasse-filling business was all about.

Our light flattened under the overcast sky. I stood next to that one black flag.

A half mile away in camp, the D8R lifted its blade off the ground. The bulldozer crept through a broad right-hand turn then faced straight down the road toward me. Not a sound came over the snow. I looked around at all the other flags. That one was safe, this one was questionable. Could something be hiding under that twenty-one feet we had drilled everywhere probing the black blobs? A faint, rhythmic clattering arose. Stretch had covered half the distance already. The PistenBully carrying the others followed not far behind.

Louder and louder, eighty-six thousand pounds clanged down our road at five miles per hour. I pulled my gloved hands out of my parka, poised to wave Stretch off. My eyes fixed on the ground beside the black flag.

The snow itself vibrated. Fifty feet away Stretch never slowed, watching me intently. I nodded to him, and then quickly looked back down. Vibrations rose into my bones. Stretch ran right over the black blob.

Nothing. Nothing at all.

Fifty feet past me, Stretch was still watching me over his shoulder. I looked up, signaling okay. In another hundred yards he stopped short of the slot's edge. We shivered with relief while the D8 idled. Whatever the black blob was, it didn't take Stretch, or me, down.

"Out there you see a forest of black flags," Eric pointed north and west as we gathered around the bulldozer. "We don't know what's in that mess. We saw crevasse signs in there. We saw black blobs. And we couldn't make sense of any of it. But what we do have," Eric pointed out a row of black flags closer in, "is a small field between us and those flags where we found nothing. No breaks, no blobs."

"Are you clear on where you can farm snow, and where you can't?" I asked Stretch.

"Yep." He nodded to the mountaineers.

Ciphers I'd worked out in the office during the northern summer showed our D8R could push a thousand cubic yards of snow per hour over a two hundred–foot carry distance. We could gather enough fill close by the crevasse edge to fill it. But we did not know how the crevasse edge would hold up to a working bulldozer on top of it.

"What do you think about pushing several big piles of snow right to the edge, and then pushing the whole pile over all at once?"

"I can do it that way, if you want," Stretch offered.

"I do want. That snow will run out in front of your blade by fifteen feet as you're pushing. Your blade is another three feet in front of your machine. That gets your main weight eighteen feet back from the edge. I'd like to see more for the time being, until I see how that edge is going to behave."

"I see what you're after," Stretch agreed.

The rest of us spotted for Stretch at the edge, our radios ready. Stretch backed toward the boundary of his farm. His tracks vanished in the flat light. In front of him he saw only flags and bodies wearing red jackets. A dozen black flags marked the edge of the slot. Two red flags, thirty feet apart, marked his dump gate on the centerline of our road.

Shaun and Eric took positions on both sides of the red flags. Russ and I crossed the timbers over the bridge, and watched from the backside.

Stretch started forward, gathering a rolling, curling pile of snow. When the toe of the pile reached the edge, I waved him back for another load. He brought up five piles before I radioed, "Everything looks good. Let's push that over and see what happens."

Snow cascaded into the slot. Billowing snow-dust rose from the void. When it settled, the bulldozer sat contentedly on its side of the crevasse, its blade five feet back from the edge.

"Have at it then, Stretch. Same way, unless one of us stops you."

The crevasse seemed to fill slower than the one thousand yards per hour predicted. We peered daintily over the edge. But after an hour into the show, Russ's radio blared: "There she is! She's a-rising now!"

A half hour later, Stretch filled it to the brim, parked his D8 on top of the snow plug, and we took the picture. We could do this job.

The day Shaun and Eric climbed out of Crevasse 2, I'd received a radio-phone call from CRREL radar expert Allan Delaney. He'd been in Christchurch the day we returned to the Shear Zone and caught a plane to the Ice that very day. He had completed the preliminaries in McMurdo and was ready to join us, but we had a couple more days of work at the Shear Zone before we could return to town and get him.

I explained over the radiophone: "Our highest priority is running a heli-copter radar survey of our crossing. We've made some devices for this. They're down at the hangar. Can you introduce yourself to the folks at Helo-Ops? You've done this kind of thing before. I don't think they have. You'd spend good time for us with the pilots discussing the mission requirements."

"Yes, I can do that," Allan said, simply.

By November 7, we'd filled Crevasse 4 and were ready to go back to Mc-Murdo. We had not one but two helicopter missions brewing.

But we awoke on November 8 to a rising snowstorm, and couldn't see the green flags leading back to McMurdo through the blowing snow. We'd planted them every quarter-mile. Looking back toward the Shear Zone, our green flags there stood out easily enough. They were planted every three hundred feet. We'd stay at the Shear Zone where we could see well enough to work.

Russ, Stretch, and Shaun hauled out the Jiffy drill and set it up over Cre-vasse 5, a hundred feet past 4. With three drillers, backs to the wind, the drilling still was not any easier. While they drilled, Eric and I manned the PistenBully, advancing our pawns. We found Crevasse 6 another five hundred feet past 5.

By midday the weather dropped from bad to worse. Back at Crevasse 5, snow swirled about the driller's parka cowls and clung to their faces. It was time to bug out of the Zone and hunker down in camp. I had a couple jobs to take care of on the way back, but I had no time to explain myself.

"Pile in, guys. Russ, you'll drive when we're ready."

Shaun helped me park our snowmobiles on top of the bridges at 5 and 4. We aligned each with the crevasses' strike, just off the road line, and covered both under their black tarps. Next, we tied off the two bridge planks to the PistenBully's tow hitch.

"Stop at Crevasse 3," I told Russ. "Drive slow."

The long planks had been painted with black epoxy, impregnated with grit for traction. We laid the planks over the crevasse bridges at 3 and 2 exactly as we had done with the snowmobiles behind us.

Back in camp I spoke over the noise of the flapping tent skin to four stony faces: "I bet you wonder what that last bit was all about?"

A man in McMurdo wanted to fly over our road with an infrared camera. His camera saw cold things as black, and warm things as white. Knowing how much colder it was inside crevasses than on surface, he hoped to find crevasses hiding under thin bridges. We had just set up a test on four known crevasse bridges. On a clear day, he'd see our sun-warmed planks and snowmobiles in white. Maybe he'd see the crevasses under them in black.

We'd go back to McMurdo when the weather let us.

The hollow, throaty wind outside blew steady. We had all served in the Antarctic enough to know it by its sounds. These sounds said "wait."

We were warm and comfortable inside the Jamesway. Each of us drifted into our personal torpors, some took up books, some napped on their cots, and some wrote letters. Fine snow whistled its way through any thin parting in the tent it could find. In little growing piles, the snow moved in with us.

At dinner, all of us sat around the long aluminum table. Metallic sounds joined the chorus. Folding steel chairs rang across the wood floor. Flatware scraped across plastic plates. Cups clapped upon the tabletop. Sullen and waiting, nobody spoke.

"You must have seen some weather in your time?" I asked Shaun, breaking the silence.

Shaun looked up from his plate to see all eyes on him.

"Well, actually that was my first job in the Antarctic . . ." he cleared his throat.

Shaun had broken in on the Ice with the British Antarctic Survey (BAS) as a younger man. He drove dog sleds for the BAS on the Antarctic Peninsula. Dogs had long been banned in Antarctica by the time the rest of us started. Shaun's first assignment had been as a weather observer on Deception Island—a quiet volcanic island the British shared with Chilean and Argentine bases.

The young Shaun disembarked the British resupply vessel, and watched the ship sail out of the circular harbor inside Deception's submerged caldera. That night he gave his first weather report to England by UHF radio: "We have snow today. And wind."

A distant dispatcher took his report.

"And we have hail. The sky is black; obscurity 100 percent." It was high Antarctic summer, with a twenty-four-hour sun overhead, somewhere.

"Did I mention we have lightning and thunder?" That was the first time lightning had ever been reported in Antarctica.

"And, oh yes . . . the volcano is erupting. We have ash and cinders falling."

Now we looked at Shaun incredulously. The eruption had clouded the skies over Deception Island, producing its own extreme weather. The Chilean base had been completely destroyed. Salvaging only the clothes they wore, and the cross from their chapel, the Chileans marched in single file around the caldera's rim. They bore their cross before them through the falling ash and cinders, hail and snow, and lightning and thunder, to the British station. Shaun painted a picture Werner Herzog would envy.

Early in the morning of November 9, we woke to a "sucker hole" in the storm, an eye of calmer weather. "Mac-Weather, this is Shear Zone Camp," I called in.

"Go ahead, Shear Zone."

"We see blue skies overhead. Ten-mile-per-hour surface winds. How you there?"

"Clearing for the moment. Thinking about coming in?"

"Yeah. Think this hole will last three hours?"

"Maybe. You got a big storm right behind it. If you get in now, you'll stay in town for a few days."

"That is our intention. Shear Zone clear."

We roused, battened down the camp, piled in the PistenBully, and raced the sucker hole across the ice shelf.

The hole slammed shut behind us at McMurdo. Five days of blizzard winds filled the town with snow, delayed helicopter flights, and pinned us down.

Stretch said good-bye in the crowded galley at breakfast. He'd redeploy soon and join his sweetheart waiting in New Zealand. Both had wintered-over in McMurdo. Both looked homeward now.

Stretch had ridden in the PistenBully with me to GAW when we gingerly searched those first twenty-three miles. That was our first trial with the radar. When he entered our project we knew nothing of the Shear Zone except what we imagined. Now he was leaving, before we had it figured out. Thinking of the long road to HFS, I thanked him for helping us get started, for going to school with us.

"Hang in there." He winked. "You'll get it."

Stretch caught a plane through another sucker hole. We'd pick up his replacement for our next trip out. Eric rotated back to the fold of mountaineers at McMurdo's Field Safety and Training. We'd take out his replacement, too. This morning "we" were Shaun, Russ, and me.

The three of us went to find Allan Delaney straight away. We'd not met him in New Hampshire because he was attached to a CRREL office in Alaska. He had seen the Shear Zone during the 1995 project. I had heard he was tough as nails; I did not expect a man so deliberately thoughtful and considerate. He was slender, wiry, and wore medium-length sandy brown hair, a trimmed brush mustache, and metal-rimmed glasses. He listened well, and gave you his full attention before he spoke.

At the breakfast table in the now-deserted galley, we briefed each other on our work in the field and his work with Helo-Ops. Allan had seen the device we made for slinging the radar under the helicopter. But he urged that we test it locally before we took it to the field. In the off-season, Helo-Ops was adamant about not fixing a hard external antenna to the skids. A sling-rig was our only choice. But our other mission involved an externally mounted infrared camera.

"And they modified the chopper's cargo basket for that?"

"I saw that, too," Allan explained. "They have cut a three-inch hole in the bottom of the basket. The camera lens looks through that hole."

Our radar antenna was housed in a one-footsquare, eight-inch-tall plastic box. It looked straight down. Any metal between it and the snow distorted the radar signal.

"Would they let us cut a larger hole in that basket?"

"They were reluctant to do that," Allan stated flatly.

"All right," I decided. "Russ, Shaun, work with Allan to get this sling-rig tested. I'm going to find the infrared guy and see what's up. See you later today."

Across town from the galley, the wind curled nastily around warehouse-looking buildings. There was no new snow with it, only old stuff beating itself to pieces, pelting my face with tiny ice grains.

The infrared guy, Don Atwood, occupied a cubicle office located in another metal-sided building and was a PhD of something. He was bright-eyed, fair-haired, and boyish with enthusiasm. I'd seen his infrared pictures of crevasses on the Castle Rock hill near McMurdo. Like stripes on a zebra, the snow-covered crevasses stood out in sharp, black contrast to the grays of the unbroken surface. We hoped infrared would show something like that on the Shear Zone flats.

"I take it you are ready to fly?" I asked.

"Just as soon as the weather lets us." Don had built a spring-damped mount to isolate his camera from helicopter vibrations. He'd tested the apparatus near town.

I briefed Don on our found crevasses and open-access holes, and how the bridge planks and snowmobiles were laid out. Then I found a vacant cubicle and settled in to write electronic reports.

Lunchtime found me back in the galley at an empty table by a window. Outside, the wind blew as stiff as ever. Gazing blankly at the weather forcing our inactivity, I played out endless mental scenarios of crossing the Shear Zone. A young man attached to the National Science Foundation broke my reverie.

"Mind if I join you?" Brian Stone asked, setting his tray on the table.

Years ago Brian performed a memorable Elvis impersonation in McMurdo. Now the tall, dark-haired, and clean-cut fellow worked for NSF's Office of Polar Programs. His open smile showed his interest and enthusiasm. I was delighted to see him again. Naturally, he wanted to know how things were going.

I explained our progress and immediate plans. I also told him my concerns for the drilling. A fifteen-feet-thick bridge did not intimidate me, but a twenty-foot bridge or thicker did. Bench cuts and a mining method called vertical-crater-retreat might work, but all that seemed too complicated for this project. It'd take a lot of time. And it wouldn't be safe.

"Do you have a hot-water drill?" he asked.

"A what?"

"A hot-water drill. The science seismic crews use them for making shot holes."

I'd seen seismic drilling at Central West Antarctica, a deep field science camp years ago. But those drills were large mechanical devices. I'd never seen a hot-water drill.

"It's small, and it works like a steam cleaner," Brian explained. "You shovel snow into a tub, a heater melts it. You keep shoveling snow into the hot water and melt more. A pump sends the hot water down a hose. The hot water comes out the end, and you melt a hole in the snow as you lower the hose."

"How deep does it drill?" I asked, noting Russ approaching our table with his own radar on.

"Well, as long as you're drilling snow, not ice, it'll drill as deep as the hose is long. Maybe a hundred feet."

Russ searched out the back of his brain: "I think I seen one of them once."

"To answer your question: no. We don't have a hot-water drill," I sighed. Russ's shoulders dropped heavily.

"How'd you like to try one?" Brian asked. Russ looked up tentatively.

"What, next year?" I asked.

"I mean right now. I think there's one on station, out at Willy Field."

"Yeah! That's the one I saw. I knew I'd seen one," cried Russ. "I think we used it once to make a hot tub!"

The promise of chucking the augers gripped both of us. Brian arranged for a seismic crew, now waiting in town for a flight to the interior, to help us find the drill and get it working. Russ broke off from his work at the helo hangar to join them. Brian may have saved the day in more ways than one. We only looked down forty feet with our radar. If some leviathan were lurking below that, a hundred-foot drill hole might find it.

After more report writing that afternoon, I was back in the galley at dinner time. Russ found us all seated together: me, Shaun, Allan, and Don. Russ danced a jig, singing, "I found it! I found it under a snow drift at Willy! We dug it out and it's on a *sled*! All we got to do is take it out there!"

"Try it out?"

"No. But that's nothing. They showed me how it works. That's all I need. I can make it work. I'll make the bits for your different dynamite tomorrow. We got to round up some glycol. Give me tomorrow to work on it."

Leaning back in my chair and smiling now, I caught Brian Stone's eye. He sat at a different table but followed the action at ours across the galley floor. I signaled thumbs up. He returned a wink and a smile.

Outside our window, snow devils swirled furiously through town.

The morning of November 11 came clear, cold, and calm. Our chopper departed McMurdo with infrared. Mount Erebus lay off to our left. The twelve-thousand-foot active volcano formed the main mass of Ross Island, and on this day every crevasse on its frozen flanks stood out with uncommon clarity.

The stony ground of White Island, and Minna Bluff beyond it, lay off to our right. These were our landmarks. Some day we might see what lay beyond them. For now, we flew over the ice shelf, following our route to the Shear Zone camp—twenty minutes in flight, three hours in a PistenBully. The storm had wiped out most of our old tracks.

I sat in the rear seat of the helicopter. Don and the pilot sat up front. Just outside the helicopter, a long cargo basket contained the camera. Don held up a small viewing screen attached to a cable that ran through the left side door jamb into the basket.

"I'll be recording everything as a moving video," Don explained over the intercom. "We'll have a running time and date stamp on the image. We can isolate stills of anything you want when we get back to the office."

Though we'd reviewed our flight plans back at the hangar, approaching the Shear Zone now at three thousand feet above the ground, the question of what to do first came up. Don wanted to monitor the camera continuously. The pilot looked back, asking, "What do you want to do?"

"Let's hover over the camp area first and see if he sees anything with the camera. We can get our bearings from there," I suggested.

"Good enough. I got the camp at twelve o'clock," replied the pilot.

Shortly, Don held up the screen so we could see the bright white images of our Jamesway and camp equipment. He was already pleased the apparatus was working. So was I.

We descended lazily to one thousand feet, targeting the two black drums next to the GAW post. Don picked them up easily.

"HFS looks just like that, three miles due east of GAW," I explained through the intercom.

We flew over the Shear Zone slowly enough to appreciate all three miles. The pilot easily spotted our black boards against the white snow, and announced when we passed over them. Don, intently watching the video screen, saw them too, in infrared.

I could do little except gaze out the cockpit window. The snowmobiles parked at Crevasses 4 and 5 marked as far as we had gone with our road. From there it was a long two and a half miles of untracked snow before we flew over the drums at HFS. Since Baby, we'd found crevasses every couple hundred feet. At the rate we were advancing our road, it would be a long time to Home Free.

After our first pass at a thousand feet, we completed two more at five hundred, and then finished off with a low pass at 250. Then we climbed back to three thousand feet and headed for McMurdo.

Back at Don's cubicle we reviewed the infrared images. At Crevasse 2, the long black board looked bright white. It pointed right toward a round, cold, black-as-night access hole fifty feet away. The grayish background of everything else showed no sign of a crevasse beneath it. With a sigh, I thanked Don for his efforts. Both of us were disappointed we'd not found a breakthrough in the crevasse-finding business.

In the galley that evening Russ, Shaun, and Allan found me at a table by a window.

"What'd you see?" they asked.

"A lot of snow in camp. We'll have to dig out first thing. Never saw a crevasse we didn't already know about. How'd you all do?"

"We fly the radar test tomorrow," Shaun confirmed.

"I need another day with the drill," Russ added.

With any luck, we'd head back out the day after tomorrow. The dull roar of myriad galley conversations long since replaced the drumming tent skin in camp. Either place, there or here, we waited.

Airborne ground penetrating radar played our last card. It wouldn't give us the map I wanted. But it would show us a line, the flight line, and it'd tell us what it saw under that line in the form of a cross section. It'd show us the kind of image our radar produced when we pushed the antenna over the snow in front of the PistenBully. But the PistenBully weighed ten thousand pounds, and I refused to run it over terra incognita to HFS. If we could fly low and fly several lines close together, we might infer something of a map between the lines. A weather-window for testing the airborne radar opened up the next afternoon.

That evening I dined quietly with Russ when I spied Allan and Shaun entering the food line across the room. "They're not smiling," I muttered.

"It was altogether unsatisfactory," Allan said when he joined our table. I appreciated his economy with language and didn't ask for details of the failure.

"So there's no hope of improving the system?"

"Not the sling." Then he added, "The chief pilot would consider modifying the cargo basket to accommodate the antenna. He hadn't committed to that when we left him thirty minutes ago."

"Thanks for trying. Now here's what I want you two to do." I looked to Shaun and Allan. "Stay in town and work with the folks at the hangar on getting that antenna mounted in the basket, if they're willing. Then test it out. If the test works, fly the mission. The rest of us are going back tomorrow, if we can."

Our new cat skinner, or heavy-equipment operator, and mountaineer were ready to go. So was the hot water drill. We were looking at digging out camp, and that would take a while, but we did have the bulldozer. The other three of us on shovels would be enough.

If Shaun and Allan were unsuccessful, we'd abandon the helicopter radar reconnaissance. They'd come out to the Shear Zone on snowmobiles, and we'd have no choice but to do it all from the ground as we had been doing.

That was the new plan. But the next day, a big blow socked in McMurdo again and we didn't go anywhere. The day after that we got out of town.

We arrived back at camp through the dregs of the storm with clear skies overhead and ground blizzards obscuring the surface.

Two of us were new to camp. Kim Uhde, the cat skinner, was also new to me. Kim came recommended by other operators in McMurdo as an artist with a blade. I welcomed him. He was a tall fellow, well-built and meaty, with sparkling, eager blue eyes that looked over a spectacular walrus moustache.

Tom Lyman, the other new guy, I'd met during my search for alpine mountaineers. His resume stood out, listing experience in geographical information systems and global positioning systems. That technical complement to his mountaineering raised intriguing possibilities for the project's future. The fair-haired Montanan had joined our group in New Hampshire for pre-season radar training. He was Shaun's age and stature.

Our camp was lousy with drift snow. Russ fired up the generator and the bulldozer while the newcomers got their briefing.

"Over here is GAW," I pointed to the four-by-four-inch post. "Everything past that is bad news, and nobody goes past GAW unless I know about it. That's where the Shear Zone lies. Out there, where all those flags are."

More than a hundred flags stood in a bamboo forest, three-quarters of a mile away. A line of green flags led into that thicket. They marked the left side of our road.

"All those other flags out there, the black ones and the red ones, mean something. We'll tell you what they mean when we go out there. For now, if you remember nothing else, remember this: the green flags will lead you to safety. If you get out there in a blinding snowstorm and need to get back, go from green flag to green flag."

"Got that," Kim drawled. "Green is good."

The wind slacked, dropping the airborne snow out of it. Towards Mc-Murdo, a wall of low gray clouds snarled over the surface. But here, a brilliant blue sky with clear horizons in three directions cheered us. We trudged around the camp area.

"And over here, this black plywood teepee-looking thing, that's our crapper. It's generally warm in there. Do your thing in a plastic bag in the bucket, then put the bag in the open drum behind the teepee. And that flag standing next to it, all by itself, that's where we pee. It doesn't look like it now, cause the ground is covered in drift. Pee there. Don't want any yellow snow anywhere else in camp because we melt the clean stuff for drinking water."

"Yellow snow over there. Got it," the cat skinner drawled again. Tom nodded, his keen blue eyes showed he, too, was taking it all in.

A line of black flags stood a couple hundred yards north of the camp perimeter, not toward the Shear Zone but in the direction of Mount Erebus, which towered over us even here.

"That's downwind generally. We've searched the ground up to those black flags. No crevasses found," I explained to Kim. "There's where you put the snow you're about to push out of camp."

"Black flags are bad," Kim nodded. "You want me to feather the snow out or pile it up?"

While the bulldozer warmed, Kim walked around his machine, chatting with Russ before he climbed into the cab. Shortly the bulldozer snorted, raising a puff of smoke, and crawled forward. The rest of us grabbed shovels and started digging out around the small stuff in camp.

The air grew uncommonly still, and the bright sun warmed us. Those of us with shovels shed our jackets while we mucked out small nooks and crannies packed with drift snow. Kim pushed our work away with the big piles he carried in front of his blade. In three hours, we had a level campsite again.

Tom and Kim explored their new surroundings while I heated up leftovers begged off the McMurdo galley and raised Helo-Ops by the radiophone.

"We're scheduled for off deck in a couple hours," Shaun explained from his end at Helo-Ops. "The antenna is in the basket. We tested it over the Castle Rock loop. It works perfectly. The pilot wants to know, how things are looking at camp?"

"Congratulations. We're mucked out and level. Blue skies overhead. The flags I'm looking at out this window are limp. Do you have ETA our location?"

"2000 hours. The pilot would like to land first in the camp perimeter and shut down. He needs to get oriented to the project."

"Understood. You take care of his orientation. And I do want you to fly in the chopper when Allan's running the radar. You may spot something in no man's land that'll be useful."

Russ, Kim, and Tom warmed expectantly by the heating stove and understood the good news heading our way. Tom asked if we had a position on the post at GAW.

Puzzled, I explained that the surveyor had been out a couple weeks before and had captured a very good position with differential GPS. I rummaged through a stack of paper next to the radiophone, found the coordinates, and handed them to Tom.

He wandered over to GAW, while the rest of us rolled a drum of aviation fuel across the yielding snow to a fifty-foot circle of red flags. We'd pushed the poles down so far that only their banners remained above the surface. It looked to us like a landing zone should look.

Tom meandered back over to us. "I think GAW has moved maybe forty feet since the surveyor was here. I can't tell exactly, but I'm certain it's moved." I spotted the hand-held GPS unit Tom had. "How long did you occupy it?" "Long enough."

Tom's finding opened a flood of possibilities. Nobody had moved the post. We knew the Shear Zone ice was moving north, but we'd not measured that yet. The surveyor's recent work was only our start. The green flag line through the Shear Zone would be part of it, too. Now Tom suggested the ice was moving three feet a day. That tweaked the pattern we imagined flying in the next hour: the pilot would fly to coordinates for HFS we'd captured over a month ago.

"Nothing we can do about it now," I shrugged. Tom agreed.

The *whocka-whocka-whocka-whocka* of an approaching helicopter also agreed.

The helicopter circled our camp, and then slowly, slowly dropped into the nest of red-flags. Heels first, then toes, its skids shimmied onto the soft snow. Billows of it pelted our faces. The engine whined. The rotors slowly turned to a stop. Our radar antenna looked down through a square hole cut in the bottom of its cargo basket.

"Nice job." I complimented as Shaun and Allan climbed out. Then recognizing the pilot who'd helped me locate a traverse route across McMurdo Sound years ago, I smiled in greeting. "Thanks for coming, Mr. Scott Pentecost."

"You bet. This is pretty neat out here. Good LZ, too," he declared, referring to our landing zone. We'd crossed paths recently at a Colorado gas station, he on his Harley, me in my truck, both of us going somewhere else.

"Allan, everything working for you?"

"Everything works fine," he said, not a word wasted.

They declined our offer of refreshments for the moment. Shaun gave Scott the briefing, and the three of them started the radar survey right away. We thrilled at watching the chopper zoom fifty feet off-deck over no-man's land.

We gathered inside the warm Jamesway when they landed back in camp.

Allan pulled a metal folding chair across the floor and slouched firmly in it, stretching his legs to relieve his helicopter cramps. I pulled up another chair and leaned forward, elbows planted on my knees. The others stood still, listening.

"We have completed seven flights from GAW to HFS," Allan reported. "One right down the line, two south of the line, and four north of the line. We have recorded the radar record of each flight, tagged at intervals with GPS coordinates."

I nodded. I got the picture.

"However," Allan went on, "I believe for windage and other considerations, some of our lines overlapped each other, particularly at the eastern or far side of the Zone. We had no reliable ground reference there to guide us."

I nodded again.

"It appears that where you are now with your road lies right in the worst of it—the most crevasses, in the densest cluster." Allan sketched a rough diagram in my logbook. My heart sagged.

He allowed that the southernmost flight line showed fewer crevasses, though he could not estimate their numbers yet. But all of the flight lines showed the densest cluster lay within the first mile and a half from GAW. Beyond that he reported an area free of crevasses for two-thirds of a mile, then another half-dozen crevasses, and then another clear area.

Finally, he explained, "There are crevasses right at HFS, but for a mile beyond that there are none. I believe that HFS is truly *home free* and once you are past there, you are across the Shear Zone."

Our road work had reached Crevasse 6, three quarters of a mile from GAW. Another three quarters might see us into that first crevasse-free area.

"Let's call that the Miracle Mile. We got to call it something. Allan, I understand your report. It's tremendously valuable. I'm not happy to learn we're in the worst ground the Zone has to offer, but I'm delighted to learn the Miracle Mile is in front of us. Tell me . . . do you see any meaningful, *qualitative* difference between any of your flight lines?"

An exceptionally good listener, Allan pondered before answering. His eyes dropped to the floor. Some time passed while he considered "qualitative" and the import of his answer. When he looked up, he said simply: "No."

That settled it. We'd go forward from where we were, in the worst of it, and hope for a happy arrival at the Miracle Mile. We wouldn't change course from straight ahead.

I walked Allan and Scott back to the helicopter. Allan would join our camp after he processed his data in town. Shaun stayed with us.

We shot the bridge at Crevasse 5, and gave Kim his first taste of filling a crevasse. He learned the meaning of the flags, the boundaries of the fill-gathering area, and where the spotter would stand. "Watch him as you come up to the edge. He's looking into the void that you cannot see," I told him.

When Kim filled 5 to the brim, he parked his machine proudly over the plug he'd just stuffed into it. "I see what this is all about now," he declared.

Moving on to 6, we set up our new hot-water drill and drilled more holes there than we really needed. Russ grinned with glee. Shaun and Tom prospected past us with the PistenBully and found 7 and 8.

Back in camp, we prepared for a trial run to HFS. I wanted to run the same transect with radar on the ground that we'd flown, but I wanted to prove we could do it safely. "Safely" meant without falling into a crevasse.

Shaun rigged a train of two snowmobiles with a Nansen sled roped between them. Those sleds—named for Fridtjof Nansen, Amundsen's Norwegian champion—were beautiful relics of bentwood and rawhide lashings. The whole sled measured twelve feet long and two feet wide. They flexed marvelously over any uneven snow surface, offering a stable ride to passenger and cargo alike.

Shaun and Tom had experience running trains like this one. Allan did, too. Russ, Kim, and I were more at home running tens of thousands of pounds of diesel-fueled equipment. I told Shaun, "Show me," so Shaun manned the lead snowmobile and Tom the rear one while I rode the Nansen as monkey-in-the-middle.

When our train circled the post at HFS, I had been shown. We didn't know how many crevasses we'd just crossed, nor where they were. We didn't fall into any of them.

From HFS, we could not see our camp. But standing atop one of the drums next to the post, I did spot it. And from that perch, I studied our tracks highlighting the surface. We'd crossed rolling country, no longer an unmarked white expanse. The rollers might be ten feet high, perhaps a quarter-mile to the crest of the nearest one. That was new knowledge, though I didn't know what it meant.

Russ and I returned to McMurdo that evening to retrieve Allan. We had him back in camp the next morning. Allan would ride the Nansen sled that afternoon.

After lunch, Kim, Russ, and I dragged the hot-water drill and a load of explosives out to Crevasse 6. Russ rode playfully upon the drill sled, now a well-warmed seat since he'd already fired up the hot water maker.

The snowmobile train started out of camp toward us, swerving to miss the drill we'd set up squarely in the middle of the road. First Shaun steered past us in a raucous yellow-and-black machine. It pushed a makeshift boom bearing the radar antenna. Shaun never took his eyes off the ground ahead. Behind him, a taut cotton rope bounced lightly over the snow. Alongside it, a black signal cable and a slack belay rope slithered by. Then the Nansen sled whispered past. Aboard it, Allan lay covered in wool blankets, his head and upper body shrouded in a cardboard box. Underneath all that he stared at a computer screen. Behind Allan's Nansen another knotted cotton rope, paired to another belay rope, snaked over the snow. Finally, Tom's snowmobile buzzed by, bringing up the rear.

"Look at how Allan's all trussed up . . . can't see where he's going." Kim remarked.

"Maybe he don't want to see," Russ added slyly, as the train disappeared into the east.

The radar survey to HFS came off without incident. The next day, Allan produced color printouts of it. Pages taped end to end made a scroll.

"We haven't seen images like those," I commented on the inverted, parabolic forms. Some were hourglass-shaped.

"I've changed the radar settings," Allan explained. "I'm not looking as deeply as you were, and I've increased the radar gain for the top five meters."

He pointed out half a dozen hourglass images that lay near HFS. Working backward, he scrolled through several pages showing flat, undisturbed stratigraphy. "That's the Miracle Mile," he explained.

"How about the road we've built so far?"

"You've gone over some features that I would like to look at more closely."

"Right. We've some questionable areas out there ourselves. But we've crossed them with the D8 already."

"That's good."

We shot the slot at Crevasse 6 in the morning, and prospected for a fill-gathering area south of our road. Mindful of Allan's claim that we were working in the worst of it, we took our time doing this. In the end, our flags and PistenBully tracks marked an irregular snow farm where the bulldozer would have no straight pushes.

I planned to head out with Allan in the PistenBully after lunch, to show him how we searched the area, and to see how he'd changed our radar settings.

"I'd like that very much," Allan said with a nod.

The bulldozer idled near Crevasse 6 in the clear afternoon. Both snowmobiles and the hot water drill were up with us, and the PistenBully was rigged for radar. For everyone's benefit, I reviewed the boundaries of the fill-gathering area and the flags and vehicle tracks surrounding it. Tom stayed at 6, spotting for Kim.

Taking a looping route around Crevasse 6, we dragged the drill up to 7 where Shaun and Russ would make holes. Allan and I went on in the PistenBully to fill in the chessboard around 8.

"I am happy you are here," I told him across the cab.

Allan sat shotgun with the radar. He looked up from the screen for a moment. "And I am happy to be here. This is a great project."

That brief exchange covered a lot of ground, but I got down to business.

"We've been holding our eyes to the bottom-right part of the screen. That's where we look for our first warning of a crevasse." Radar imagery scrolled across the screen from right to left. As we moved forward, the image continuously revealed what the radar antenna saw under it. "If we see a reflector down there, we call it out. If we see a vertical black image enter the screen right after that, we call *stop*. What part of the screen do *you* watch?"

Allan considered my question. "A reflector in the lower right *will* give you an early warning of a crevasse. However, I tend to watch the upper right, and mostly the top few meters. If I see the surface layers begin to dip, then I believe I am looking at a sagging crevasse bridge."

He showed me how to focus the radar on the shallower portions of the snow. We'd not been watching for sagging surface layers since every bit of surface here looked flat. It was flat. And he did *not* mention black voids.

"I have compressed the image to accentuate sagging if it appears." His new settings made crevasses far more recognizable on the radar screen. But compressing the image introduced a new variable affecting safe search speeds for the PistenBully.

Until we'd run the helicopter survey, and then completed the snowmobile transect, we'd had no idea what lay out in front of us. I figured our chessboard approach was the safest, most methodical way to enter unexplored ground where crevasses might hide.

"I have never done it that way," Allan told me. "But I believe your ideas are sound."

"But now that we can cross the Zone in snowmobiles, I'd like to lay out the green flag line all the way to HFS. If we do that, we can dispense with this chessboard and stick to what's right on our road. What do you think?"

"I think that is a reasonable approach, too."

My radio squawked: "Hey, can you come back here and pull this drill up to number 8?"

We spun the PistenBully around and followed our own tracks out of the chessboard, having found several more crevasses off track. As we pulled squarely up to the road, I asked Allan, "Look out the window to your right, will you please? Make sure nobody's coming."

Allan looked to his right. "Nobody's coming."

I grinned. We were in the middle of nowhere in Antarctica, and he laughed at my fun. I liked this guy.

We dragged the hot-water drill up to Crevasse 8 where I dropped Allan to work with Russ. The drill would be our best friend when were actually probing for voids. I wanted Allan to get a feel for that. We'd shoot the access hole at 7 before quitting time. I wanted him to see that, too.

Shaun went with me to fetch the dynamite, now stored on top of an old navy sled parked near Baby. Heading back, we passed Kim and Tom at 6. They might finish there in another hour.

The next morning brought overcast with no wind to the Shear Zone. Against the indistinct shadows our many colored flags, brightly painted vehicles, and even our own bodies clothed in reds, blues, and blacks resembled a pointillist painting in progress upon a plain white canvas. The soft snow brought an audible hush to the place.

We started our day gathered around the access hole at Crevasse 7. Allan saw how our mountaineers explored the voids and learned how and what hard information we collected from that work. All of us had a role in the exercise. Shaun and Tom descended into the crevasse. Russ and Kim tended their ropes. I took notes from information Shaun radioed up. Allan observed. We all hauled the mountaineers out when the job was finished.

Through the rest of the morning we shifted into other jobs. The skies had cleared. Tom spotted for Kim while he finished just a "leetle bit more" work filling Crevasse 6. Russ and Shaun drilled the slot holes at 7. Allan and I prospected past 8 and located Crevasse 9. It was a narrow crack, thinly bridged, just big enough for a man to fall into.

I planned to switch crews in the early afternoon so the mountaineers could get some time with Allan. Russ had finished the slot holes and returned to camp on a snowmobile to work on the generator. Shaun had a bit more work stowing the drill. I told him Allan and I would be right back.

We ran down to the powder sled in the PistenBully. Passing Crevasse 6, I looked out over the fill-gathering area again. Tom had left his spotting post and was down in the borrow pit, pulling perimeter flags out of the snow. I thought that curious.

"You about done dressing it up in there?" I radioed to Kim.

"Yes. I'll park this thing on the road in a few minutes," he radioed back.

"Come on up and join us at number 7 then. We're getting the explosives now." Then Tom could join Allan for the rest of the afternoon, while Shaun and Kim helped me load and shoot.

At the powder sled, Allan and I started loading fifty-five-pound boxes of dynamite into the rear cab of the PistenBully. Our radio squawked. It was Tom at Crevasse 6. He spoke the words I most feared to hear:

"The D8 has broken through a crevasse and is stuck in it."

|6| Crossing It Right—
Year One

"You need to come out here right away."

Linda! Mechanically, I radioed back to Tom, "Copy that. We'll be right there. Stay off the radio for now." Our frequency could be overheard in Mc-Murdo, and we didn't need folks in town getting spun up just yet.

"Shit! Allan, unload this dynamite."

From the PistenBully approaching Crevasse 6 we spotted the bulldozer tipped improbably onto its right side down in the borrow pit. Kim and Tom stood upright on high ground, outside the pit.

I parked atop the fill plug and walked slowly toward them, looking back down on the bulldozer. Its right track had broken through a bridge. The dozer had skated sideways before it stopped, blocked against the opposite wall. Had it stopped sliding? The crevasse lay just outside the borrow pit. A few flags remained around the fill-gathering area.

"You guys all right?" My eyes betrayed my flat voice.

"We're both okay," Tom said. "I had him jump off. Didn't want to mess around with ropes."

With its right side sunk, the bulldozer's left side reached for the sky. Some jump.

"I rolled a bit," Kim volunteered.

Questions could come later. Everybody was safe for now.

Shaun was still working by Crevasse 7. I waved, holding up my radio. Over the distance separating us, he couldn't see into the pit. Either his radio was off, or his batteries were dead. I keyed mine anyway, beckoning at the same time: "Drop what you are doing and walk over here. Now!"

Shaun arrived, taking in the scene with a pair of astonished eyes.

"We all see what has happened here," I spoke quickly, before anyone else could. "I'll say it for all of us: *this . . . is . . . serious.* First, none of us is hurt. That is good." Improvising as fast as I could, I continued, "Now, we're going to get that bulldozer out of that crevasse. We don't know how we're going to do that, *yet.* But we're going to figure it out. Shaun, stay here with Tom and Allan. Find out what you can about the nature of this crevasse and the position of the bulldozer in it. Do it safely. Allan, sweep the area with one of them again. See if we can find safe access to the rear of the dozer . . . not just for us, but for another bulldozer. Take your time. I'll be back in an hour or so. Kim, come with me on the snowmobile."

We slowed down by the generator in camp. "Russ, I need you to go out to Crevasse 6 and look over a problem. No great hurry, but please do go."

"Something broke?" he asked.

"Not exactly . . . "

Inside the Jamesway, Kim waited awkwardly while I raised the heavy equipment supervisor in McMurdo on the radiophone. "Gerald, we have a situation that requires the use of the other D8R you've got, the one with the big winch on it. Can you oblige us?'

Gerald Crist instantly decoded my message. In his always cheerful manner, he replied, "I understand perfectly. We'll divert that dozer right away. It's headed out to Pegasus Field now. It'll be at your location in six to eight hours. I'll send you an operator you know."

That was that.

Russ roared out of camp on our other snowmobile. I turned to Kim. "You doing all right?"

"Yeah . . ." In measured syllables, he asked, "Am I fired?"

"Good heavens, no! I am *not* going to fire the man who has at this moment gained the most experience of any of us working around these crevasses!"

Kim half-stepped back.

"Look, this is not going to happen again. You're not going to let it, right?"

"R-right." Kim nodded slowly, waiting to hear what came next.

"We'll go over all this tonight. For now, you need to be away from that scene."

Kim agonized over it all, but were he out there he'd be crawling all over his dozer, trying to figure what to do next. And he'd probably hurt himself.

For now, I needed Kim standing by the radio. We had another bulldozer coming. We had a well-flagged route. But the other guy had never traveled it. Kim could help a brother cat skinner. And if there were any change in plan, I needed to know.

"If anybody on that radio asks, tell them all is well. Because all is well. For now." But if we lost one man, or dropped one piece of equipment down a crevasse, then it was all over. So far we'd done neither.

"Got it."

"And get over what you're feeling. Right now, you're our most valuable player." My adrenaline was up, but I hoped my tone was reassuring. "While you're manning the radios, would you prepare the evening meal? We'll need that, too, please. I'm going back out to see what the fellas have come up with."

"I understand. And . . . thank you."

We had a new job now.

Ralph Horak arrived at camp with the second bulldozer. Next month he'd accompany the French on their six-hundred-mile traverse to Concordia. This evening, we planned out how we'd get past our twenty-fourth mile.

I stood near one end of the long dinner table. Behind me the scene, diagrammed on a whiteboard, hung from the partition separating our bunkroom from the common room. Reconstructing the events showed us that everyone but Russ and Ralph had a hand in the close call.

Shaun, zealous to remove extraneous flags "cluttering" the fill-gathering area, ordered Tom to remove them. The sideline where the dozer had strayed out of bounds wasn't flagged well enough in the first place. We'd laid down PistenBully tracks along that sideline, settling on those as a boundary. Tom knew the dozer was cutting the sideline close, but failed to caution Kim. I, seeing they were nearly finished, failed to halt the operation when I observed Tom removing flags. I failed at least to question him. Removing the rest of the flags left the fill-gathering area virtually unmarked, *except* for the PistenBully tracks.

After establishing shared culpability, I faced Kim. "You got greedy, didn't you?"

"Yes. Yes I did." Kim stood at the opposite end of the table. He rolled his eyes to the ceiling, replaying his memory. "I was nearly finished, and I just wanted a little bit more snow from my sidewall. I knew I reached out past those tracks."

"Thank you." Our eyes met, acknowledging his truth.

I brought the group back into the discussion. "We have learned quite a bit here. Surely no one wanted this to happen. This was an *accident*. All of us had a hand in it. Now, we're each going to have a hand getting us out of it."

Flags were a serious matter, particularly important when we worked in flat light or whiteout. I made a new rule.

"From now on, the removal or placement of any flag in the Shear Zone will only be done with my knowledge and at my direction."

All nodded. We invented how to pull this job off as we went, but not all of us were equally versed in each other's professions. Cat skinners were naturally inclined to cut boundaries close. That's how they showed off their skill. I made another rule.

"We will no longer flag a fill-gathering area by placing a flag on top of a crevasse we happen to find. We will set the flags twenty feet in for margin."

And generally mountaineers were minimalist, low-impact folks. A Caterpillar D8R and several tons of dynamite were anything but. I made my third rule.

"Dozer operators, do not expect a mountaineer to understand what you're doing with an eighty-six-thousand-pound machine. Talk to them. Tell them what you're doing. Remember, they are spotting for you to save your life. Now, let's brainstorm how we get that Cat out of the trap tomorrow."

Allan interrupted, "I am not exempt from responsibility in what happened today. I want to share what I have learned."

"Go ahead."

"I have learned the interpretation of a radar display showing sagging surface layers over a rising diffraction pattern, and showing no black void, should not be interpreted as *no void*. I believe I misinterpreted some imagery."

We'd seen radar images that had the form of a crevasse, but lacked any black void in their interiors. The space where black should have been was filled with chaotic reflections. We supposed those were produced by blocks of collapsed bridge material plugging the void. Now, seeing more crevasses opened for inspection than he ever had seen, Allan said that was not necessarily so. He wasn't involved in the support contractor's hierarchy, but he generously bought-in with us.

That evening we worked out our rough solution for rescuing the dozer. As we shuffled to our cots, I approached Kim with an afterthought: "Be careful to walk your dozer out of that hole *only* under tension from the winch cable. If you slip your tracks at all, you'll chew up the snow and grind yourself down farther than you are now."

I was no cat skinner of Kim's caliber, so I apologized. "I just needed to say that."

Kim peered off into tomorrow's future. He saw it. "Thank you for that reminder. I needed to hear it."

Ralph backed onto a mound of snow he'd built near the rear of Kim's dozer and stopped at the top. The extra height gave his winch mechanical advantage for lifting Kim. Allan and I had flagged a precise route to get to that point. The site for the mound lay perilously close to yet another crevasse.

Each player rehearsed his or her role. I gave my last instruction: "Stay off the radios as much as possible. That's not for McMurdo. It's for us. Unnecessary chatter will break our concentration."

Realizing only then I had no role for myself, I muttered, "Now what do *I* do?"

Kim adroitly answered, "Your job is to watch everybody."

"Right you are." Allan and I withdrew the PistenBully to a safe spot on the road, well out of the action.

Ralph paid out the winch cable while Russ walked it back, hooking it to Kim's tilted machine. Kim swallowed hard, climbed back aboard, and started his engine. Tom and Shaun watched from both sides of Kim's bulldozer for any new failure at the crevasse edge. I fidgeted with the radio mike in my hand and ran one last radio check from our overlook. Then I radioed: "Okay, Russ. It's your show."

With both arms outstretched, and using hand signals that mechanics and operators understood, Russ stood like Stravinsky on the snow. Both bulldozers revved, snorting black smoke. The exhaust cleared, and the first dark puffs drifted, wraith-like, across the snowscape under the overcast skies. Russ's left hand scribed tight circles in the air. The winch cable stretched. His right hand beckoned "come to me," his fingers pinching "little bit at a time." At the cable's first steady tug, Kim's bulldozer shuddered, then sank. Russ sliced his hands across his neck. Both dozers stopped.

Shaun radioed, "A slight, not a great change in the situation. Maybe dropped three inches."

The bulldozers revved again. Russ caught both operators' eyes, and then gave the downbeat: "Now!"

Kim backed slowly against the taut winch cable, first clawing up, then teetering at the crevasse edge. A moment passed. Heavily, he tipped level. Ralph spooled cable until Kim footed on stable snow. Both operators stopped, then bowed to each other through their cab windows. When Ralph slacked the cable, the show was over.

Allan beamed with pleasure in the PistenBully, congratulating me.

"Congratulations, each of you!" I radioed, my heart still racing. I hadn't let go of the mike. "Let's get our equipment back onto the road and have some lunch."

By 1100 hours both bulldozers idled back in camp. Any lingering responsibility Kim felt dissipated in our shared pride.

"You saved our bacon," I told Ralph.

"Aw, hell, it's nice working with you again, ol' Buddy. But I'm gone. I can get back just in time for a hot meal tonight in the galley."

Ralph tracked past our camp perimeter flags, headed back to town. The day had turned gold for us.

That same afternoon, the McMurdo surveyors showed up at the Shear Zone in a red, track-driven pickup truck. Jeff Scanniello, the chief surveyor, and I had worked with one another over several years. We held each other in high regard. He was a bearded, rugged fellow with a sharp wit and sense of humor. Jeff would've stopped for a trailside chat with Ralph. He stepped out of his truck in camp, asking simply: "How's it going?"

"No . . . problem," I answered. Our eyes met. He knew. But we'd get right to work.

Jeff came to plant our first milepost at GAW+1. Its location lay between Crevasses 7 and 8, in ground we'd already proven safe. When he set the post with global positioning instruments, our green flag line ran close to his mark.

We'd extended that line through all our chessboards using only the red-flag back sights Jeff located for us in early October.

"Eight feet off in a mile. One and a half thousandths. Not bad for eyeballing," I stood by my green flag, three paces away from his post.

"Hah," Jeff shot back. "The only time you're on line is when you cross it."

I conceded, laughing, and we discussed plans to set the second mile post. We still couldn't see HFS from the first one, but I thought we might from the next. It'd lie in the Miracle Mile. I wanted to use the mile posts for sights and run our green flag line right between them, all the way to the end.

"Copy that," Jeff acknowledged. "Next week?"

I wasn't so eager to push on to the Miracle Mile. When we found Crevasse 9, the Miracle Mile seemed within reach. We might advance from one crevasse to the next, right into it. But now I heeded Allan's confession. We looked again at the questionable areas and black blobs we'd found weeks earlier. With the hot water drill and Allan's radar expertise, new crevasses appeared on our roster. We *had* missed some.

So we started back at Baby. We ran radar lines across it with the PistenBully at every imaginable angle. We ran parallel to it, our tracks straddling the crack. Only when the antenna passed directly over it, from any direction, did we see a clear crevasse image on our screen. Our New Hampshire training had taught us that a side-scanning cone of influence radiated down from the antenna, and contributed to the radar imagery. But that wasn't true here.

Russ cautioned us, "It's the ones that sneak up on you from behind that will get you. Your radar's way out in front. Before it sees a crevasse your tracks are already over it!"

We started filling in the gaps between our numbered crevasses. First, we discovered Crevasse 3.1 crossing part of our road. It pinched to a close just short of the green flag line. Radar run directly along the flag line failed to detect it, yet five feet south the radar showed it plain as day. We opened an access hole in it and sent Tom down to see what was really there. From inside the crevasse, he reported yet a deeper, intersecting crevasse below it.

"It is extensive," Tom said. "Perhaps twenty feet wide, and I can see light in the distance." Again I feared monsters hiding below us.

When we shot the slot, intending to fill it no matter what, Russ called our attention to something behind us: "That one just sneezed!" Powder smoke wafted up from another access hole in another crevasse not far away. They *were* interconnected.

Hunting crevasses became less like stalking big game and more like hunting unseen devils. The more we looked down through the snow, the more complicated the Shear Zone got. Allan's helicopter flights had found us in the worst of it. I felt the project slipping away, wondering whether we could really understand the place.

"It's a son of a bitch," I declared. "But even if we don't get to HFS this season, we're going to bomb-proof everything in our way as far as we *do* get. We're not going to leave bad work behind us."

Weather didn't help. Frequently our light flattened so that we couldn't see our own shadows against the snowy surface. Moving anywhere in the Shear Zone was like drifting in a cloud. Vertigo played its tricks. Crevasse edges disappeared. We didn't dare run the bulldozer at those times.

When the weather was poor, we advanced the cause some other way. Sometimes we followed flags into the Zone and drilled and blasted. Sometimes we sent a mountaineer down an access hole. Often we stayed in camp waiting for better weather. Shoveling drift snow claimed a lot of our time.

By Friday, November 22, we worked back to the black flag that marked where I'd watched Stretch and the D8R enter the Shear Zone. Now Allan's radar showed us a distinct crevasse-form there: an hourglass shape. The surface layers of the compressed image sagged into the neck. Below that, the whole image flared into a wide bell. The bell was filled with chaotic reflections that we no longer trusted. This was Crevasse 3.4.

The hot-water drill found a small void below this questionable area. At twenty feet down, the bit dropped two feet through air, and then found solid snow again. We continued drilling solid to forty feet before we pulled out of the hole, puzzled.

"What do you want to do about it?" Russ and Kim asked, manning the drill.

"Shoot it," I snarled. We drilled and shot the five-spot pattern.

When the smoke cleared, we looked down through an irregular chimney, just big enough for a man enter. At its bottom was a tiny black hole. Shaun roped up and lowered himself down the chimney. Crouched at the tiny hole, he looked into the blackness, then he turned to our expectant faces waiting above: "There is an immense cavern here."

"*Now* what do you want to do?" Russ and Kim asked again.

"More holes. More powder!" I bellowed, finally glimpsing the monster.

When the air cleared from the second blast, we cautiously looked over the crater's rim into the biggest, blackest hole we'd ever seen. Powder smoke curled around in its darkness. To a man, we gaped in disbelief. "Jeezus it's big."

"We'll let that one air out," I told the mountaineers, business-like. "That'll do for today." *How could I have sent Stretch over that?*

The next morning, when he returned to surface from the immense cavern, Shaun reported the enlarged access hole lay against the side of a huge room that spanned twenty-five feet. The underside of the bridge sagged deeply into the void, adding another ten feet to the thickness we had drilled. The void ran as far as Shaun could see into the gloom, with no end in sight on both sides. We measured its depth at 110 feet. Crevasse 3.4 deserved a special name, like Baby had a name.

This one we named Mongo.

We had a day or so to think about Mongo. That afternoon we decamped for McMurdo. Two new CRREL people had arrived. I wasn't sure what for, but Mongo would have to wait until we brought them back.

Monday our numbers briefly swelled by four. The CRREL investigators joined Allan. Jeff Scanniello and his helper came out for the day to locate the next milepost.

Kim, however, took seriously ill once he got to camp. I raised Jeff, who had already planted the new post and was on his way back to McMurdo, on the VHF radio. "Survey 1, we have an important package that needs to get back to town right away. Can you meet us, and take it in with you?"

I rushed Kim, and extra fuel for Jeff, across the McMurdo Ice Shelf in the PistenBully. Shaun followed in a snowmobile. Somewhere in the middle, Kim transferred to Jeff's speedier truck, and Shaun returned to camp. I followed Jeff into town at my own pace and stayed there for the night. On arrival, I dropped by McMurdo General.

"They're not going to send me off to Christchurch," Kim spoke hoarsely, rolling his head sideways on the gurney. "But I'm going to be here for a few days." He sounded rough and looked worse.

"I'm glad you are going to stay put."

"But I want to go back camping with you all."

"I want that, too," I assured him. "But I'm going to take another operator out tomorrow. Give yourself a couple of weeks. If the doc says okay, I'll bring you back. You can believe it."

Brad Johnson, Kim's replacement, was an amateur mountaineer, expert blaster, and a fine dozer operator. The handsome young man could help out in nearly every aspect of our work. Meanwhile, the arrival of the new CRREL investigators in camp had come as a surprise. I asked them bluntly that evening, "What are you doing here?"

They'd assumed I knew. With the bearing of an affronted Spaniard, dark-eyed Jim Lever explained, "We've been engaged to come to the Shear Zone to determine crevasse bridge strengths . . . to gauge safety issues for heavy vehicle crossings."

"Aw, Christ! So that's it," I laughed. "George Blaisdell said I'd have answers to my questions on that subject by Thanksgiving, but I thought he'd be sending research from the CRREL library. I didn't realize he was sending out two bodies." Did we have enough food for them?

We got over the awkward moment with straight talk. Jim and his partner, Russ Alger, a husky, jovial fellow from Michigan's Upper Peninsula, discussed their needs for field support. I considered how to accommodate them. For my part, I described our progress across the Shear Zone.

"I've no intention of crossing a bridge based on anyone's stamp," I responded to their caution. "I intend to find every crevasse that stands in our way, drop its bridge, and fill it. What you *can* tell me is how deep to drill."

Apparently I made no sense. It was a dense point. We'd seen questionable images, but they hadn't. Nor had they seen our drill.

"Suppose you tell us something about bridge strength that relates its thickness to its span. We can determine both those dimensions by drilling. Now we come to a questionable area under our road. We drill it to a certain depth, and we drill a line of holes across it. Say we don't find a void. Your calculations *could* allow us to walk over that questionable area without actually knowing what it was because its thickness and widths met your strength criteria."

They got it conceptually, but they'd have to see it. It was then Jim's turn to ask the challenging question. "You stated that you crossed Mongo at least one dozen times with a D8, both coming and going. And you stated that a D8 is most likely the heaviest point-load that will ever cross the Shear Zone. That is valuable information. How would you like us to deal with that?"

I hadn't considered the politics of embarrassment before. "You tell the truth."

We got along fine from then on. Tom worked full time with Jim and Alger, looking out for their safety, and assisting in their technical investigations. They'd work in designated areas well clear of other activity.

While we filled crevasses and prospected out to 12, Tom and the CRREL engineers exposed a bit of the bridge at Crevasse 6. Using that, they derived thickness-span ratios that could support our ten-thousand-pound PistenBully.

Emboldened by their findings, I sent Allan and Shaun in the PistenBully to retrace our radar survey past the second milepost, now that we knew exactly where it was. We could see the post at HFS from there. They'd have a visible target and could steer very close to where our road would actually go. Allan's next printed record showed us for the first time exactly where and how many crevasses we'd have to cross. He also showed us several new questionable areas.

So we were taking little steps, one at a time, since we started over. HFS was still a long way off. But Allan was now scheduled to redeploy. We'd miss him, but he'd be leaving us far better equipped to fend for ourselves.

On the afternoon of November 28, Allan and Shaun set off for McMurdo on a pair of snowmobiles. We who remained at the Shear Zone saluted Allan's departure with a very large blast in which we neatly dropped the bridge over Mongo.

The next morning, Mac-Weather announced a three-day storm was moving into the area. We went into McMurdo ourselves and found Allan had already caught his flight home.

As investment in our project's future, I'd planned to rotate as many mechanics, mountaineers, and equipment operators through the Shear Zone operation as practical. Russ knew that when he sat out this time. But the enforced break did him no favors. He was not comfortable around the bustle of McMurdo.

Shaun also stayed behind. He'd fly home on family leave and be gone for two weeks.

The storm that ran us into town passed. On Tuesday, December 3, we returned to camp with mechanic Rick Pietrek. It was his turn. The tall, beefy Wisconsinite had served many years in Antarctica. He brought with him his friendly presence and enthusiasm for our project.

Morning in camp opened with bright, clear skies. I threw the whole crew, CRREL engineers included, at completing the green flag line.

Besides guiding us through the crevasse field, the green flags played a dual role as a strain grid. The moving ice shelves would carry our road northward, but we couldn't predict how fast the road might move, nor how it might warp. Back in Denver I'd planned the strain grid to monitor that movement over time. Periodic surveys at each flag station would show how the road deformed and what it might take to maintain it.

"Every three hundred feet," I reminded them. "That's every hundred yards. Plant them at least a foot and a half deep. And plant them as 'doubles': two green flags together, one banner just below the other. We're getting so many flags out here now, you can't tell at a distance which is which. Doubles will stand out."

The crew split in two. Both teams carried three-hundred-foot cloth measuring tapes and bundles of green flags on eight-foot bamboo poles. Jim, Alger, and Tom took a tripod and level with a telescopic sight. They covered the span from the second mile post to HFS with the PistenBully. Rick, Brad, and I took binoculars. We used snowmobiles to cover the gap between the first mile post and the second. At day's end, a line of flags stretched in front of us to our goal . . . something other than illusory, white plains.

"We've done ourselves a great good," I congratulated us at dinner. "Flags every three hundred feet to HFS. Now we know exactly where our road is going, because we can see it. Think, for a moment, of all the steps we've taken just to get—"

"Did you say three hundred feet?" Tom interrupted. "We used the meter side of the tape . . . ours were every hundred meters."

The effect on the strain grid measurements would be negligible. But I realized then, profoundly, I had a whole new set of people to work with.

"Very well," I said, calmly. "We have green flags every hundred yards from GAW to GAW+2. From GAW+2 to HFS, we have flags every hundred meters." Smiling, I asked Jim and Alger: "You guys ever work for JPL?"

Following their befuddled silence, Tom volunteered: "Jet Propulsion Laboratories. Lockheed-Martin gave them miles. JPL read it as kilometers. Or vice versa. They missed Mars on account of it."

We all laughed.

By December 10, Jim Lever and Russ Alger had completed their studies. On that day we filled Crevasse 6.1, finally passing the one that sent us back to the beginning on November 19.

A quick trip to McMurdo got our two CRREL friends back to catch their plane home. Brad had another field commitment, and also left our crew. Kim, recovered now, rejoined us, packing his guitar this time. That spelled promising evenings in camp.

Another CRREL radar man, Steve Arcone, had by the sheerest chance come in from another field assignment. He could come out to the Shear Zone should we want that. With Shaun still on leave we had space and provisions enough in camp. Steve could only help us.

But a lot of folks wanted to scope out our first steps on the "Road to the Pole." While in McMurdo a few weeks earlier, Dave Bresnahan brought up the subject. He was then running things from NSF's "big chair." He decreed who would go out and who would not.

"That's a dangerous place, and we still haven't got a handle on it," I explained. "If you want artists and writers to come out, just say so. But know that when we are working everybody's got a job, and nobody's got time to guide strangers. If strangers come out, I will shut down everything and walk them around."

"John, I want *you* to understand that NSF would like to get some pictures. It would be more than a courtesy of you to have some photographers visit." Dave remained firm.

"Right now they'd see a bunch of us wondering what in the hell is going on. I don't think the foundation wants pictures of *that*."

"How about a daytrip out there? Can you be ready?"

"How about a couple of weeks from now?"

"That'll be fine. I can tell them to expect something. And that you're on board with it."

That day was coming. But on December 11, only five of us returned to camp in the PistenBully.

Back in the saddle, Kim filled a new crevasse we named Strange Brew. Its radar image had showed a screen-full of chaotic arcs and parabolas, the likes of which we'd not yet seen. Tom made sense of it when he rappelled into it. Crevasse 6.1 had split. The piece we called Strange Brew ran underneath our road for a hundred feet before it turned again and crossed it. For that hundred feet, our road itself was the bridge.

After Strange Brew, Kim jumped over to Crevasse 7 and filled that one the same day. In crossing it, he brought the bulldozer to the post where it touched our first mile.

"Somewhere out there," I tilted my head toward HFS, "not far, is the Miracle Mile. Inside that Miracle Mile is our second milepost, our next stop. There's one more thing to do here, before we call it quits for the day."

We took the picture.

In the morning, the PistenBully and hot-water drill came to a new crevasse just past the milepost. We'd recorded only a black blob here, but now it was Crevasse 7.8.

Tom cautiously entered the void after we shot our access hole. Fifty feet down, he hollered back to his rope tenders, "Haul me out."

Clambering over the lip of the crater, he explained loud enough for everyone to hear: "There's not enough light down there. And it's still pretty gassy."

"Very good. We'll open a bigger hole. Maybe we'll shoot the slot and have done with it," I said.

Tom approached me quietly then, his eyes big as saucers. "This is a really big crevasse. It's bigger than Mongo. This one is really, really big!"

I smiled. "Yes. But we know where it is. We have found it. Next, we are going to fill it with snow."

Tom felt he hadn't got his message across.

" . . . And then we're going to drive over it, and go on to the next crevasse, which is Crevasse 8. We know where that one is, too. Then we're going on to Crevasse 9 and slam it shut. All *bigness* means is it'll take us longer to fill. We're OK, Tom."

We shot the slot that afternoon, and found huge blocks of broken ice walls had plugged off the south half of the big crevasse. The void aired out immediately. There was plenty of light in there now.

Tom rappelled into it again, descending near the blocks. He explored delicately around them. "I think these blocks came off an intersecting crevasse," he radioed.

"Okay. Come on out now. We'll shove some snow into it tomorrow, and you can walk down the snow pile," I radioed back.

Kim, who'd been tending the ropes, observed dryly: "It looks like I'll only have to fill half a crevasse here."

Kim was exactly right. The fallen blocks held back all the snow he pushed into the slot. He only had to fill the north half. From the time he walked the bulldozer out from camp, Kim took three and a half hours to fill and cross 7.8. Add an hour to that for the time Tom explored down the spill slope, and the whole job was done by noon.

Kim went on to Crevasse 8 after lunch. He filled that in another two hours.

We advanced to Crevasse 9, the narrow crevasse Allan Delaney found. Here we drilled a series of blast holes along both sides of the crevasse. Loading them all with dynamite, the shot slammed the walls into the void. Kim smoothed out our work.

"Three crevasses bagged in one day," I grinned. "You are a mighty crevasse-hunter, Bwana Kim."

The really, really big crevasse earned a nickname that day, too: Personal Space. An attractive female research assistant, bearing a striking resemblance to actress Sandra Bullock, may have inspired it. Apparently one of our crew had attempted to get close to her. She warned him against invading her "personal space."

We were into naming things, and a jolly mood prevailed that evening in camp. Right before dinner, Steve Arcone walked around the front of the Jamesway where the short, curly-headed easterner surprised me in the act of coiling the day's climbing ropes.

"Who the fuck are you—Gene Autry?" he cracked.

Steve's abrasive New York humor was foreign to most of our company, certainly foreign to the Shear Zone. I "got it" moments later and started laughing. "Go on," I growled, keeping my eyes to the ground. "Get inside."

The mood carried through dinner. Three crevasses in one day. "You find them, you fill them. *It's a simple concept,*" Rick Pietrek summarized for us.

Kim got out his guitar after dinner and hit a lick. He played all over—Beatles, John Perrine, Chicago Blues. One at a time, he roped each of us into song.

The wisecracking New Yorker revealed an unexpectedly melodious voice. Steve had just accompanied Kim through a round of "Alice's Restaurant" when he started in on "Love is Blue." Here, though, his vocal chords stumbled.

"Blue . . . no, too low . . . blue, no, higher . . . blue, no, too high . . . blue . . . blue . . . blue, blue."

"Who the fuck are you—Bing Crosby?" I nailed him.

"More powder. More detonating cord. And we need to groom our road. Can you help us out?" I radioed to Gerald Crist. On this fine day, I hated to break our momentum to go into town for supplies.

"We can do that," Gerald answered cheerfully. "We have a fellow here this morning just waiting for something like this to come up. I'll send him out with a tractor and a trail drag."

By morning, we'd flagged the snow farms for 10, 11, and 12. At lunch we set up the hot-water drill for their access holes. By afternoon, my old partner Marty Reed showed up with a tractor from McMurdo.

Marty was now the McMurdo blaster. Looking like an Okie turning off Route 66, he had boxes of dynamite lashed all over the outside of his tractor. He brought John Penney with him to rotate for Rick. John showed up his first year at Pole with a face full of hair and a shaggy topknot. The burly mechanic came back to Pole, after an R&R excursion to McMurdo, sporting a mohawk. Now he showed up at the Shear Zone shaved completely bald. John brought boxes of fresh vegetables and eggs.

Rick and John turned over special knowledge of the mechanical items in camp while Marty and I stowed the explosives on the old navy sled. Late afternoon, Rick climbed aboard the tractor returning to McMurdo with Marty.

Just before he shut the cab door, Rick turned to me and hollered: "It's a simple concept!"

✧ ✧ ✧

Sunday brought sleep-in, eggs for breakfast, and a gray overcast. We'd not take out the bulldozer, but the boys wanted to blow something up. The holes were already drilled . . . and it was Sunday. We made an expedition of it.

The five of us blew access holes in Crevasses 10, 11, and 12, and we explored inside Crevasse 6, easily walking down the fill plug's slope to the bottom. A paper-thin gap between the plug snow and the icy crevasse wall prompted debate: Was the crevasse dilating, or was the snow plug shrinking as it set up? In the cavernous blue-whiteness, Steve studied minute details of the crevasse walls. He pointed out contorted folding in its icy layers, epiphanies before his eyes he had only imagined from the radar. When we came out, the wind came up, so we left our field of play for camp and an evening feast.

Monday's overcast again wouldn't allow us to take out the bulldozer. But we could see the flags well enough to send Tom into the access holes, and to drill for slot blasting. When the afternoon weather cleared, Kim walked the bulldozer out and filled Crevasse 10. Tuesday he filled 11 and 12, and then we decamped at noon.

Bordering on frenzy, we were seizing crevasses one at a time, right down the green flag line, closing on the Miracle Mile. But Steve had to go home now too. That meant another trip to McMurdo, and *progress interruptus*. Steve had kept us in stitches. He certified our radar practice. He explained the puzzling black imagery. We educated him about the side-scanning cone of influence. We'd lose this guy who had helped us, and we'd probably come back with tourists.

✧ ✧ ✧

"We can take visitors," I confided to Dave back in town. "We have bridges already drilled out, ready to shoot. When we shoot, they can get some nice pictures of smoke and fly-ice. They can take pictures of the bulldozer pushing snow into a crevasse. If you like, we can set aside a day to walk them through all the operation."

"Some of them wanted to stay with you for a week." Dave upped the ante, jolting me.

"Can they cook?" I recovered.

"I don't know . . ."

"In that case, the answer is *no*," I was quite firm. "We just came back in to drop off Arcone and get a shower. We're heading back out tomorrow . . . early."

"What would you say to a helicopter bringing some out for a day?" Dave could order a helicopter.

"We can handle that. You should come, too."

"We'll see. I'll let you know through Mac-Ops."

I found Russ Magsig in the galley for dinner. He looked haggard from his prolonged stint in town and pleaded for escape. I wanted Russ for the three-year show and couldn't afford to break his spirit. Tomorrow we'd go out for a short stretch, but we'd be back. "When we go out again after Christmas, Russ, you'll go with us."

Having my promise, Russ visibly relaxed. Only then did he ask, "How's it going?"

"We just stuffed 12."

Russ brightened. "Stuffed 12? It really is going good then?"

To whet his appetite, I threw back my head in imitation of the great Civil Rights leader, half-singing, half-chanting: "I can seeeee . . . the Miracle Mile. . . . It's a Laaaand of Milk and Honey!" Then I lowered my gaze. "I appreciate your patience, giving the others their turn. But I want *you* with me when we go into the Miracle Mile."

We sealed our compact with a nod.

Four of us returned to the Shear Zone Wednesday morning, same crew but missing Steve Arcone. We went right to work drilling and blasting access holes in Crevasses 13, 14, and 15. The next day brought high winds and blowing snow. Same the day after. We did what we could during the sucker holes. Otherwise we mucked storm drift out of camp. The storms that kept us mucking also kept the helicopters away. Visitors never showed up.

The weather broke by noon on Saturday. Bwana bagged Crevasses 13 and 14. Shaun, back on the Ice from family leave, hijacked a snowmobile from town and rejoined us in the afternoon. When he'd left us for home, we were dealing with Crevasses 3, 3.1, and Mongo. Now we were fast approaching the Miracle Mile. Shaun's return added that much more mass to our momentum.

Sunday we bagged 15 and drilled access holes in 16, 17, 18, and 19. The Miracle Mile started just past 19, but we wouldn't cross into it that day.

Monday we returned to McMurdo. Tuesday and Wednesday were Christmas holidays in town—two days off and a feast.

Gerald Crist in McMurdo asked if I were ready to rotate dozer operators. But I thought we were going to win this one now. I'd not snatch defeat from the jaws of victory with an unknown.

"Mind if I keep Kim?"

"Not at all." Gerald understood perfectly.

Bwana Kim came back out. So did Russ. Shaun, too, with another mountaineer from the McMurdo stable. This one was new to the Shear Zone. Allen O'Bannon was a tall, fit fellow with the look of John Lennon sporting a stubble of whiskers.

Straight away we ran out to the crevasses and blasted the next four access holes. Through two days of high winds and blowing snow, we got our mountaineers into all four. We blasted the slots at two of them, and we would fill those when the dozer could come out.

Sunday, the weather broke, and we pounced. Kim bagged all four crevasses, crossed 19, and rolled into the Miracle Mile.

The D8R stopped long enough for the picture at the second milepost, then rolled all the way up to Crevasse 20 at the far side of the Mile. Between us and the post at HFS, six more crevasses blocked our way.

We returned to McMurdo for the New Year holiday. When we when came back, we'd finish the job.

Russ and I sat down in a quiet corner of the galley.

"There's one more mechanic at the Heavy Shop that signed up for duty. The first-year guy. Brandon."

"Yeah . . ." Russ saw what was coming. "He's a good kid."

"We're going out there to stay until we finish the job. I'm going to take the kid. You're going to stay in town."

Russ sighed with resignation. He didn't see what was coming next.

"While you're in town I want you to scout the old navy sleds parked at Willy. See what we can put together for a road trip. We're going to finish this job, and if we don't screw up, we'll finish early. Early enough to get out on the Ross Ice Shelf and grab a few more miles before McMurdo closes for the winter."

Russ saw his future, then, and liked it. "Let the kid be with you at the finish. He deserves it."

Back at the Shear Zone, marginal weather devolved to crappy weather, which then improved to poor. That day we filled and crossed Crevasse 20. which we named Snap. Crackle soon followed.

"More powder!" I called into McMurdo on our radiophone. We were running short of dynamite again. Brad came out with a load of explosives. On January 8, Pop went down. Then we buried Crevasse 23, not stopping to name it.

Shaun and Allen prospected thirteen miles southward past HFS. They found not one crevasse.

January 10, Bwana filled Crevasse 24 in two and a half hours. He bagged 25 in another three. Then he mowed down 26. Seconds later, he brought the D8R to the post at HFS.

We climbed atop the bulldozer and raised our American flag.

From camp that evening, I transmitted a digital image of the scene to our project counterparts at NSF, and to my bosses at McMurdo. The straightforward message that accompanied it read: "January 10, 2003, at 5:30 p.m.: The D8R arrived at HFS, and traveled a half mile beyond it. You may say we have crossed the Shear Zone."

The Ross Ice Shelf was open for business.

Winning those three miles from GAW to HFS took from October 31 until January 10. One thousand miles of unexplored terrain lay between us and Pole, and our mission called for a round-trip in one season.

Yet we crossed the Shear Zone earlier than expected. With a light traverse train, we headed out onto the Ross Ice Shelf and flagged another one hundred miles of trail. Russ went with us. We turned around at a place we named SOUTH.

Another pair of CRREL investigators showed up. Tom accommodated them with study time in the Shear Zone before we broke camp all together.

Sometime in February at Pegasus Field near McMurdo, I shuffled along with other day-dreamers waiting to board a jet airplane home, staring blankly at the snow.

Dave Bresnahan strode across the runway toward the plane. He placed a gentle hand on my shoulder, turned me around and looked me right in the eyes. "Outstanding! I congratulate you on a stunning season. Well done!"

To the moment of stepping onto the airplane, I'd not heard anything like that from anyone. I thanked Dave for his courtesy. We shook hands.

Onboard the plane, I strapped into my jump seat, and began shutting out the ice world. My wife was pregnant with our second child when I'd left for the Ice. She was due in April, and I'd told no one here. I couldn't risk losing focus on the safety of my crew. I found peace now dreaming of homecoming, of the love of my wife and son, and wondering what new life grew in her swollen belly.

My eyelids drooped. A young man with a Marine-like bearing approached. He gave his name, stating forthrightly, "I am interested in your project. What can I do to get involved?"

His appeal sounded different from the eager, gung-ho requests I'd become used to hearing. Many wanted kicks blowing things up and jumping down crevasses. Some wanted their names associated with the grand project.

"Here're two paths to get you into the traverse business. You get a job next season with the equipment operations group, or you get a job with the heavy shop. I plan on hiring out of those two departments. Do you have a resume?"

He had one. I glanced through it and saw something about command of an amphibious assault vehicle company. "I will support you," he told me.

We learned a lot about Shear Zone dynamics over the years. This first year we looked down a straight road. It didn't stay that way. It got crooked.

Strain grid measurements said GAW moved north at 2.3 feet a day. That's 840 feet a year. HFS moved slightly east of north at 3.75 feet a day, or 1,370 feet a year.

Spreading between GAW and HFS accelerated. Our last measurements showed the distance growing 160 feet a year. Most spreading manifested in plastic deformation, stretching the ice like taffy. But annual radar surveys detected new cracks appearing. We observed growing separation between some crevasse walls and their fill plugs. Perhaps 20 percent of the spreading manifested in new crevasses and the dilation of old ones.

Safe crossings demand vigilance and maintenance. That includes keeping up the flags and monuments. We measured annual snow accumulation in the Shear Zone: 1.6 feet. Our flags would be buried in a few short years. Anyone who heads out there and finds no flags, no markers, will have to start all over again.

|7| Crossing the Ross Ice Shelf—Year Two

"How far did you get?" asked a voice over the Iridium phone.

"All is well." We were warm, had plenty of food and fuel, and nobody was hurt.

Sheltered in our living module, we enjoyed ample power from the energy module behind it. These red, metal-clad buildings came right off French floor plans. We even called them "modules" because the French did. But our modules, and the sleds under them, had been built for us in Alberta, Canada. The living module, ten feet wide by thirty-five feet long, had two bunkrooms at either end. Each bunkroom held two double bunks. A phone-booth-sized communications cubby and a twelve-foot-long galley separated the bunkrooms. Our energy module, ten-by-twenty-five-feet long, contained two 35 kW generators. It held a snow melter, two sinks, a shower, a compact marine washing machine, an incinerating toilet, and a fuel pumping station. Outside both modules, electric outlets provided "hitching posts" where we plugged in our tractors to keep them warm.

"Come on . . . you can tell me . . . How far did you get?" The Iridium phone offered confidentiality not available through VHF.

"All is well," I repeated. *You don't need to know anything else.*

It was the same message I transmitted daily to Mac-Ops over the VHF radio. Our daily report stated our condition and declared our intentions for the next day: either "remain at this location" or "advance on course." It detailed the day's weather and gave our coordinate position. A change in coordinate position, if it changed, told all. Mac-Ops distributed transcripts through the e-mail network, but that we were still in VHF range told anyone listening that we had not gotten very far.

We were still at SOUTH on the Ross Ice Shelf, wallowed in soft snow. The steaming summit of Mt. Erebus on Ross Island and the stony tip of Minna Bluff on the continent still peeked over the horizons behind us. A bright sun glared down through a deep blue sky and burned hard upon our living module. Snow on its black metal roof melted. Inside, Stretch, John Penney, and James McCabe—an old Ice hand but new to our project this year—shifted pots and pans, catching rare liquid water that found every open seam in its new construction. Outside, I swept snow off the roof, boggled by the sudden heat. The heat was *not* in the brochure, and the growing swarm of footprints around our camp said we'd not moved off this spot for days.

Last year we charged the hundred miles past the Shear Zone in two and a half days to get to this spot. This year it took us seven. *Proven technology, my ass!*

In the beginning our project had only three instructions: establish a haul route from McMurdo to South Pole, execute a round trip traverse along that route in one season, and deliver "meaningful" cargo to Pole. Do all that in three years, of course. But myriad layers of authority held a stake in our project, and the rules of engagement multiplied.

Before we'd ever seen the Shear Zone, Dave Bresnahan had called me in Denver. "As you begin your big equipment procurements, Erick wants to make sure the project uses proven technology only."

"Proven technology only . . ." I repeated, leaning back in my caster chair. Technology hadn't been proven for a South Pole traverse. "What does that mean?"

"It means 'off-the-shelf equipment.' He doesn't want to invest in experimental designs."

Heavy cargo sleds, off the shelf, were made in Germany. The manufacturer had bankrupted. Another German company acquired the rights a year later. It could produce the sleds, but its two-year delivery didn't do our three-year project much good. That same summer, the French came to our rescue. Since they'd been in the traverse business for years, their custom sled designs satisfied proven technology.

Tractors were another matter. CRREL engineers had proven that bulldozers with segmented steel tracks were too slow for the two-thousand-mile round-trip. Bulldozers offered no great return in cargo delivery. So we looked at agricultural tractors with continuous rubber-belted tracks. These offered speeds like we wanted, and they were strong pullers. But these were not small tractors. An operator climbed up stair steps with guard rails, and onto a side deck, just to get into the cab towering above him. Caterpillar made a dual-track model called a Challenger, painted yellow of course. Case made an intriguing four-track model called a Quadtrac, painted red for contrast, naturally.

At purchase time, when Dave's call came, Caterpillar had just sold its Challenger line to another company. The new owner discontinued the old line and wouldn't produce the new models until it was too late for us. That played well for trialing a Case Quadtrac.

George Blaisdell and I flew to Prudhoe Bay, Alaska, to inspect a Quadtrac fleet used there by a seismic exploration company. The model needed modifications for our project, and the manufacturer cooperated. So, because Case tractors were used on the North Slope, they became proven technology.

Meanwhile, an NSF accountant vetoed the Case. At the time, she occupied the big seat at McMurdo. It was a "one-off model," she said. Caterpillar-brand equipment otherwise dominated the USAP fleet. Parts interchangeability and inventory simplicity argued for Caterpillar. But the new Challengers, whenever they were ready, would have completely different engines and transmissions. They'd be one-off, too.

I wanted to try Cat *and* Case. We didn't know which would work best. We didn't know the terrain. And we didn't know how many tractors it took to move just *us* to Pole, let alone cargo. The best cargo tractor and the best pioneering tractor may not be the same model. In the end, Case overcame the accountant's veto simply because it was available. We called the big red tractor *Quadzilla*.

Judy Goldsberry found our second tractor on a lot in Makoti, North Dakota, where she lived when she wasn't the foreman at Williams Field. It was a new Challenger of the discontinued series. We fitted it with a hydraulic knuckleboom crane, like the French did, and we named it *Fritzy*.

Our D8R with its huge snow blade would be slow, but because we already had it, it became proven technology, too. We christened her *Mary Lou*, after Judy's twin sister.

Our fourth tractor was an odd looking machine, modified from the discontinued Challengers. A six-passenger cab perched on top of its engine. A flatbed deck with a fifth wheel hitch fit on the rear where the standard cab used to be. It pulled a train of tracked trailers. CRREL thought it might become the ultimate traverse tractor. We latched onto it to test the fifth wheel system. And, because the USAP had purchased it already for other purposes, it was also proven technology. We named it the *Elephant Man*.

Fritzy and the *Elephant Man* disembarked the ship a month after we completed the Shear Zone crossing in February of 2003. *Quadzilla*, along with our entire sled fleet, arrived at the start of the next season, October 2003, in the bellies of United States Air Force C-17s.

A lot of us showed up on those C-17s.

James McCabe had been out of the program for a couple years. When Stretch learned McCabe was coming back as an equipment operator, he wrote two words to me: "Great score!" Russ Magsig demanded the snake-eyed Texas skinflint bring cigars. I knew the dry-witted Texan would be a popular choice.

Stretch had been on the Ice since August. Same with Russ and John Penney. The CRREL contingent—Jason Weale, George Blaisdell, and later Allan Delaney—arrived in October. Buddy Truesdell and Richard Sievert, representing Case, trained our crew on *Quadzilla*. Herb Setz, master sledmaker from Alberta, came in to supervise our sled assembly. Our sleds had arrived in pieces. Throughout October in McMurdo we built sleds, we trained, we radared the Shear Zone, and we tested tractor trains.

The trick with tractor trains was to strike the right balance between the tractor's ability to pull, called "draw bar pull," and the sleds' resistance to being pulled. We measured both pull and resistance by linking scales between the tractor and the sleds. Pull and resistance were only partially related to the equipment's gross weight.

We wanted more pull than resistance, naturally; otherwise we'd get stuck. So the character of the surface, where tracks met snow, became a factor, too. We figured the towed load should equal no more than 90 percent of the tractor's draw bar pull. That became our "load planning tool." We measured the towing resistance for each sled on snows near Williams Field, and we added sleds in a train until the sum of their resistance neared 90 percent.

In early November we shook down our tractors on a local traverse, sixty miles across the frozen seawater of McMurdo Sound to Marble Point. At the end of that line, we delivered bulk fuel to a helicopter refueling station. *Quadzilla*, *Fritzy*, and the *Elephant Man* made the trip.

McMurdo Sound was ice hard, and we enjoyed great traction over most of the route. But when I drove the *Elephant Man* over one snow-covered patch, the tractor reared back under the heavy load bearing down on its fifth wheel. Pure blue sky took over my windshield. The rear of my tracks ground deeply into the snow, and we stuck.

That was not a good sign. Deep snow covered the Ross Ice Shelf.

"When are you going to go?" everyone in McMurdo asked.

"When we're ready," we always answered.

I wouldn't launch until we *were* ready. We loaded our sleds, married our sled trains, and settled on the order we'd head down the trail and how we'd stagger our tracks to compact the snow.

"When are you going to be ready?"

"Soon."

At the end of day shift, November 16, I passed out cigars and we enjoyed an outdoor smoke. The afternoon was calm and sunny at our staging area on the Sea Ice Runway. We stood around with nothing left to do.

"Are you ready?" I asked James McCabe.

James squinted in the bright sun. "Let's go," he nodded.

The others bought in: "Ready." "Let's go." "I'm in."

"Then take tomorrow off. Meet here after breakfast day after tomorrow. We go." Grinning, I added, "Our hearts are pure. Our cause is just. The time is now."

Across McMurdo Sound, the Royal Society Mountains pierced the sky in crisp detail. Morning operations at the Sea Ice Runway got under way. The still air buzzed with humming engines. Forklifts carried pallets about the frozen sea surface. Cargo handlers loaded airplanes. LC-130s taxied across the parking apron to the fuel depot.

We gathered on the ice by our machines. The station padre offered up a tractor-prayer. David Pacheco, a large and gentle man who accompanied the padre, gave us an inlaid wooden cross, handmade from his home in Peñasco, New Mexico. When we hitched to our loads and lined up in the order of march, I hailed the control tower:

"Tower, South Pole Traverse requests permission to transit the apron."

"Proceed as requested, South Pole Traverse."

Allan Delaney and Allen O'Bannon led the way in the PistenBully, dragging a long rope tethered to two snowmobiles, each lashed down on plastic sheet–sleds. Stretch and the D8R fell in line. He pulled a long train beginning with our module sleds. These two alone weighed over ninety-nine thousand pounds. And behind those he pulled three more supply sleds at thirty thousand pounds each. John Penney, who'd captain the radar and flagging team once we passed SOUTH, rode with me. We slipped into the line with the *Elephant Man*, pulling two trailers on its fifth wheel. Each trailer carried a five-thousand-gallon fuel tank. They were partially full, and we hoped to deliver them empty to South Pole as cargo. Russ followed us with *Fritzy*, pulling three three-thousand-gallon fuel tank sleds. James McCabe and *Quadzilla* rode drag, pulling five three-thousand-gallon tank sleds. All together, we weighed 772,000 pounds, moving out at four miles per hour.

An hour and a half after leaving the runway, we climbed the thirty-foot rise from the sea-ice onto the McMurdo Ice Shelf. The Shelf road, a compacted snow road rather than an ice road, led to Williams Field skiway at the city limits of McMurdo. We stopped along the way to hitch up trail grooming "drags" behind our sled trains. These were an assortment of long, heavy pipes and anchor chains we had staged a few days before. The drags leveled bumps and filled ruts made by our passage.

At the city limits, a group of well-wishers cheered us with balloons and signs bearing encouraging words like "Party on, Dudes!" We stopped to share their fun and stand for photos.

Crossing the city limits after checking out with Mac-Ops, we headed onto the less-traveled path to the Shear Zone. James strayed off the track at the first turn, and *Quadzilla* wallowed up to its belly pan in the soft, virgin snow. Russ unhitched *Fritzy* and went back to pull James out of his mire, still within sight of Williams Field. But no one was looking. The well-wishers had gone back to town.

Nobody witnessed what happened after we passed over the horizon.

"Split your load and go on up to the Shear Zone camp. We'll come back for the rest tomorrow," I radioed James, behind me, as the blizzard swelled in front of us.

We were headed for disappointment this year. I just wished I didn't know that on this first day. *Quadzilla* couldn't pull all five tank sleds over the soft snow. The *Elephant Man* had enough trouble with its twinned trailers. Russ pulled both of us into camp with *Fritzy*.

Four days later we shuttled our fleet across the Shear Zone and started south. Harsh truth struck again. The *Elephant Man* made a quarter mile riding nose-high before we, I, and it got stuck. Angry, I unhitched my second trailer and left it. We'd pick it up on our way back to McMurdo, someday.

Launching again with the D8R leading, *Fritzy*, the *Elephant Man*, and *Quadzilla* all broke traction through the day, grinding their tracks into the soft snow. Each time a tractor wallowed-in another tractor unhitched and went back to unstick its stranded companion. We made less than fifteen miles, slogging forward at two miles per hour. At day's end, Russ had left a half-load several miles behind us.

The 90 percent load planning tool wasn't working.

Several thought our slow pace, lined up as we were behind the bulldozer, didn't give the momentum needed to avoid wallowing-in. So the next day I ordered the other tractors to lead while Stretch brought up the rear. The strategy worked. We stuck less, and we advanced between three and four miles per hour. When Stretch caught up at the end of the day, we'd covered another fifteen miles. Happy about that, I walked back to the D8R that hauled our home.

Then I spotted the wreckage: two containers mounted on Stretch's trailing sleds now lay on the snow with all their tangled sled pieces still linked to his train. Their tracks extended well over the horizon. Stretch had dragged them that way for miles. He could never have noticed that, for he couldn't see around the living module from his cab.

No one had witnessed this wreck, and I'd never considered a repair job like this on the trail. The crew gathered around it, one at a time, thunderstruck.

Fritzy's crane helped in the heavy lifts. In two hours we'd rebuilt one sled, discovering the culprit turntable pin had snapped in two. We carried spare pins. These were case hardened steel, two-and-a-quarter-inch diameter by two feet long. But what forces could break such a pin?

"We figured this one out," I sighed. "Let's call it a day, and go eat." The other sled could wait till tomorrow.

From that day on, the D8R always took the lead. The other tractors ran packed close behind it. And we watched each other, hawk-like, for signs of trouble.

A new snow form appeared over the next few miles that became our bane for the next hundred. These were long, narrow hummocks of hard, dense snow. In flat light we saw nothing of them. Windblown snow filled the troughs between the hummocks so that their tops appeared level with everything else. A tractor passing over the top of a hummock might not leave a mark on it. But on plunging into the fluffy traps between them, the tractor wallowed-in. When that happened, we all stopped to help.

We hadn't seen these snow forms the year before during the dash traverse. We were too light then to notice them. But this year we were heavy, and we noticed every one. At an evening meal Russ volunteered an explanation.

"When my uncle and I'd be plowing a field, and the tiller hung up on a rocky ledge we couldn't see, we'd jolt to a stop. I always fell off the tractor. My uncle called them *dorniks*. I think that's German." Russ had been raised on an Ohio farm.

"Dornik" is of Gaelic origin. It means a buried fieldstone one might use to build a dry stone wall, something that would stop a plow. Dornik stuck for us, and as an epithet it fit. When John Penney called out on the radio: "Fucking dornik!" everybody knew what he meant. The whole fleet halted and we went back.

But even helping was not easy. The stirred up snow made terrible footing. We worked cautiously around stuck tractors and broken sleds, checking that everyone stood safely out of the way before making a big move, or a heavy lift. Still, we fell down a lot.

To get that first hundred miles to SOUTH, we even traveled at "night." When the sun sat lower on the horizon and the temperature chilled, we thought we'd find a firmer surface. That was an illusion. We still got stuck. And I stopped counting the number of times it happened.

Crossing the Ross Ice Shelf wasn't going to happen for us this season. And hauling cargo to South Pole was sheer fantasy when we couldn't even pull ourselves. None of us had any idea a snow swamp lay ahead, waiting to swallow us whole.

We dragged ourselves into SOUTH seven days after crossing the Shear Zone. In camp we discovered a cracked pinion seal on *Quadzilla*. Repairing it required a spare part from McMurdo. Since we were immobile without it, I radioed to McMurdo, hoping a Twin Otter ski plane might fly the part to us. And we waited.

For days a cloudy ceiling stretched from one horizon to the other, disappearing into dim shades of gray on gray. A plane would never attempt the landing. One day a Twin Otter flew over us. We heard it, but we never saw the plane through the pall. It refused even an airdrop.

While footprints around our camp multiplied, we studied the terrain that hobbled us. Allan Delaney produced a snow sampling kit. We dug test pits near our camp, measured snow densities, and studied snow crystal structures. We dragged sleds and measured rut depths. In one test, we discovered the *Elephant Man* worked better as a pulling tractor using its hitch pin than it did using its fifth wheel. After that, I sidetracked *Elephant Man*'s remaining fifth-wheel trailer and hitched the tractor onto a pair of fuel tank sleds.

But still we waited at SOUTH.

Allan Delaney was nearing the end of his time with us. If the resupply flight came, he'd go back to McMurdo on it. Apparently the weather wasn't going to allow that flight, so we came up with a new plan.

SOUTH lay a hundred miles from the Shear Zone camp. A flagged route led the way. There we'd left a shelter equipped with food and snowmobile fuel. After discussing emergency contingencies, we agreed we could execute our plan safely. I notified Mac-Ops, and then sent O'Bannon and Delaney back to McMurdo on our two snowmobiles. O'Bannon would return a couple of days later with the needed part and a replacement radar man.

Delaney had stuck with us through tough days on the trail this year, and more recently through the edgy days of waiting. He'd worked brilliantly with us the year before when we forged the Shear Zone crossing. When he started his snowmobile, I hailed him. Allan turned around.

We who stayed stood outside the living module, saluting Allan with slow, rhythmic clapping.

"Thanks, fellas," he said.

Three days later, out of the north, a pair of bright headlights bobbing independently in the washed-out distance defined our horizon. Within ten minutes, two snowmobiles roared into camp, shut down, and two tired faces looked up.

"Norbert Yankielun, welcome," I greeted the tall, clean-shaven, bald-headed man I'd met at CRREL HQ a year ago. He looked haggard and ready to stop.

"Allen, thank you," I turned to O'Bannon, as Russ and John Penney eagerly took custody of the spare parts. "We're still on a night shift cycle here. We'll get you some food. You guys take twenty-four. When you're rested we'll try it again."

A raging blizzard had socked in McMurdo. Allen told me my boss's boss in McMurdo was disturbed that I launched the snowmobile expedition in the first place. "It didn't bother us," Allen explained. "We waited at the Shear Zone until the weather let us go in."

"Yep, that was the plan," I concurred. "We knew our capabilities. We let Mac-Ops know we were coming. That's all we needed to do. And now you're back. Take your rest, pardner."

While Russ and John completed *Quadzilla*'s repairs, Allen and Norbert adjusted their sleep cycles. Then, fully seven days *after* we arrived at SOUTH, we were ready to roll again.

Following a new towing plan, James and *Quadzilla* hitched to the living and energy modules. The rest of the sled fleet apportioned among other tractors, Stretch and the D8R hitched to four fuel tank sleds in line. That should have been an easy pull. But when the tank sleds dug into a bear trap flanking a dornik and pulled down the D8, we stared, dumbfounded. Stretch, James,

Russ, John Penney, and I grimly dismounted our tractors. After some time and more reconfiguring, we all got back on our feet and made camp two hundred yards farther south from where we had camped for seven days.

"Well . . . that didn't work," I muttered to the wastelands.

Norbert had been observing all this. He asked me, "Has it been like that?"

"Yes."

Norbert heaved a sigh, apprehensive for his future with us.

We cannot have been an easy group for Norbert to walk into. Our hopes for the season faded daily. The terrain whipped us. "Existing technology only" whipped us. We were beat up.

But Norbert made the best of it. He'd brought an amateur radio set with him, keeping us in touch with world news. He won our best cook contest. And one evening, he lectured us on synthetic aperture radar, the sort satellites used. The white metal door at one end of our galley became his whiteboard. Norbert covered it with multicolored-diagrams worthy of a New York graffiti artist.

But after the experience with the D8R and the dornik, I threw in the towel. We had to change what we were doing. We'd depot some loads here and along the way. We'd pick them up on our return. We'd get lighter going south, breaking trail as best we could. And we'd hope the compacted trail would set up behind us for our return.

"We'll keep heading south until we consume half our fuel or half our time, whichever comes first," I declared the next morning in the galley. "Only then will we turn back north. But to make any southern progress at all, we're going to start shuttling our loads. We'll have to be smart about it, but that's what we're going to do."

Others surely thought the same thing, but I had to declare it. Even though we'd sidetracked some loads two hundred yards back at SOUTH, we still couldn't advance what we kept all at once. Shuttling meant moving a portion of our loads forward, and then going back to retrieve the remaining portion. For every mile won, we'd cover three. We'd pay a high cost in fuel to do that. We'd also pay in spent emotions. But this was the change I had to make.

Not every tractor would be involved in shuttling, so there was the added challenge of finding constructive work for those who weren't engaged. At our next camp, sixteen miles beyond SOUTH, Stretch and James went back to retrieve two loads. Russ and John Penney remained in camp working maintenance chores and coordinating radio comms with the dispersed crew. I joined Norbert and Allen on the radar team, and we flagged the next twenty miles forward. Though we hadn't seen a twenty-mile day since departing the Shear Zone, this next stretch held suspect terrain where hidden crevasses might lurk. When we rejoined the camp at day's end, I had good news.

"We never found a crevasse. And we've proved a hundred-foot-wide safe corridor for the next twenty miles. And . . . we never saw a dornik all day."

The dorniks lay behind us now. But the days got warmer, the snow got softer, and we wallowed more and more pushing south through the snow swamp. One day a tractor could pull two fully loaded fuel tank sleds. The next day it could only pull one. Bewildered, we altered our shuttling plans as the conditions changed. And, we got very good at rescuing stuck tractors and repairing broken sleds, quickly.

On passing one hundred miles from SOUTH, we planted a tall wooden post into the snow and stood for a photograph beside it. That photo showed a weary, unsmiling crew standing in flat light with no horizon.

Farther down the trail, a failed fuel injector disabled one of our tractors. Again, we didn't have the spare with us. A crew rotator flight would soon swap out Allen O'Bannon, but this time we wouldn't wait for the plane. We fit plastic skis under the disabled tractor, and then dragged the *tractor* forward. The surprising success of our improvised rescue skis got us talking at dinner again.

Russ started it. "I think we need to try hover barges."

"What'd they do with *Maxine*? They retro-ed it in '93," I chimed in. "You think NSF would go for that again? Hah! Proven technology only." *Maxine* was a small hovercraft purchased by the USAP. It'd been trialed on the Ice during the late 1980s and early '90s. NSF scrapped it.

"No, no," Russ insisted. "I'm talking about hover *barges*. Barges, not hovercraft. A big barge with an air cushion under it. It don't take much air, less than five psi. You move big printing presses around warehouse floors with aircushions. That'd work here. Just load up a barge and turn on the air. We'd pull the barges with our tractors. Nothing to it."

"It'd work until the wind came up. Blow you all over the place," James observed.

"Yeah, or until you crossed a crevasse and the wind dropped out from under you. Then what do you do . . . fill the crevasse up with air?" I speculated.

"Or until you had to go up hill . . ." McCabe again.

"Yeah, but all you'd have to do is get to the base of the mountains. You could drag everything the rest of the way from there, just like we're doing now. On a hover barge, I bet you could move ten times as much as we're moving now." Russ was right, of course.

"Ten times nothing is nothing." Stretch brought us back to reality.

"But it sure is nice to think about." Russ again.

"I wonder how big you can get that plastic? I wonder how heavy you could load it," I mused.

"Man, that stuff is sure slick," Russ said.

We dreamed of floating unimaginable loads across the Ross Ice Shelf, effortlessly. We conjured wonderful designs using technologies not proven.

While we dreamed, the Twin Otter caught up with us. Mountaineer Scott "Scooter" Metcalf stepped off the plane to replace Allen O'Bannon. Scooter was fit. He wore a short black beard and mustache and a topknot of curly dark hair. He stood five-and-a-half-feet tall. The rest of us were all six feet, or over. A shorter fellow among towering grumps in close quarters might find himself uncomfortable.

We stayed in camp for a day to adjust Scooter's sleep cycle. Russ and John Penney dealt with the fuel injector.

When the tractor was ready, James and Stretch took *Quadzilla* and *Fritzy* back twenty miles to retrieve a load. They arrived back in camp for lunch, and then advanced that same load another twenty miles forward. While they were gone, Norbert picked up news on his amateur radio that Saddam Hussein had finally been captured. None of us liked having our marines and soldiers killed in Iraq, but now we cheered. I passed on Norbert's news when the shuttle crew came within VHF range.

James's tired voice radioed back: "Finally, some good news." They'd covered eighty miles that day only to return to the exact point where they started.

At two hundred miles past SOUTH we planted another wood post, and again we stood for a photo in the flat light that wouldn't leave us. While the crew slept that evening, I placed a red mark on a particular day later in December on the wall calendar in our galley. The next morning Scooter immediately noticed the red mark and demanded to know what it meant.

"It's a red mark, Scooter. That's all. It's a red mark," I curtly replied.

Seven miles past our last post, things changed. We'd been sidetracking pairs of fuel tank sleds across the swamp. As one tank emptied, we left it on the snow along with a second full tank to guarantee our return fuel. Now only two full tank sleds remained, which we could haul forward all at once. No more shuttling.

On Christmas morning, the distant mountain fronts of the Transantarctics gleamed above our southern horizon, our first clear day in weeks. We made an unprecedented thirty miles, and in the process we crossed the 180 degree meridian in latitude S 82° 25'. Russ sleuthed out that since we had crossed the dateline, we could have Christmas again. The next morning we did: we slept in.

After waking, we shared candies and packages from home that the Twin Otter had brought along with Scooter. Personal Christmas cards read aloud cheered us. We passed out tokens from the folks in Alberta who'd made our modules. Wooden backscratchers I purchased from a rubber-tomahawk store back home went 'round to everyone. Now we could reach back inside our heavy coats and go after an itch.

I found a quiet moment later that morning and called my wife using our Iridium phone. She answered her cell phone from Preservation Hall in New Orleans. It was intermission at the jazz music venue. She, our son, and our brand-new daughter were passing through on their way to Grammy's house in Florida for the holiday. I'd had no idea, but I had a great laugh.

That was only a brief escape for me. We started down the trail again that afternoon in calm weather, watching as the mountains grew clearer and larger. The snow felt firmer under my tractor. Were we coming out of the snow swamp, or was it just the lighter loads? Perhaps those mountains made some kind of local weather, better snow. Perhaps it was all a phantom.

But that same afternoon we only made twelve miles. It was our worst day ever. Three pineapple lockdowns on our container sleds broke. These were nearly indestructible devices that tie the container van to the sled base. When the last one broke, we were out of replacements. After cobbling a solution of heavy chains and sacrificed tools, we again picked ourselves up and got on down the trail.

James was dogging Stretch's module train in *Quadzilla* when he screamed out on the radio: "Stop, Stretch! Stretch, stop! Stop!"

All our trains halted. We dismounted again and surveyed the damage. Another turntable pin had snapped in two, this time on the energy module sled. The module balanced precariously on its undercarriage. A false move would bring it to the ground. If that happened, we had no means of lifting it back onto the sled chassis; *Fritzy*'s crane was not up to it, so the wreck would have had to stay in the middle of the Ross Ice Shelf.

Come alongs pulled the undercarriage pieces back into alignment. Through a hole we cut in the bathroom floor, we dropped the replacement pin into the turntable. The energy module was again secure on the sled chassis. We had dodged a serious bullet, and we thanked God for the Texan's vigilance.

That evening's e-mail brought me a startling Christmas message from the big chair in McMurdo. It was the NSF accountant, again, demanding an exact accounting of our disappointing performance against our preseason expectations.

We'd been busy that day repairing pineapples and turntable pins and were presently exhausted. We were committed to going as far south as half our fuel or half our time would allow. But we had discovered a region of exceptionally soft snow forcing us to shuttle, and that had consumed an inordinate amount of our onboard fuel supply. While we'd hoped to reach the base of the Leverett Glacier, I doubted we would accomplish that this season. In as much as we were traversing unexplored ground, I couldn't predict how far we might get.

That evening's report to Mac-Ops gave our condition: "Situation desperate. Odds against us. Just the way we like it."

The next day, we made thirty-one miles with no shuttling. The day after that we made it another fourteen, arriving at a point designated RIS-1 on the proposed route. It was our first targeted point on the Ross Ice Shelf, and it lay 397 miles from the Shear Zone. We had enough fuel to advance another twenty-five miles.

But this was December 28. Red ink on the calendar marked the day. "Here," I declared, "is where we turn around."

Here was where we confronted our disappointment, but *here* was where we acknowledged we had done our best. The mountains beckoned us south, but over the next two days we rested.

Norwegian Roald Amundsen had cached whole seal carcasses on his depot journey in 1910, the year before his dash to the Pole. He'd intended to use them as food, both for his men and for his dogs. Since he didn't know how much snow might accumulate in those spots, he planted the frozen seals head first, upright and sticking well out of the snow. That way, he stood a better chance of finding them the next year.

Following Amundsen's lead, we cached two thousand green trail flags and sixteen long wooden posts the same way for next year's use. The half-dozen bundles of bamboo poles and posts resembled the plinths of Stonehenge. Scooter called it "Boo-henge." One of the posts we held back, planting it at RIS-1. We stood beside it for the photo.

On December 30 we turned our backs to the mountains and headed north. We'd been forty-two days getting to RIS-1. If it took that long to get back, we'd have just enough time to winterize our fleet before we caught a plane ride home.

Northbound we made forty-six miles one day, thirty-three miles another, then forty-three miles, thirty-three miles, and thirty-eight miles . . . unthinkable daily distances for the southbound traverse. Every shuttle mission had packed and groomed our trail surface. The snow had set up into a proper road. Now we flew down that road, and the scene was thrilling. I rode with Norbert one day in the PistenBully, off-track, just watching the heavy fleet running down the flag line. Our four tractors and their sled trains packed up like coursing hounds bounding down the trail, each one keenly looking after the other.

By January 5 we'd gathered up enough of our sidetracked sleds that we started shuttling again. Two days later we camped thirty-two miles shy of SOUTH. That night our Iridium phone connected with two CRREL engineers in McMurdo waiting to join us on the next Twin Otter flight. Jim Lever and Russ Alger had come back, planning to conduct crevasse bridge studies with us in the Leverett region.

"Jim, we won't be getting anywhere near there this year. It hasn't been pretty in this snow swamp. We're heading back to McMurdo now. We know what a lot of our problems are. We need you guys to characterize this snow and put the engineering touch on our mobility issues. Can you shift gears and do that for us?"

"Yes, we can. When would you like us to do this?" Jim had caught wind of our difficulties in McMurdo. Perhaps he thought he and Alger might wait for us there.

"Immediately. We'll wait for you at our present location."

The Twin Otter arrived the next day. Jim Lever, Russ Alger, and mountaineer Matthew Szundy climbed out. Norbert and Scooter climbed in and went home.

"Bresnahan tells me NSF doesn't place a lot of stock in our anecdotal information," I explained to Jim. "We need you guys to legitimize our findings with hard engineering data. Let me show you the kind of things we're talking about."

Stretch took *Fritzy* and a train of four tank sleds around in a circle. Jim rode in the cab with Stretch and watched. When the sleds swung inside the broad circle, their skis rose out of the tractor tracks onto virgin snow. The train pulled easily. When Stretch pulled straight, the skis plowed deeply into the tracked snow and bogged *Fritzy* down.

"Jim," I continued, "we saw this during the pre-launch exercises in McMurdo. Blaisdell was there. Herb Setz, too. It was counterintuitive for sure, but it was plain: we had to get the skis out of the tractor ruts! Herb and I hit on some design changes to pull that off. It was too late then to do us any good this year. But after this season, we'll be fighting just to have a next year. You can help."

Lever and Alger rigged a V-shaped yoke of two long, heavy-duty towing straps. We hitched the four-sled train at the vertex, and two tractors, one each at the wide ends of the V. Placing a load-sensing device at the vertex, they directly measured the towing resistance of the sled load. The tractors took off, separating enough to draw the sled train through the virgin snow between them. The measurements indicated the towing resistance was 50 percent, exactly half the resistance of the sled train when towed in the tractor tracks.

"Jeez, I knew it was easier, Jim. But I didn't know it was *that* easier!" I exclaimed. That was exactly the kind of information we needed.

"Now try this: as you can see, we can't pull everything we've got down the trail. That's why we're shuttling. When our engine-load monitors in the cab show 80 percent to 95 percent, we get high traction slip and we're going down. At our slow speeds, we have no reserve power to blast through the bog. When our engine loads run 65 percent to 70 percent, we rarely get stuck, and we have plenty reserve."

Through a complex analysis, the CRREL engineers elucidated the mechanisms of our immobility. They produced a new load planning tool that resulted in zero "immobilizations." The new tool targeted 65 percent available draw bar pull on virgin snow.

We now spent half of our return time to McMurdo conducting CRREL's expedient tests. We were exhausted, but the CRREL boys were courteous enough to hold their freshness in check while we limped back. Once, they witnessed us repair a broken sled. John Penney unhitched *Fritzy* and backed it into position next to the sled. Stretch grabbed the ladder and secured the heavy chain to the top of the container. Russ fetched the parts, James grabbed the hand tools, and I ran *Fritzy*'s crane. No one said a word. From damage detection to back on the road, the whole process took only thirty minutes.

Lever apologized, "We should never have sent you out at 90 percent draw bar."

"Jim, it was a lot of things. Not just draw bar," I allowed. "We could always drop sleds. Mainly it's this three year rush . . . just not enough time to be thoughtful. You pay for that one way or another. And you have got to be that much more vigilant for each other's safety. Three years is a dangerous pace."

On January 17 the traverse arrived back at the Shear Zone camp. We'd collected all our sidetracked sleds and trailers along the way. Over the next five days, we continued mobility testing in the camp while some shuttled partial loads into Williams Field. We were still operating on the "night" shift.

On January 22 we collected the remaining sleds at the Shear Zone camp and went in together.

"Mac-Ops, Mac-Ops. South Pole Traverse," I radioed.

"Go ahead, South Pole Traverse. This is Mac-Ops."

"Mac-Ops, South Pole Traverse has arrived back at McMurdo with all souls, tractors, and sleds."

After sixty-six days in the field, we arrived back in McMurdo deeply fatigued. We'd take two days off, rest up, and then demobilize and winterize the fleet.

An accounting for our less-than-hoped-for performance had been ordered, and I prepared for the captain's mast. The matter was postponed several times and later deferred all together. It'd resurface when I sought funding for next year.

This year we advanced the face of the trail 425 miles from McMurdo. We returned with three thousand gallons of fuel. Counting shuttling, we covered 1,485 miles all together. That is equivalent to the distance from McMurdo to South Pole, and half way back, with enough fuel to complete the round trip.

It was *all* there. But we could not get *all* of it going south at the same time.

On February 7, 2004, I boarded an LC-130 in McMurdo bound for Pole. At Pole, I met George Blaisdell. George now worked full time with NSF and was in a position to arrange an aerial reconnaissance. Together we boarded another LC-130 and flew over the entire proposed route from Pole back to McMurdo. Once airborne, we took observer positions in the cockpit.

We flew over a vast region of patterned snow on the Polar Plateau: sastrugi, elongated ridge-like features carved in the surface by wind and blowing snow. Sastrugi are generally hard, sharp angled, and make for rough travel by foot, ski, or tractor. We'd seen mild sastrugi down on the Ross Ice Shelf, at most a foot high, but ski-adventurers told of monstrous sastrugi on the Plateau. From the cockpit three thousand feet above them, I thought I saw some monsters.

Farther along the Plateau, as we neared the headwall of the Leverett Glacier, a field of open crevasses bore directly off the port side of the airplane.

"How far would you estimate those crevasses are?" I asked the pilot, figuring him a better judge of distance from his airplane than me.

"About seven miles."

"Copy seven. Would you capture our present position by GPS, please sir?" I asked the navigator.

The navigator read off our coordinates. Later in McMurdo I combined those two pieces of information and plotted the crevasse field on our route map. The plot fell exactly on a proposed turning point. *That* was a point to avoid, not a place to go.

Circling the headwall of the Leverett Glacier and then descending to one thousand feet above surface, we identified many crevasses in the headwall cirque that I'd seen earlier in RADARSAT imagery available from the Canadian Space Agency. There were no unpleasant surprises here, just lots of unpleasant crevasses. Our planned route up the headwall still looked like the best one.

Swooping down the Leverett, again I saw no surprises: glazed, icy, wind-blown surfaces, but no blue ice fields that'd give us new kinds of traction problems. Our predecessors in the mid-nineties who'd targeted the Leverett, had selected well.

Toward the bottom of the glacier a low cloudbank obscured the Leverett's confluence with the Ross Ice Shelf. The cloudbank forced us to climb. From our new height we saw the cloudbank nestled along a broad sweep of the Transantarctic Mountain fronts. It extended well out over the Ross Ice Shelf, but it broke up in the area of RIS-1, our farthest point south.

There were our tracks, where we'd turned around, and where we'd gathered up for camps, all this against the expanse of the snow swamp. We'd taken that ground and held it. And now I was proud of us.

But the cloudbank . . . My official report of the Airborne LC-130 Reconnaissance reads:

> The same cloudbank that thwarted effective visual reconnaissance of the lower Leverett region also obscured the Transantarctic Mountain front and the proposed traverse route from L00 to RIS-5 through RIS-2. There is nothing to add to route-planning knowledge for that segment from this reconnaissance flight.

Underneath that cloudbank hid ground that nearly stopped the whole project. It was the ground we later named "The Shoals of Intractable Funding."

|8| That *Word*:

Ruminations on the Meaning of Road and the Influence of Terrain

The word *came down in a phone call* during the northern summer a year earlier following our first season's success in crossing the Shear Zone. Its impact carried over through the entire project, and waxed especially acute the year of our disappointing advance across the Ross Ice Shelf. The *word* denied the very nature of our project.

I had been seated at my manager's cubicle in the Denver office and reached for the handset, glancing first at the "Caller ID."

"John Wright speaking. That you, George?"

My phone offered a choice of several ringtones. I'd selected a woman's voice that mechanically but pleasantly asked, "Are you there? Are you there?" I usually caught myself at the last second, amused, before answering, "Yes, I am here." Thus, most of my phone conversations began with a smile on my end.

"Good morning," came the familiar and cheerful voice of George Blaisdell in Washington, D.C.

After an exchange of pleasantries, George came to the point, "John, we need you, along with all of us, to refrain from using the word 'road' in connection with the South Pole Traverse Project."

A telltale tik-tik-tik-ing of a computer keyboard sounded in the background of my earpiece. George was multitasking. I was bewildered.

"What's up? We built a road across the Shear Zone, and we're going to build a road to the South Pole."

The National Science Foundation was crafting the environmental documentation for future traverses. The word had New Zealand and Australian environmental coalitions spun up about a highway cutting across the continent. "Road" conjured images of traffic. It misdirected attention from the numbers of LC-130 turboprop flights we might save. Attention that would be better focused on the fuel savings and emissions reductions for cargo delivered by a surface traverse.

Yet a photo of our D8R Caterpillar loading onto a U.S. Air Force C-17 in New Zealand appeared in the Christchurch newspaper last year. Its caption proclaimed: "*THE ROAD TO THE POLE!*" I thought that language came from the NSF. I thought it expressed high-level, programmatic brio.

"George, the French have been running a traverse for years. The Russians run from Mirny to Vostok. The Australians, the Germans, and for all I know the Japanese and the Chinese programs all run traverses. Is this opposition directed at their programs, too?"

"No . . . it's pretty much directed at us. We're the biggest kid on the block, and people like taking shots at the United States."

George was an engineer with a specialty in snow and ice pavements. We were making a road, a road made of snow. And we were going to traverse it with tractors and sleds, just like those other programs did. I couldn't imagine someone of George's background *not* calling a road "a road." Now he pressed me in the unique way a program officer at NSF could lean on a contract worker.

"I need your cooperation to not use the word '*road*.'"

"What word shall we use in place of '*road*'?" I chortled, an edge to my voice.

"We don't have one for that. 'Traverse' works. 'Route.' 'Trail.' All I can say is: In *this* office we will not use *that word* in connection with the project."

"George, you're a messenger here, right?"

"That's right," he allowed, gratefully.

I gripped the phone, feeling my jaw tense. "Message delivered. This is big. I need to think about what it means. Talk later?"

"Any time," George agreed.

I hung up and, leaning way back in my chair, stared at the office ceiling. *No more frontier attitude . . . don't want any cowboys . . . don't call it a road . . . What does it mean?*

An image of another guy in the executive branch came to mind. He looked me right in the eyes through the television screen. "That depends on what the meaning of the word 'is,' is." Nobody wanted duplicity associated with our project.

I shook my head, rising from my ergonomic chair to take a stroll outside. I might find fresh air, and clarity.

The day was pretty and fresh. The few clouds brought soothing, long views of the Front Range Mountains to the west. My thoughts wandered as I strolled through the parking lot. Imagine grabbing the radio in the middle of the Ross Ice Shelf: "Stretch, I must insist you not use that word."

We all built roads. And that's what we called them. Don't get off the road. Got to work on the road. We didn't run helter skelter over the sea ice on those Marble Point traverses. We built and groomed a road from the snow resting on top of the sea ice. When the snow road set up, curing into a hardened surface, we flew across it. Deadheading back we covered the sixty miles in three and a half hours. Because we had a road.

I could tell the crew, "NSF does not want us to call it a road, this thing we're building to run our tractors on." We'd still call it a road. And I'd suffer their snickers for a short while during the season.

But in presentations to folks in the contractor's office, to folks at NSF, and at times to journalists, I had to be on my toes because "road" was instinctive. It reached far back into collective human memory. The road to perdition. The swan's road. Road as "way." Don't go down that road. Take the high road. Road map. Asphalt road. Macadam road. Dirt road. Snow road.

What are the consequences of not calling a road a road?

George Orwell described "Newspeak" in his classic future fiction *1984.* Newspeak deliberately limited vocabulary's range for the masses. In that future world Newspeak eliminated nuance and shades of meaning from interpersonal discourse. Argument, opposition, debate, all vanished. That was Big Brother's object.

There were no Big Brothers here. There were just people like George, Dave, me, Russ . . . we wanted this traverse to become reality. Who were we fooling?

If we weren't building a road after all, then we were just driving a tractor over a map. On paper we'd arrive at South Pole in no time. But we had to break trail first, and we had to build a road-in-fact to make that trail stronger and smoother. Across the street, orange State of Colorado dump trucks were busy maintaining the road.

Build. Maintain.

If we took away "road" from the language of our project, then we ignored the fundamental nature of the project. And we confronted unreal expectations for it.

Unreal expectations for time and money . . . those are the consequences of not calling a road a road.

I told Dave this was not a three-year project.

Our road was made of snow.

Most animals in groups will not wander aimlessly across a snowfield, breaking their own trail. Breaking trail is hard work. With a herd of caribou migrating across the snow-covered coastal plain of northern Alaska, for example, one caribou in front works his way through knee-high snow. Each following caribou beats the trail down more and more. The trailbreaker's job rotates once in a while, but the herd moves forward in a long thin wedge, compacting the snow, making the path stronger. By its own traffic the herd makes a road.

The United States Antarctic Program builds fine snow roads. With vigorous effort, we've even built snow pavements that support a loaded C-17 cargo jet on wheels. There's not much to it in concept: compact the snow. Get on top, and stay on top. Drag and groom the surface. Smooth it and keep drift snow down. The hard part is breaking trail in the first place.

It *was* hard, but even in the last year of our project my boss's boss stunned me when he casually dismissed our efforts, reducing them to: "It's just a matter of time and distance."

"Well," I countered dryly, nonplussed, "there is the small matter of terrain."

We had CRREL mobility engineers working with us throughout the project, combining their ideas with ours, to derive mechanical mobility solutions. But our mountaineers often gave our best insights into the nature of the terrain that impeded our mobility. Their contributions were important to us. Because of them, I can now speak somewhat authoritatively about it.

For example, near surface, the snow is porous. Air transpires through the mass. When the local weather is stable over a long time, individual snowflakes re-form into angular grains, like sugar crystals. The grains do not immediately bond with their neighbors but remain a loose aggregate of tiny beads. Snow scientists have technical names for this snow form. When we found ourselves in vast areas of the stuff, we called it a "swamp."

Mountaineer "Scooter" Metcalf had joined us in the second field season when we were stuck in the Ross Ice Shelf swamp. We didn't understand it as a swamp at that time. All we knew was our tractors sank in it, our sleds broke in it, and for us to make any headway across it we had to split our trains and shuttle. When Scooter stepped off the Twin Otter, he stepped into a group of frustrated stiffs wooden-headedly slogging south. His voice carried a high-pitched edge, mimicking a wise-cracking comic, and we adjusted to our new seventh man.

Scooter spent his first day on the trail riding with me in the *Elephant Man*.

"They tell me in McMurdo you're a pretty serious guy . . . a no-nonsense boss," Scooter opened the conversation while I was busy.

I'd just started the *Elephant Man* rolling, pleased we hadn't wallowed into the snow right away. His question hung a bit longer before I looked across the cab. "Well, that's McMurdo."

"They told me you're hard to get along with," Scooter said, staying on point.

"Then that depends on who *they* are."

Many people would say that. I preferred keeping an amused distance there. But this was not McMurdo. I needed to rope in Scooter right away.

"I'm glad you're here, Scooter. Understand, though, you have walked into a scene where we are finding and solving problems daily. Some we can solve now. Some we can't solve this year. There's not much you can do about that. But I've got some problems you can help with."

"Problem solvers, eh?" Scooter interjected, gazing through the windshield past the colorful tractors against the featureless white ahead.

"That's right." I looked across the cab at him until he looked back at me. "Do you know anything about us?"

"Not really. This is my first time on the Ice. You guys are all Ice veterans. I've heard some names, and what some people say about them."

"Like I'm hard to get along with?" I looked ahead again.

"Yeah. Like that. And that you never smile," Scooter cracked back.

"That's my *face*, Scooter." I sighed. *Elephant Man* was still on top of the snow. "We have two superb mechanics. Russ Magsig has been coming down to the Ice since Christ was a corporal. He's got phenomenal experience down here, and we all learn from him. Russ will rarely sit down and talk with you, though. Pretty much a hermit. John Penney served several years at Pole as chief mechanic. I worked with him there. John is articulate, keenly intelligent, and you should credit him with far more 'stuff' than you might if you thought him 'just a mechanic.' You'll be working with John Penney. He's captain of the flagging crew, and he's a natural teacher. You'll wind up rotating through different jobs on his crew."

"That's the radar crew in the PistenBully?"

"Right."

Norbert ran the radar on that crew. He came out, like Scooter, to a group that was beat up already. They'd have that in common. Norbert would teach Scooter how to run the radar.

We jostled over the snow at three miles per hour, staggering our tracks with the tractor in front of us. "Then you've got James McCabe and Stretch Vaitonis. Both of those guys are superb equipment operators. Both are gentlemen of the highest caliber. If you think redneck, rough, and crude when you think heavy equipment operator, then you think wrong when it comes to those two."

"What about you? What should I think when I think *you*?"

"You're finding that out right now." I caught his eye across the cab, again.

We weren't a military operation, and I didn't expect blind allegiance. We were an egalitarian group. Individually we were an introspective lot, relishing time alone in our cabs, left to our own thoughts. But we enjoyed fellowship and banter at the end of the day. With all the experience we'd amassed, and the unknowns we faced, everybody's input was equally valuable. I happened to be the headman, and I made the decisions when a decision was necessary. If I made a dumb decision, every one of these guys would say "Fuck you!" I would, too.

"Have you made a decision yet?" Scooter asked, still sounding smart with me.

"I have."

"Well . . . ?"

"We're going to keep going south until half our time or half our fuel runs out. We're going to find out what it takes to cross this damn Shelf. And then we're going to turn around and go back. That is my decision."

A long silence followed as the *Elephant Man* lunged forward over the virgin snows. Soon enough, Scooter would see a tractor sink or a sled break. Then he'd stand off to the side and watch us fall into our routines.

We already speculated on the roots of our disappointments. Popular culprits ranged from soft snow and high ambient temperatures to tractor tread and sled designs. Meanwhile, we were stuck with it for the year. Virgin snow lay in front of us, and behind us lay no road but that which we'd built. Putting a fully loaded, even overloaded, traverse fleet into the trail-breaking business had been a mistake. NSF expected we'd make it to the top of the Leverett this second year. We'd be lucky to get to the base of it.

"What would you like me to do besides run with the flagging crew, John?" Scooter asked.

"One component of our difficulties *is* this soft snow. You mountaineers have your own take on snow, and I need some of that. I want you to do your mountaineering thing and teach me what you learn about it."

"Like dig snow pits? I can dig snow pits for you!" Scooter sounded enthusiastic now. We'd dug a few pits back when Delaney was with us, but we hadn't kept it up.

"Excellent, Scooter. Meter-deep pits ought to do it. Our troubles are in the top two or three feet. We've got to work hard to sink farther than that. I'll ask Norbert to help you."

From that day on, we had snow pits at every campsite. Scooter and Norbert measured snow densities and temperatures down the walls of their pits. They correlated that data to the snow layers they exposed.

We didn't have a rammsonde, the standard snow science penetrometer for measuring the unconfined, compressive strength of snow. Instead, Scooter used a mountaineer's trick for empirically deriving the same information. He measured resistance to penetration along the pit walls by jamming things into it. A knife measured the hardest, most resistant end of his scale. A pencil, then a finger, then two fingers, four fingers, and, finally, a fist graded down to the soft end. Scooter and Norbert went the extra mile by including measurements of our rut depths near each pit.

One flat-light day, I looked around the module sleds and spotted Scooter's head floating in the whiteness two hundred feet away. Just his head. Floating nearby, at Scooter's chin level, Norbert's crouching form took notes. Towering above all, Stretch patiently leaned against a floating shovel and stared down at Scooter. The colorful phantasms drew me over.

"What do you see in this one?" I asked from the pit's edge. Scooter's incorporeal form had now materialized into his entire body down in a hole.

"This is the stuff that's giving you troubles." He scooped out a handful of grainy snow near the bottom of the pit wall, and held it out on his black gloves. The grains were the size of small BBs. "This is TG snow. Uniform-sized, facetted."

"TG?"

"Temperature gradient. It's weak stuff."

"That's like what Delaney showed us from his little core tubes. It doesn't stick together," I recalled.

"Yeah. Well, most of this pit wall is TG snow. But see this thin layer here?" Scooter pointed to a layer three inches thick, a foot below the surface. Its finer grains stuck together, laminated. "This is WF snow. It's stronger. You want more of this stuff," he declared.

"What's WF?"

"Wind fucked . . . It's my own term. Some call it wind slab. Stand over here on this edge of the pit."

I stepped where he indicated and the ground gave way under my weight. The WF slab cracked. The TG material supporting it collapsed, spilling a pile of icy BBs onto the pit floor.

"See?" he asked.

"QED," I answered.

"Right. Whatever that means. Anyway, all the pit walls show mostly TG snow below the surface crust. Just a few thin WF layers. Altogether, that don't support squat."

"Copy that, Scooter. Then the best we can hope for as long as we're in this stuff is to smash it down, and hope it sinters into some sort of pavement by the time we turn around and go back."

"Road building is your thing. Snow pits are mine."

✧ ✧ ✧

Back in the living module I pulled out a couple of references from our traveling library and opened them for Scooter and Norbert on our galley table. One was a thick copy of Albert Crary's glaciological studies from his late-1950s science traverse, when he'd circumnavigated the Ross Ice Shelf. I turned to the contour map on which he'd plotted snow strengths.

"Crary distinguishes between hard and soft snow on this map. The contour lines have numerical values. He doesn't give their units, but I think they derive from rammsonde measurements."

Norbert and Scooter studied the map. Crary's track ran around the edge of the Ice Shelf. All his snow strength measurements came from along that track. We were cutting across the middle of the Shelf, where Crary didn't go. We had crossed his track back near the Shear Zone. We'd cross it again somewhere up ahead.

"You see these closed contour loops he's mapped around the middle? Where we are right now?"

Scooter and Norbert nodded. Those contours indicated what Crary believed would be the softest, weakest snow. He had to extrapolate those values over a hundred miles because he wasn't here.

"Scooter, do you think your TG snow is the same soft, weak stuff Crary was talking about?"

"I want to look over this report more closely," Scooter said. "But I think so."

"If it is so," I speculated, "then there's hope that we'll come out of this swamp. Up here closer to the mountains, where Crary went, the contours show a harder surface. Now let me show you this other one."

The other report was only a half-inch thick. It collected contributions to a traverse conference held in Washington, D.C., in 1994. NSF sponsored it and CRREL hosted it. The list of attendees named French and Russian traverse experts, Caterpillar tractor dealers, and other snow vehicle manufacturers. Names like Dave Bresnahan and George Blaisdell rang familiar.

"Check this name," I turned the page. "Russell Magsig."

Their eyebrows rose. I added, "Our Russell has been in on this for a long time. Respect that. But here's what I want to show you now . . ."

The next section represented glaciologist's contributions. I'd never met Robert Bindschadler or Gordon Hamilton, but I had heard their names around the program a lot. Their notes described criteria for selecting the Leverett route across the Transantarctics. We were not there to debate that. We were going to test it. But their list of criteria included features they thought should be avoided: abundance of crevasses, steep slopes, blue ice, and "depth hoar."

"Scooter, the alpine mountaineers in my home town are always talking about weak depth hoar layers at the base of the snow pack. They predict avalanches on account of it. As I understand, that stuff is pretty much the same as what you've been digging here?"

Scooter nodded, his eyes wide open and attentive. "Right. The old timers used to call it depth hoar. These days we call it TG, and the process that makes it is kinetic metamorphism. It ain't going to avalanche on this Shelf, of course, but it's the same stuff that collapses under your tractors as you squirm through it."

"Thank you. I thought so. Those glaciologists thought depth hoar should be avoided. And I reckon we know why, now. You put those guys together with Crary's projections and you have this big swamp. Had I understood that ahead of time, I might've made a strong argument for building a road across it first, before we brought out heavy loads to break trail."

Scooter cocked his head. "Hey, nobody can blame you, John."

"Blame's beside the point. That's dinosaur bones. I'm looking at that three-year schedule to complete, and wondering how big this swamp is."

We got our first indication on December 27 that second year, still headed south. Quite suddenly in the afternoon, all our tractors started riding up on top of the snow. The overcast that obscured our skies for weeks rolled back. Golden glints of sunlight reflected off the distant mountains now rising for the first time on our southern horizon. Scooter invited me over to his snow pit that evening. I dropped down beside him.

"Look at this, John." He pointed out the various layers exposed in his pit wall.

"No BBs. Is this all WF snow?"

"A lot of it is. But look at these layers with the finer grains. This is equitemperature stuff."

"What? ET, now?"

"Just another name. But check this . . . it's bonded. It doesn't spill."

I stood up in the pit, studying the new mountains. "You suppose they have anything to do with this snow being here? I'm talking about weather and wind up close to them. Not like those foggy doldrums behind us."

"Could be. There's a lot more to learn."

"If we've just come out of three hundred miles of swamp, then that would be wonderful."

But we would wait a year to find out. The next day was December 28. There was a red mark on the calendar. We turned around to run back on the road we'd built behind us.

Snow accumulates in Antarctica to such an extent that, over time and depth, it compacts itself under its own weight. It squeezes the air out of its mass until it becomes dense ice. When that ice cracks, you get a crevasse. If you're building a road across Antarctica, crevasses are a terrain problem that will slow you down, or kill you. We understood this, and sometimes our knowledge flowed back to the mountaineers.

Matthew Szundy had rotated in for Scooter as we retreated from our farthest south. His boyishly handsome, clean-shaven, and smiling face loudly proclaimed: I am ALERT!

During our retreat, we stopped at a place we called the George Trend to explore for crevasses that might be lurking there. Blaisdell had called my attention to a satellite image where he noticed a staggered array of linear features cutting across our path. If the features themselves weren't crevasses, they might be telltales of crevasse country. Our outbound trip proved that a hundred-foot-wide, twenty-mile-long path through the George Trend was free of crevasses. That was good enough for us then. But on our return, I wanted to see if we could actually find a crevasse there.

Matthew and I went exploring in the PistenBully. He ran the radar, and I drove. Over two days we ran one-mile squares on both sides of our trail. Cloudy skies gave us no surface definition. I navigated by GPS. But even had there been clear skies, we had no landmarks. At 120 miles from the Shear Zone, the peaks of the Transantarctic Range hid below all our horizons.

While we mapped out one of our western squares, the clouds broke a tiny bit. A shaft of bright sunlight struck the snowfield in front of us, and cast an oddly curved shadow on the snow. I broke Matthew's concentration. "I don't believe my eyes. Do you see what I see? Is that a *hill* in front of us?"

Matthew looked up from the radar screen and out the windshield: "You don't believe your eyes? That looks like a hill to me."

"What's a hill doing out here?" Matthew was new to the Ross Ice Shelf. Did he get how weird that was?

"Maybe we're in a trough?" he suggested.

That would mean we were in a bottom, looking up, with another hill behind us. And we hadn't felt any slope-change by the seat of our pants. We'd never have seen this hill if it hadn't been for that shaft of sunlight.

We went ahead to find out what the radar saw. Matthew reported the stratigraphy beneath us rose as we started climbing. It flattened out as we crested the hill. That meant some sort of fold lay below us, an anticline of sorts.

We continued into a broad, sunlit stretch of flat ground.

"STOP!" Matthew cried.

I let go of everything. The PistenBully automatically stopped.

"I got a crevasse," Matthew turned the computer screen toward me.

He was on it. The clear black needle-form in the radar image was probably ten feet in front of us now. It looked narrow, like a crack we could drive over. But it was too small to account for what we'd seen on the satellite images. I looked right into Matthew's bright blue eyes.

"Good job. You know, I teased those CRREL guys all the way from the Shear Zone out to RIS-1. They never found a single crevasse on the open Shelf. But here, on your first day out, you found one! You are *good*, man! You are *much* better than those CRREL guys!"

"But I thought finding no crevasses *was* good?" Matthew puzzled over my praise.

"Finding no crevasses *is* good, but it didn't stop me from teasing them. Now I'm teasing you."

Matthew laughed uneasily. He was brand new to our haggard mob and needed to fit in right away. He knew his routine job would be running the radar and looking for crevasses. He'd dealt with alpine crevasses as a guide, but these were Shelf crevasses. And our job was to get tractor trains through, not paying clients on foot.

That evening in our galley, long after the crew retired to their bunks, I slouched wide awake on the galley bench. All the scenes of our ignominious defeat in the snow swamp replayed for me on the ceiling. I plotted solutions, but I wondered if NSF would receive our horror stories as whining complaints or as lessons learned. Matthew surprised me as he stepped in from outside.

"Hi, John. You're not asleep?"

"No, I am cogitating."

"Me, too. Cogitating. Been thinking about crevasses," Matthew confessed.

"Have a seat?"

He dragged the caster chair out of the comms booth and sat across the floor from me. My legs stretched across to a stool on the other side of the galley table.

"I'm concerned about these crevasses. I'm not sure we're paying enough attention to them," Matthew said. I saw where this conversation was headed.

"Well, that's actually an old joke," I replied.

Matthew's neck straightened. "What?"

"A *very* old joke," I repeated. "You know the story of the blind men and the elephant?"

"Yeah, I know that story," Matthew said, probably wondering if he was getting through to me at all.

"Okay. One blind man says an elephant is like a tree. Another one says it's like a wall. And another one says it's like a snake . . . You with me?"

Matthew smiled at the twist his earnest conversation had taken. I was going to enjoy this.

"Well, I'm talking to my hometown Rabbi," I continued. "Marvin Paioff, the smartest man I ever met, and our conversation turns to Jews' preoccupation with anti-Semitism. 'Marvin,' I said, 'I had a college buddy named Jeff Schwartz. We shared an English literature class together. Every time we had to write a paper, I'd explore my favorite theme of medieval knighthood. Jeff would explore anti-Semitism. So it'd be 'The Value System of the Red Cross Knight in Edmund Spenser's *Faerie Queene*,' for me. For Jeff, it'd be 'Anti-Semitism in Chaucer's *Wife of Bath's Tale*.' Now, Marvin, that's what Jeff was interested in. Exploring anti-Semitism. He did it every chance he got. And I explored chivalry, every chance I got . . . until I understood it to be licensed hypocrisy. But I've noticed over the years that many of my Jewish friends have Jeff's same infatuation with anti-Semitism. Why is that?' Do you know what he told me?"

Matthew, thoroughly lost, was nevertheless intrigued. "I have no idea what Rabbi Paioff told you."

"He told me the same thing I just told you."

"What?"

"That it's a very old joke. And he asked me if I knew the story of the blind men and the elephant?"

"But what's the joke?"

"Oh . . . you want to know that?"

"Yes!" Matthew demanded.

"Okay. I was wondering. A U.N. delegation studies the elephant. When they're done, they write up their reports. The United States representative turns in his: *The Use of Elephant Manure as an Agricultural Crop Enhancement.* The German's report is titled *The Elephant as a War Machine.* And the Frenchman writes about *The Love Life of the Elephant.* You know what the Israeli's paper is?"

"No," cried Matthew, now grinning from ear to ear.

"*Anti-Semitism and the Elephant.*"

"Aw jeez," he laughed. "I thought we were talking about crevasses!"

"We *are* talking about crevasses. Haven't you been paying attention?"

Matthew gestured with open palms and open mouth, as if to say, "What? What?"

I took a more serious tone. "You're a mountaineer. You've seen a jillion crevasses. You're a crevasse expert. If you're like other mountaineers, you figure you've got a lock on crevasses. Am I right?"

"Yes," Matthew said forthrightly, now more engaged with the subject. There was no backing down in him. No false modesty. He was going to work great for us.

"Okay. Matthew, you're a mountaineer, and you've got a lock on crevasses. Think about old, gruff Russell. He was in the Shear Zone when *Linda* went down. He saw that huge bulldozer disappear with two guys on board, so Russell knows something about crevasses."

Matthew's attention grew.

"Think about Stretch. Stretch has run that eighty-six thousand pound D8 Cat right up to the very edge of crevasses. Right there in the Shear Zone, last year . . . He filled them full of snow and drove over them. Stretch knows something about crevasses. And those two guys are in their bunks, not twenty feet away from you."

My point began to dawn on Matthew.

"Now me," I said. "I have a feel for how huge masses of material behave under stress. And I've studied and studied this route. *I* know something about crevasses. My first choice is to *avoid* them. Our problem is we've got to find the crevasses before they find us. My second choice is to destroy them. Like we did in the Shear Zone. You're a mountaineer, and a damn good one I understand. *You* know something about crevasses, too. But you haven't got a lock on them. See what I'm getting at?"

Matthew nodded deeply.

"We *all* think about crevasses *all* the time," I said. "And you can be sure every one of us is scared to death of them. That's why I'm up late at night and can't sleep. I'm looking ahead to the Kelly Trend, wondering what crevasses may be lurking there tomorrow."

Matthew sat back in his chair. I never moved my legs, or changed my slouching posture. I wanted to relax, and I was doing a fine job of it.

"I've enjoyed our conversation, John," Matthew said before retiring to our bunkroom.

"I have, too, Matthew. I'm glad you're with us," I complimented him. "And if Jeff Schwartz were here, he'd have something to tell us about anti-Semitism and the crevasse."

Matthew went to bed, laughing. An hour later, so did I.

Back in the "real" world, Raymond Lilley, an Associated Press writer from Wellington, New Zealand, reached me by e-mail while I was still in McMurdo. We'd just concluded the second year's slog across the Ross Ice Shelf, and I would be heading home soon to the real "real" world. The contractor's manager of public communications referred Lilley to me.

Lilley's beat included the USAP's doings, particularly those emanating from Ross Island. New Zealand claimed the island as its territorial dependency. The first 640 miles of our route to the base of the Leverett Glacier started at Ross Island and ran right across New Zealand's claimed sector. The traverse project was big news.

Lilley's interest was not one of territorial encroachment. The Antarctic Treaty Nations set aside all such issues when they agreed how nations should get along on the continent. Instead, the issue of public interest for Lilley ran toward the boldness of our undertaking, the environmental consequences of ongoing traverse operations, and the historical nature of the project. New Zealanders were particularly fascinated by the project since their man, Sir Edmund Hillary, had been the first to drive a tractor to South Pole. Fifty years later, here come Americans talking tractors in terms suggesting traffic.

Lilley asked good questions, referring to that which we were building as "road." Answering him challenged my lexicon as I sought to avoid using *that word*. Excerpts from the e-mail interview ran:

Lilley: What was the toughest part of the road-forming?
Wright: It is all work, and none of it easy. Last year it took us 3 months to go 3 miles across a crevasse field. The tough part of that was the tension of working in a place full of dangerous, hidden crevasses. This year we went out to 425 miles across the snows of the Ross Ice Shelf. That was breaking trail . . . a long, slow slog in soft snow. The toughest part of that was always urging for more distance and having our hopes thwarted by the soft snows.
Lilley: Will that work stay in place, particularly through the shear zone?
Wright: Yes. I need to qualify that. The improved surface—marked by bamboo poles with flags—will remain compacted and harder as a result of our work. It will stay in the same place relative to the flags. But "in place?" No . . . the Ice Shelf on whose surface it is built is dynamic . . . in slow, fluid motion. So, the improved surface we built moves with the flow of the Ice Shelf. We have measured 6.5 feet per day in places. But as the ice moves, it takes the flags with it, and so we know where the improved surface is . . . next to the flags. "Particularly through the Shear Zone?" Our passage through the Shear Zone—made last year—remained intact and fit for passage this year. The passage was about 1,000 feet farther north than when we left it last year (due to Ice Shelf movement), and about 100 feet longer (the ice had stretched). We located 5 new crevasses on our crossing. These were juvenile features, not big enough to require mitigation . . . yet. We keep our eye on these, as well as the other 32 we dealt with last year.
Lilley: What is the length of the ice road now, after two years driving/forming it?

Wright: 425 miles.

Lilley: Do you have a guesstimate of the time pole trips will take once the road is through?

Wright: Early feasibility projections performed by engineers at CRREL (US Army Corps of Engineers—Cold Regions Research and Engineering Laboratories) in 1999–2000 estimated 20 days outbound and loaded, and ten days return deadheading—a 30-day round trip. Any update on that estimate should await the actual completion of the passage.

Lilley: How different are the tractors you use from the Fordson tractor Sir Ed Hillary and the expedition used to reach the pole?

Wright: I thought Sir Ed Hillary drove a Massey Ferguson? Anyhow . . . "how different are they?" You have seen Hillary's. Pretty small. Not meant for cargo delivery . . . that wasn't his purpose. I believe he was hauling his own expedition supplies and air dropping supplies as well. Not unlike a "science traverse" today. Conversely, we're aiming to haul not just stuff we need, but a whole lot more stuff that is needed at South Pole. So we have heavier tractors, heavier loads, more horsepower, the advantage of modern engine and tractor technology and far more years' experience in the Antarctic environment than did pioneer Hillary. My hat's off to him.

Lilley: Do you think the pole road an attainable goal? (What I mean by this is whether, given such obstacles as the shear zone, bad weather, etc., it can become a functioning road in your estimate?)

Wright: Yes.

Lilley: Is it possible/likely the road could be used outside the strict summer season?

Wright: Doubtful. The limiter would be the unavailability of emergency support in the winter months.

Lilley: Does the "road" have a working name?

Wright: No.

Lilley wrote an eight hundred word piece that incorporated our interview, adding text and quotes from other sources concerned with environmental impacts. Among the more interesting speculations were those for environmental impacts of incidental tourists who might want to use the road. Lilley's article went out on the AP wire under the title "Ice Highway being cut to Earth's

Last Frontier." Other news media picked up the story, and the headline freely changed as local editors adapted it to local interests. An *Arizona Republic* article, printed in Phoenix, called it "Interstate 10 Below." A friend at home told me radio announcer Paul Harvey decried the idea as a dumb waste of U.S. taxpayers' money.

After Lilley's article came out, NSF amended its public communications policy. Henceforth, all public statements about our project would be cleared through Peter West of the NSF's Office of Legal and Public Affairs. West addressed a large convention room filled with Annual Planning Conference attendees. He explained that of all media inquiries he fielded for NSF at-large that year, over 60 percent of them focused on the South Pole Traverse project.

Meanwhile, I never called it a road. Not to Lilley anyway. Remote Oversnow Antarctic Dragway worked. R.O.A.D. But that depended on what the meaning of the word *road* was.

At some point politics' swamps and jargon's crevasses would stop progress altogether. We needed to get back to pioneering the real thing.

|9| Farthest South— Year Three

"Burma-Shave alert!"

Operators in six tractors motored south across the snow-covered infinity toward a stark blue-on-white horizon. Each turned up their radio volume and waited. Green flags on bamboo poles ticked by every quarter mile. One by one, each marker harkened back to days when some of us delighted in finding verse by the side of the road.

The radios squawked again: "Roberts climbs . . . In lofty places . . . Has close shaves . . . On Everest's faces . . ." Then a pause: "BURMA-SHAVE!"

"Score!" another radio sang out.

"Maybe a seven."

"Six."

"Nah, that's an eight or nine. Good to the last strop!"

That so many of us appreciated Burma-Shave jingles betrayed our average age.

The going was much better for us this third year across the Ross Ice Shelf. This year we needed distance, and we were getting it. We cruised over a well-packed trail. Only six inches of new snow covered it in a year. Get off the trail, and we were back in the swamp. But staying on it, we turned in record fifty-mile days. Not once did we shuttle a load. We were happier this year. It showed in our banter. Last year we hailed one another by a tractor's fleet number. This year we were *Fritzy, Elephant Man, Quadzilla.*

Fritzy was mine this year. It was the dual-track yellow tractor with the rear mounted knuckle-boom crane. Fassi, an Italian company, made the crane. Russ

Magsig could never quite remember Fassi. But *Fritzy* stuck well enough with him. That worked for the rest of us, too.

Russ ran the *Elephant Man*, the modified dual-track yellow tractor with the crew cab mounted above the engine that I'd run last year. *Elephant Man* was ugly, but it took its name because it pitched and rolled like a howdah on an Indian elephant's back.

Brad Johnson took *Quadzilla*, the red, articulated four-track Case. Our strongest puller, other than the bulldozer, *Quadzilla* mimicked the mighty monster's name.

Stretch's D8R bulldozer went by *Mary Lou*. All the historic D8s at McMurdo took the names of cherished women: *Linda*, *Rebecca*, *Mary Ann*, *Pamela*. Ours held to that tradition, taking the name of Judy Goldsberry's twin sister.

Judy ran a tractor we borrowed from the McMurdo fleet. We never named #283.

We were still two days away from our farthest south at RIS-1, but we'd arrive a day ahead of schedule. We'd sleep in and play for a day, waiting for the small Twin Otter to land beside us. When it came, we'd switch out Mike Roberts and Russ Alger. They'd been good comrades.

A few days before, we crowded into our mobile galley waiting out a snow storm. Mike Roberts gave us an engaging lecture on climbing Everest. The lanky mountaineer had been to Everest's top more than once. With his lecture, he took us all there. His stature among his peers was world-class. His bearing as a human being brought out the best in all of us.

We'd lose a lot of laughs when Alger boarded the plane, too. Alger installed instruments on our sleds to monitor their response to terrain. One morning he fiddled with pitch-and-roll sensors on the living module, delaying our morning's launch. Russ Magsig quipped, "We have just enough technology to stop progress all together!" Alger giggled. He never spoke a cross word, or lost his sense of humor.

Outside *Fritzy*'s elegantly curved, tinted window glass the cold lands and green flags rambled by. I relished our high spirits, but I could not recall starting another Ice season already exhausted. I had tried the meaning of "full support for the development of the South Pole Traverse."

✦ ✦ ✦

Traverse know-how eluded the United States Antarctic Program. It had developed the finest polar airlift capacity of any nation, but it had abandoned long-haul surface traversing decades ago.

Existing technology didn't work on the virgin snows of the Ross Ice Shelf. We'd proved we couldn't pull all our loads with four tractors last year. We needed a fifth. That tractor sat in McMurdo, scheduled to be dismantled and flown to Pole in pieces on three LC-130 flights. We could drive it intact to Pole, if we could get it. Simple.

Instead, NSF ordered a study of matrixed scenarios: the use of a fifth tractor, on one hand, weighed against fuel delivered by air to four tractors in the deep field on the other hand. My study concluded only the fifth tractor eliminated shuttling and refueling delays. Two days before its release, Erick Chiang and the accountant declared: "There will be no fifth tractor for the South Pole Traverse."

George Blaisdell had arranged a CRREL study demonstrating the complete traverse could be managed with only four tractors. But those engineers' sharp-pencils admitted no margin. They had not broken trail across the swamp.

One slim possibility remained: use of another McMurdo fleet tractor on the trail, while McMurdo used South Pole's tractor until time to fly it to Pole. In late September, days before we deployed to the Ice, I called Dave Bresnahan.

"Dave, we have a nonsense situation here. We have won a fifth McMurdo tractor. And we have a fifth tractor operator. Judy has completed her physical qualification and all other paperwork. She's scheduled to depart North Dakota to join us on traverse. Her ticketing deadline is two days from now. Human resources here will not allow the travel department to ticket Judy because they're waiting for official hiring approval from the accountant in your office. Can you get me some word from NSF—like *now*—so we can get Judy to the Ice?"

Judy Goldsberry, a ranch woman from Makoti, North Dakota, wanted to "go hell-ing around the continent" with us. When she gave up ranching in Makoti, she worked as an equipment operator on a pipeline crew. Then she moved into town and taught physical education in the public schools. These days, during the northern summers, she helped run a horse packing business on the Maah Daah Hey Trail in the Roosevelt National Park. During the southern summers, Judy worked on the Ice. The last couple of years she'd been the heavy equipment foreman at Williams Field. She'd often seen us off with a friendly word at the city limits as we ran back and forth to the Shear Zone, working our way across crevasses.

I met Judy on the road to Williams Field skiway my first year in 1993 when I'd stuck the blaster's truck in soft snow. Judy then patrolled the road with packing and grooming equipment, and she stopped to pull me out. Being new to the Ice, I braced for the hard time McMurdo hands usually gave a newcomer. The dark-haired, lean woman got out of her tractor and showed me kindness instead. After pulling me out of my wallow, she explained how the flag lines on the Willy road worked.

I remarked on Judy's instinct to kindness years later, and thanked her for it.

She smiled back, explaining, "Oh, I just loved that job! People are *nice* to you when you're helping them get unstuck." Judy was a good hand. And tough.

This year, Judy flew down to McMurdo on the same plane with me. It was early October. Right behind us came U.S. Air Force C-17s bearing our improved sled parts. Our hopes for success turned on these parts and the fifth tractor.

Two days away now from the farthest south of our second year at RIS-1, lumbering toward that blue-on-white horizon, recollections of time wasted invaded my cab. Outside, on our compacted snow road, everything—*everything*—we did to improve our mobility after our disappointing second year worked. But beyond that wooden post at RIS-1 lay virgin snow and no trail. Somewhere ahead lurked a crevasse field we didn't know much about.

"Alger!" I radioed the radar team ranging in front of the heavy fleet.

"Go ahead, *Fritzy*," Alger drawled with accents of Michigan.

"When you guys get to our campsite at the end of the day, sweep a broad circle around the camp flag, a couple hundred foot radius. We're going to do that every day from now on. We'll call that our camp circle. If you don't find any crevasses on that circle, then we'll pull into it and make camp. Do you understand?"

"You betcha, *Fritzy*."

Route planning consumed me in the off-season. The land could kill us. Historical works from the earliest explorers, reports from 1950s science expeditions, opinions from modern glaciologists, maps both modern and old, and all the latest satellite information I could get my hands on went into route planning. Two-week excursions into matrixed analyses that nobody read wasted time that would've been far better spent making sure my crew survived.

Terrain assessments often pointed to regions of crevasse *probability* rather than certainty. I'd briefed the crew on suspected crevasses ahead. But with our mixed backgrounds, probability meant different things. The ultimate crevasse hazard, however, meant the same to each of us. Alger's PistenBully tracks would say, "stay inside this circle," a safe perimeter everybody could grasp at a glance.

"John, I could smell the fear on you guys this morning when you brought up the snow swamp. Last year must have been just horrible." Judy caught me outside, attending to *Fritzy* on the morning of November 30. We were breaking camp at RIS-1, starting our tractors and rigging for travel.

"It was. You understand we're going onto virgin snow? We travel close from now on. Watch that train in front of you. If a sled's breaking, we need to catch it before the whole thing collapses."

"I got that loud and clear," Judy acknowledged, moving off to #283.

We'd arrived at RIS-1 four days earlier, fully one month ahead of our arrival the year before. Ahead, ice-covered peaks of the Transantarctic Range broke up our formerly smooth horizon. While we waited for the Twin Otter, we spent a breezy day under clear blue skies tending to camp chores and playing.

Brad, Mike, and Stretch flew a colorful, two-handed parasail kite my wife and kids had given us. Brad, flying the kite, stepped onto one of our slick recovery skis. Soon that kite pulled three grown, giggling men, one after the other, around the camp circle, riding the three-foot-by-ten-foot plastic sheet like a surfboard.

John Penney launched his remote-controlled model airplane and flew it overhead. He'd attached a lightweight digital camera under its wing. From that day on, when weather allowed, we enjoyed seeing oblique aerial photos of our camp on his laptop.

The Twin Otter brought Jim Lever and our replacement mountaineer Susan Detweiler. She was a svelte, muscular woman wearing long brunette tresses. Her eyes, her whole bearing, said, "I'm here to help." During the next day in camp, the newcomers learned the ropes.

John Penney captained the radar team on a training mission to lay out the next several miles of trail. All three team members had to coordinate their work, and that required practice. Jim and Susan were new to the business. Jim operated the PistenBully, navigating the course I gave him. Susan rode shotgun with the radar, looking for hidden crevasses. John ran behind them on a snowmobile, pulling a wooden Nansen sled loaded with green flags. At day's end, John pronounced his team good to go. Green flags, planted straight and on course every quarter mile, marked the safe path.

On the morning Judy smelled our fear, we launched the heavy fleet down John Penney's nine miles of newly flagged trail leading south. We didn't find crevasses that day. Within two hours, a fierce head wind blowing horizontal snow found us. We hunkered down at the end of John Penney's flag line with nine miles made good. The Leverett Glacier sat 230 miles away.

The blizzard stayed with us through the next morning. Drift snow buried our fleet. We dug out, fired up our tractors, and pulled our camp into the wind. Then we hunkered down again, expecting sooner or later the storm would blow itself out. But it didn't. We logged one hundred yards that day.

"*Fritzy*," my radio squawked. Susan's voice.

"Go ahead, Warrior Princess."

Susan was new to heavy equipment. When we were still at McMurdo, she and Mike Roberts led us in a training session at a "practice crevasse" near town. I took Susan out there in *Fritzy*, our shared cab time an opportunity to review my expectations for her on the trail. Since we'd taken a shortcut, we arrived at the practice grounds ahead of the others. I introduced her to *Fritzy* and its crane. She unshyly took the controls. After the others joined us, she and Mike took over. We spent the rest of the afternoon working with knots and webs of rope, raising volunteer bodies out of the makeshift snow trench. Susan won our unanimous thumbs up.

"*Fritzy*," she radioed now. "We have a strange image on our screen. You should look at it."

"Copy that. All halt," I radioed the moving fleet. We stopped just over a hundred miles south of RIS-1. The radar team had been flagging new trail a mile ahead of us. Susan brought back the image. When the red PistenBully pulled up opposite my yellow tractor, third in line, I dismounted to see what she'd spotted.

"Good catch," I complimented her when she showed me the screen. In a field full of crevasses, the image was so small it would've been insignificant. But after miles of boring flat stratigraphy beneath us, Susan saw something different: a vague discontinuity in the layers twelve meters below the surface. That was deep.

"Susan has found something," I radioed to the others. "It's not a crevasse, but it is some kind of disturbance. And it's well below us. We're going to proceed, but be ready to stop again." Then off radio, and looking to Susan and Jim in the PistenBully: "Let me know immediately if you see any more of that stuff."

Two miles later, Susan radioed back, "*Fritzy*, we have more, and they are shallower."

"Make the camp circle!" I closed my eyes, sucking in a deep breath through clenched teeth. The day was December 4, 2004.

During the off-season, George Blaisdell had reviewed RADARSAT satellite imagery of the area. He inferred that a crevasse field might be lying around here. The imagery didn't show crevasses, but it did show flow patterns where mountain glaciers merged with the Ross Ice Shelf. Icy turbulence at those confluences could make crevasses.

Now we camped fifteen miles short of our next turning point. Blaisdell had hoped RIS-2 might be located in crevasse-free ground south of the suspected field. And I nursed a hope of avoiding the field all together by steering right to his point.

The next day, with the mountains tantalizingly close, we launched the ten-thousand pound PistenBully toward RIS-2. Jim Lever's earlier studies in the Shear Zone had shown us what bridge thicknesses would support that light machine, and we had the skills to judge those in advance while we moved ahead and to stop if we had to. But none of that relieved the creeps we felt for crossing over a bridged crevasse.

I rode in the back of the PistenBully, looking over Susan's shoulder at the radar images. In those fifteen miles, we crossed over more than a hundred bridged, hidden crevasses. These were serious, not just deeply buried sign. RIS-2 sat right in the middle of them. I'd not risk running the heavy fleet over that ground without investigating each one. And there was not enough dynamite on the continent to blow them all. We'd have to find a way around.

"We're going to be here for a while," I announced back in camp. "Prepare for a siege."

That evening, I placed a note in a bottle and cast it into the e-mail ether. It might find Dave Bresnahan. He sat in the big chair in McMurdo then. My message read:

> We're camped fifteen miles short of RIS-2, on course RIS-1 to RIS-2. Between this place and RIS-2 we have encountered many crevasses. RIS-2 lies squarely in crevasse territory. We are seeking a route solution around whatever is in front of us with means we have at hand. Can you enlist George Blaisdell to review satellite imagery for the same purpose?

For the next six days we camped on the brink of this crevasse field. The first three of those days we explored ever more south and east, toward the base of the Leverett. I ran the PistenBully. Susan read the radar. Stretch and Judy followed us on snowmobiles, flagging our track. Our prospecting loops covered ten miles by fifteen miles. Everywhere we looked, we mapped hundreds more hidden crevasses under that featureless snow surface. We found no sign of a passage through them.

Those same three days, Russ and John Penney stayed in camp anchoring our communications and attending to maintenance. Jim Lever and Brad Johnson stayed back, too, running mobility studies on safe ground. After three days, those four grew dangerously bored waiting for a new direction. I'd been stalling. Now I needed work for all of us to do together.

The next morning, we departed camp toward RIS-2 with the PistenBully pulling our hot water drill on a makeshift sled. Two in the PistenBully, two riding the drill, and two each on snowmobiles brought all eight of us into the crevasse field.

We drilled bridges to gauge their thickness and span. We measured snow strengths with the rammsonde penetrometer that we carried with us this year. We mapped the courses of the hidden crevasses with our radar. And we built complete pictures of several crevasses, combining their radar images with the drilling profiles and bridge strengths. We learned a great deal about the crevasses in that particular area, but because of the sheer number of them our efforts to evaluate each crossing were futile. Over six days we found no joy on the ground.

But my note-in-a-bottle had found its mark. Dave had caught George in transit from the United States to New Zealand. George was headed for Mc-Murdo where he'd take his first turn in the big chair.

When George learned of our trouble, he contacted two NSF grantee glaciologists. Both were attached to NASA, but both were familiar with our region of the Ice Shelf. They introduced George to ASTER satellite imagery, newer stuff than RADARSAT offered. ASTER—Advanced Spaceborne Thermal Emission and Reflection Radiometer—was a joint U.S.-Japanese earth-observing satellite launched in 1999. ASTER used both thermal and visible light spectrums, rather than microwave radar. And it offered higher resolution imagery. ASTER showed elongated, narrow shadows in our region.

By the time George arrived in McMurdo, he had ASTER imagery in hand. In a great stroke, he arranged collaboration with McMurdo's geographic information systems (GIS) analyst, Jessica Walker, who had also been a vital player in my preseason route planning. She knew our proposed route and the nuances associated with it. She magically called up all manner of digital information on her computer and transposed it onto our maps. ASTER gave her exactly the type of information she could use.

George and Jessica became our "eyes in the sky." Using our Iridium link, I sent them ground truth from our own ground-based radar to calibrate their interpretations of ASTER's images.

"What I'm seeing here appears to be shadows cast by sagging crevasse bridges. There are a lot of them surrounding RIS-2," George explained over the Iridium phone. "Do you see sagging bridges on the ground where you are?"

We already knew there were a lot of crevasses around RIS-2, but we didn't see sagging bridges at ground level. And I was pretty sure we saw crevasses with our radar where ASTER didn't see any.

"Keep the ground truth coming in. The glaciologists think there is a crevasse-free gap in the field, and a clear path to the Leverett south of that. I'll keep studying the images." George had just arrived in McMurdo. He had a lot of business on his plate besides ours.

Meanwhile, we'd exhausted our strategies for a route solution on the ground and readied to leave the area. Our inability to advance frustrated us. I planned to retreat north a few miles, and then run southeast toward the Leverett, staying well north of the crevasse field. We might get sixty miles in one pitch, and we could shuttle the camp along that baseline. From any point on the baseline we could safely launch the PistenBully southward, seeking to penetrate the field. Making sixty miles by itself would be a welcome change.

"We really haven't looked west yet," Russ observed.

West took us away from the Leverett. But there was no good reason *not* to look west while we were here.

Blinding white-yellow sunlight flashed through the PistenBully's windshield. The antenna boom lurched skyward. We buckled, slipping backward through the broken lid of a crevasse. I gunned the engine as we desperately clawed our way up to flat ground. For long minutes, Susan and I stared ahead at the right-wise horizon. Neither of us said a word.

The westerly course took us out of sight of camp, out of VHF radio range, and down into a rolling ice valley. Brown, tan, and red strata in the mountains ahead displayed an unreal clarity through partings in their icy mantles. The day was brilliant and calm.

We'd passed over deep crevasse sign in the first two miles. At a prearranged turning point, we turned south and found sign more frequently. All looked like everything else we'd seen in the preceding days. I looked over to Susan. "Shall we see what we have here?" She looked back through wide-open eyes, like mine.

Susan roped us up, tying off to the PistenBully. We looked gingerly into the blackness of the hole behind us. A four-foot-wide crevasse hid beneath a strangely thin, broken bridge.

I called back to camp on the Iridium phone. "Judy, we are turning back for your position. When we get there, we'll break camp and move north a bit.

Pass the word. We'll head your way just as soon as we figure how to get back across this crevasse."

"Copy all," Judy acknowledged. But she understood what had happened, adding, "Be careful."

Still roped up, Susan and I probed the snow with long, thin poles to locate fissure's hidden course. We'd crossed it squarely. A hundred feet to the west it narrowed to two feet. We re-crossed it there.

Once on the camp-side of the crevasse, we turned the radar back onto it as far as the antenna would reach. It showed us an image unlike any we'd seen. It lacked clarity. There was no inverted parabolic shape, no sign of a bridge or sagging surface layers. Yet there *was* an image, and we'd missed calling stop.

Outside the idling PistenBully, Susan and I stretched in what warmth the summer sun offered. We wasted no thoughts on recriminations. We read each other's eyes, gauged each other's breathing. The picturesque horizon spread south of us. When smiles eventually appeared, our adrenaline had run its course and we returned to camp.

"We're not going that way either," I told the others, gathered in the galley. "We'll talk about what happened tomorrow morning. For now, let's move out. We're going to try something else." And my message to McMurdo that evening said simply, "There is nothing more for us to do in this place."

We retreated ten miles from that first faint sign Susan spotted on entering the territory. Ten miles seemed a safe enough margin, and we named the new camp FORK. Behind us, more than two hundred flags marked abandoned trails through the maze of crevasses. Among them was a wooden post, planted at RIS-2, bearing the name "McCabe." James McCabe from Texas had toiled with us the year before. He was unable to rejoin us this year, and we missed him.

"CHRISTMAS CONTEST—$1,000,000 prize for the best drag design for our purposes."

The announcement appeared on the white board in our galley the next morning at FORK. A "drag" is a trail-grooming device, dragged behind a tractor or a sled. Our makeshift drags bogged us down. The million dollar prize for a better design got everybody's attention.

"For us to design one, you got to tell us what the purpose of the drag is," Russ complained.

"Yeah . . . but the prize is as much for what you *think* our purposes are, as for the design itself." I left it at that. Russ grumbled. But now we were thinking about something besides crevasses. And the promise of movement today lifted our spirits.

We reached the end of the baseline two days and sixty-four miles later. Since we were already there, I decided to explore the ground south of us. Our whole fleet turned directly toward the base of the Leverett Glacier, a coordinate location for us, since it was still too far off to see. Within five miles we halted at our first crevasse. Prospects of another siege brought us down again.

We explored much as we had near RIS-2. But unlike there, where ten miles revealed a hundred hidden crevasses, here we found twice that number. To test how efficiently we could evaluate crevasse bridges in a single day, we targeted eight, but completed only six. A southern passage here was as futile as ever.

"George, are you seeing any crevasses immediately south of our position?" I asked our McMurdo eyes.

"I see clusters of crevasses perhaps twenty and thirty miles south of your position. But I see none on the ASTER imagery where you are now." George shuffled un-gridded photo mosaics, a work in progress, around his desktop trying to answer my questions.

"Copy that. We're going to prospect here a little longer," I signed off.

Outside the living module near *Fritzy*, a droop-shouldered Russ Magsig duck-footed his way over the snow toward me. His head hung down, swinging side to side. He wore a plaintive look. "We can always go back to the Skelton and try it from there."

The Skelton Glacier, much closer to McMurdo, was the pass Sir Edmund Hillary chose for his historic tractor traverse to Pole in 1957–1958. It was way over there and certainly not for us this year. And, it was riddled with crevasses. Hillary had found plenty. Evans's crew in 1995 went there and found exactly what Hillary found. The Skelton made a distant second choice to the Leverett. The only reason the Skelton had made the list of candidate passes was that Hillary *had* done it. But we sought a safe, repeatable route, not a risky one. And now I saw depression creeping into camp.

At our morning briefing the next day, I laid out our situation: "We are here. Our job for this season is to find a way to the base of the Leverett Glacier.

We are safe, we have plenty of food, we are warm, and we have fuel. We are not going to leave this region until we've exhausted all our efforts, or spent half our fuel, to get to the Leverett base. Consider going back to McMurdo before we've done all we could. Do you really want to go back to McMurdo at all? We're in a mighty fine place, right here in the middle of nowhere. And we have an interesting problem to solve. Maybe we'll find a solution."

Grim faces nodded in silent assent. Putting it *my* way, not one of us wanted to go back to McMurdo.

Our eyes sent in a detailed description of a route segment on the far side of the crevasse field. As far as ASTER could determine, it was crevasse-free. And it was within reach of the PistenBully so long as we staged extra fuel forward. If we could cross the crevasses in front of us, we could test ASTER's findings. But should anything happen to the radar team, none of the heavy tractors could safely follow us to the rescue.

We made a plan for exploring a triangular loop that crossed the field. The opposite leg of that triangle was the ASTER segment. It might take two or three days to carry out the plan, though my daily reports simply said we were prospecting.

The first day, Judy accompanied Susan, Jim, and me in the PistenBully. Judy ran the radar under Susan's watchful eye. Susan kept tally of the crevasses we crossed. First, we retraced our path toward the base of the Leverett. We'd already identified 214 crevasses on those ten miles. At the end of the line we staged a drum of fuel and called the place DRUM. From DRUM, we turned a westerly course toward one end of that distant, ASTER route segment. Judy called sixty hidden crevasses along the next five miles before we turned back for DRUM, and then camp. As we got out of the PistenBully, she remarked, "This is just like hunting rattlesnakes!"

For the whole prospecting loop, we'd take our two snowmobiles with the PistenBully. The snowmobiles gave us a way to return to camp in an emergency. We didn't plan to run them. But we'd tow them with enough fuel onboard to cover the distance.

Should the PistenBully fall into a crevasse with the snowmobiles towed closely behind, they'd follow it in. So we rigged a two-hundred-foot-long line of heavy, knotted tow-rope. It hooked to the PistenBully on one end and to a pair of slick plastic sleds on the other. The sleds, lashed side by side, bore the two snowmobiles. A webbing of heavy cargo chain formed the hitch to the sleds. When the PistenBully pulled the sleds, the tow rope and the chains rode taut. But, if the PistenBully stopped, the chains fell slack.

In the safety of our camp circle, we ran the PistenBully at full speed then stopped abruptly. The snowmobile sleds overran the chains as we'd hoped. The chain-brake dragged the whole package, with one passenger on board, to a stop in twenty feet. That satisfied us.

On the clear morning of December 19, we loaded mechanic's tools, emergency medical gear, and spare fuel onto the snowmobile sleds. For our second foray, the party included me, John Penney, Susan, and Jim Lever. Russ, Stretch, Brad, and Judy remained in camp. That division placed one mountaineer, one emergency medical care provider, and one mechanic with each group.

Jim ran the PistenBully. I rode in the back, looking over Susan's shoulder at the radar, and logged the numbers of crevasses. John Penney rode atop the snowmobiles. We refueled at DRUM then turned a new course to the other end of the ASTER segment. Over the next twenty miles we found continuous crevassing. But two miles shy of our target, we ran out of crevasses. The ground was clear. We arrived at the turning point, still no crevasses, and planted four red flags on bamboo poles.

Next, we steered directly along ASTER's route. The radar showed flat, undisturbed snow beneath us over the entire ten-mile course. No crevasses. At the next turning point we planted another four red flags. Then we turned toward DRUM to close the fifty-mile loop.

We ran two more miles before finding another crevasse. From there on, we found them continuously. After refueling at DRUM, we ran the remaining distance into camp.

Russ came out to greet us. He'd been worried.

"Pretty good news," I told him. "There're a lot of crevasses out there, but we got to the other side and *that* ground is clear."

We now had *some* solid ground truth for ASTER.

Still, I wasn't going to bring the fleet across that ground, despite the Promised Land we'd just glimpsed on the other side. But ASTER had seen a breach

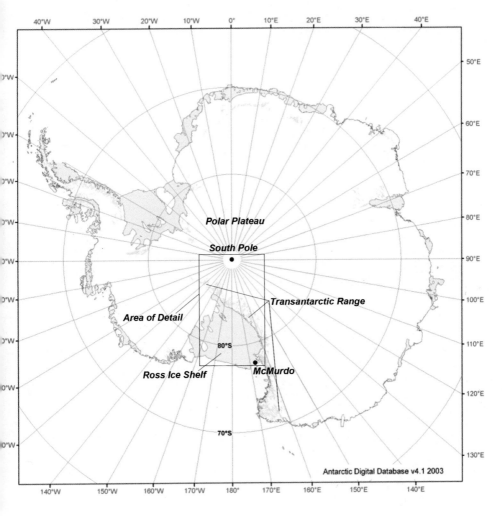

Generalized map of Antarctica showing features of interest for *Blazing Ice*.
(USAP Antarctic Photo Library, Antarctic Digital Database/Jessica Walker, 2003)

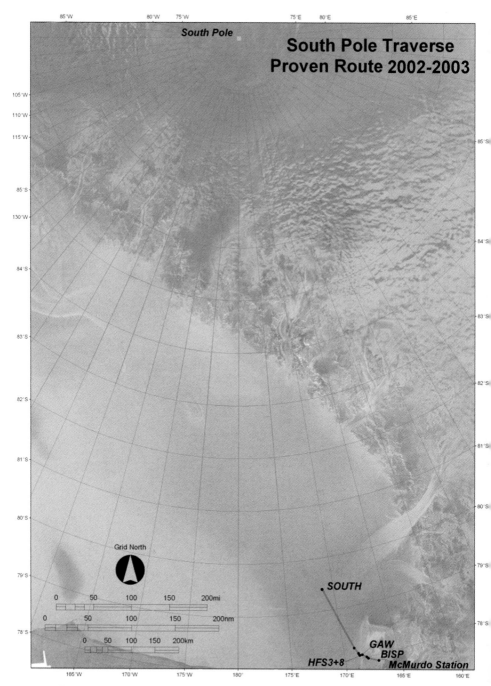

South Pole Traverse Proven Route 2002–2003. (After USAP map drawn by Jessica Walker 2005–2006 with route data provided by John H. Wright and surface data provided by Canadian Space Agency)

The post marking the start of the South Pole trail on the McMurdo Ice Shelf at the intersection with the Black Island road. Mt. Erebus, the active volcano that forms the main mass of Ross Island, lies in the background. The author stands beside the post. (John H. Wright, 2002)

A 10,000-pound PistenBully adapted for crevasse detection. Note: twenty-foot boom extension with inner-tube at its end. The ground penetrating radar antenna rests in the inner-tube, looking down. A cable delivers the antenna signal to a radar reader inside the cab. (Russ Alger, 2002)

The blast that finally opened Mongo to reveal the immense cavern first glimpsed through a tiny hole by Shaun Norman. (Russ Alger, 2002)

Mongo revealed after blast. The author retrieves gear from the top of the crevasse bridge. Note the featureless background terrain, beneath which lurk myriad hidden crevasses like Mongo. (Russ Alger, 2002)

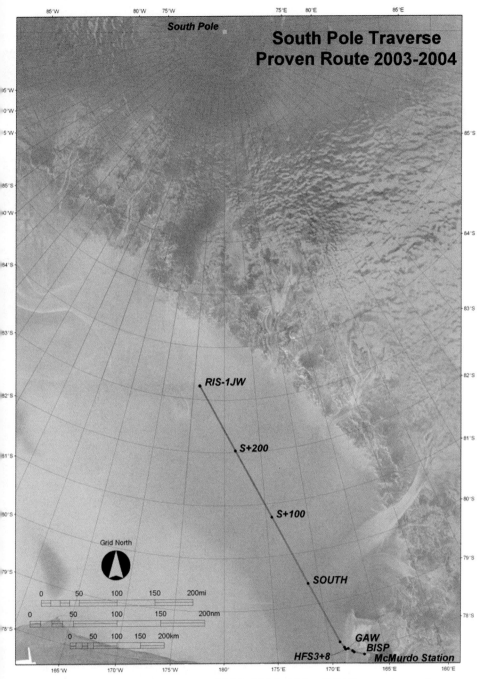

South Pole Traverse Proven Route 2003–2004. (After USAP map drawn by
Jessica Walker 2005–2006 with route data provided by John H. Wright and
surface data provided by Canadian Space Agency)

The 85,000-pound D8R Caterpillar bulldozer pulls a five-sled train across the Shear Zone. Behind the D8, in order, are the living module, the energy module, the refrigerator van, the flat rack van, and the spare parts milvan. (Traverse Crew, 2003)

The 51,420-pound Kress modified Caterpillar Challenger-95, which later came to be known as the *Elephant Man*, departs McMurdo with two tracked trailers loaded with 5,000-gallon fuel tanks intended for South Pole Station. (Traverse Crew, 2003)

The 41,440-pound Caterpillar Challenger-95, fitted with Fassi crane, pulls a reconfigured load across the Ross Ice Shelf. The tractor later came to be known as *Fritzy*. (Traverse Crew, 2003)

The 56,100-pound Case STX Quadtrack—*Quadzilla*—pulls a shuttle load of two 3,000-gallon tank sleds across the Ross Ice Shelf. James McCabe inspects his tractor. (Traverse Crew, 2003)

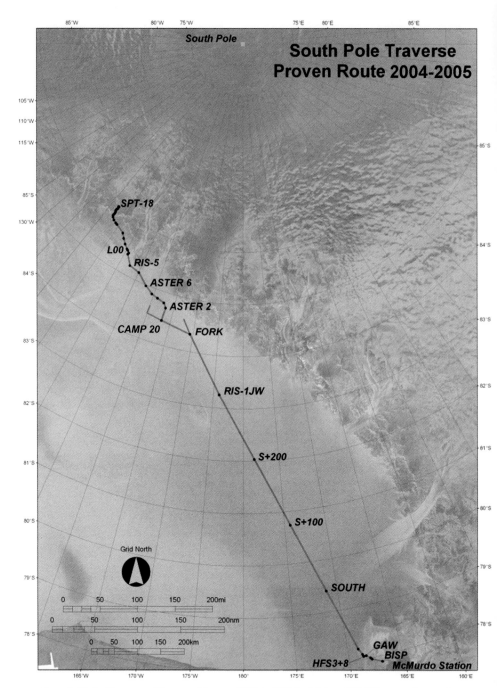

South Pole Traverse Proven Route 2004–2005. (After USAP map drawn by Jessica Walker 2005–2006 with route data provided by John H. Wright and surface data provided by Canadian Space Agency)

Traverse camp at the foot of the Leverett glacier. The Transantarctic mountain fronts form the horizon. Note the camp circle indicating the safe camp perimeter. Radio-controlled model airplane pilot, John Penney, stands to the far left in the circle and captures this photo from a wing-mounted camera in his model airplane. (John Penney, 2004)

The traverse fleet moves up a street on the Leverett glacier. Note the ice falls in the background, and open crevasses in the middle ground. (John Penney, 2004)

In a ponderous and stately event, the D8R, pulling the living module and energy module, and the *Elephant Man* pulling the refrigerator van and a fuel tank sled, crest the headwall of the Leverett glacier topping out onto the polar plateau. The rock mass to the left is the foot of Mount Beazley. The rock mass to the right later bore the name Magsig Rampart. (Jim Lever, 2004)

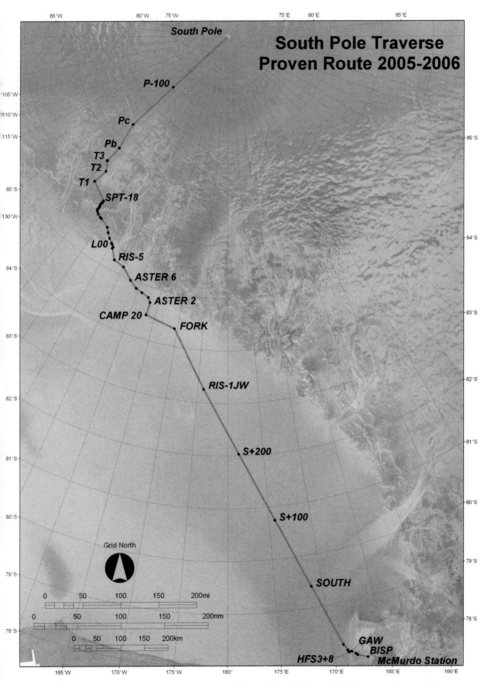

South Pole Traverse Proven Route 2005–2006. (After USAP map drawn by Jessica Walker 2005–2006 with route data provided by John H. Wright and surface data provided by Canadian Space Agency)

The South Pole Station's snow haul trailer, and the flat rack sled loaded with a skid-steer track loader are two items of deliverable cargo destined for South Pole in the fourth year of the project. (Traverse Crew, 2005)

A Twin Otter intercepts the traverse while on the Ross Ice Shelf. Dave Bresnahan delivers a disc containing vital declassified information on the route ahead from the National Geospatial Intelligence Agency. Unwittingly, he brings forms from the contractor's human resources department relating to the use of the McMurdo e-mail system which we must sign. Richard "Stretch" Vaitonis signs his form using the author's back while Dave Bresnahan looks on. (John Van Vlack, 2005)

The crew tends to *Quadzilla's* injury during the climb up the Leverett glacier. Pictured from left to right: John Van Vlack, Russ Magsig, Greg Feleppa. Note that full sun and the absence of wind make for short-lived t-shirt weather. (Traverse Crew, 2005)

The PistenBully encounters miles and miles of hard, wind-sculpted sastrugi. (John Van Vlack, 2005)

Sundogs, haloes, glories, and a burning sun pillar accompanied us all day long when we finally came out of Sastrugi National Park. (John Van Vlack, 2005)

A 13-mile track, the road we unabashedly built for the D8R, leads from our camp to South Pole Station on the horizon on the morning we went all the way. A British Antarctic Survey Twin Otter gave us a fly-over that morning and took this picture. (BAS, 2005)

Fritzy, with the author at the controls, pulls the crippled Caterpillar MT-865 Challenger the final miles into South Pole Station. (Traverse Crew, 2005)

The crew poses by the marker indicating 90 degrees South on the day after Christmas. From left to right, tractors: D8R, *Fritzy*, and the *Elephant Man*; standing: Greg Feleppa, Richard "Stretch" Vaitonis, the author, and Brad Johnson; kneeling: Russ Magsig, Judy Goldsberry, John Van Vlack, and Tom Lyman. (John "Scotty" Jackson, 2005)

The traverse fleet returns to the outskirts of McMurdo, joining the well-traveled Williams Field road. White Island forms the background. The Concept is proved. (George Blaisdell, 2006)

in the crevasse field some distance back. The evening of the day we saw the Promised Land, I asked our eyes in the sky what ASTER saw due north of that breach. George said it appeared to be clear, but twice we'd camped near crevasse-riddled ground where ASTER saw nothing.

We retreated along our baseline to a point due north of the suspected breach. We called the place CAMP 20 for the date: December 20. Brad scribed that name into the top of a post and, after signing his own name at the bottom, planted the post upright in the snow.

I lay awake contemplating the effect of failure on our third attempt to penetrate the field. The stoic crew had accepted no joy for our every effort over the last weeks. If tomorrow's attempt failed to find a way, then we were all out of ideas. Our return to McMurdo wouldn't be a happy one.

The next morning, Jim, Susan, and I launched a prospecting mission into the breach while the others remained in camp. With each mile forward our hopes swelled. We found no crevasse sign along those first twenty miles, and stopped at a point designated ASTER 2. It lay marginally on the south side of the crevasse field. There we planted four red flags and swept a small camp circle around them. The ground was clear.

Our tracks showed we'd just climbed up a broad ice valley about five miles wide. We hadn't seen that or felt it when we crossed it. Now we stood on high ground, looking back on it, anticipating success.

Then we turned southeastward, toward the ASTER segment we proved two days before. Three miles out we crossed two discreet, deeply buried crevasses. We searched out their courses, and the area around them. No other crevasse sign lay anywhere near.

"Brad, we've done pretty good here," I called back to camp. Brad was on comms duty. "We only see two crevasses. I need you to prepare the next monument posts. Label them ASTER 2, 3, 4, and 5. We're running low on fuel, and turning back for camp now. See you in a couple of hours."

Uncertain of my message, Brad asked, "Did you find a way through?"

"You make the posts, Brad. We'll plant them. We're all coming through tomorrow."

On our arrival back at CAMP 20, Russ once again duck-footed his way over the snow to me. This time he grinned ear to ear, his head down and wagging back and forth in joyous disbelief.

"We just now got lucky," I told him, shaking hands under a gray sky.

That evening I spoke to George in McMurdo. "We've found two isolated crevasses at ASTER 2 plus 3.5 miles toward ASTER 3. We saw no other crevasses in the area. What does ASTER see?"

George came back. "I see two, very faint crevasse traces, and no other crevasses nearby. They appear a half mile east of the location you gave."

"What is the date of the ASTER imagery?"

"December 2002 to January 2003."

That was plausible. Two years, a quarter-mile movement per year, nothing else around it. We'd measured a half-mile a year at SOUTH, well back on the Shelf. We had our second solid ground truth.

On December 22, the heavy fleet lumbered through the gap, halting short of the black flags marking yesterday's finds. Where hundreds of crevasses had stymied us for weeks, now we stopped for two.

Susan, Jim, and Judy captured their images, measured the strength of their snow bridges with the rammsonde, then returned to the living module to reduce the data.

The rest of us dragged out the hot-water drill. Across the first bridge, we drilled a line of five sixty-foot deep holes. They all drilled solid snow to their entire depth. Not one found a void.

Across the second bridge, another five holes in line bottomed at ninety feet. One found void at eighty-eight, but landed in solid snow again two feet later. All the other ones drilled solid to their entire depths.

Now we'd drilled both bridges far deeper than the thicknesses our radar predicted. And we didn't find any great void. Possibly the crevasses had squeezed shut since they first formed, but our task wasn't an academic one. Facts were facts. I didn't wait for Jim's data. I unhitched *Fritzy* from its load and drove the forty-two thousand pound tractor across the crevasses.

"These two have just been proved safe," I declared. "Let's stow the drill, eat lunch, and get down the trail."

We broke out over crevasse-free ground toward the red flags we planted days before. Passing those the next day, we made camp at ASTER 7 on Christmas Eve. But for those two isolated crevasses, the entire course from CAMP 20 to ASTER 7 was clear.

That eloquent phrase John Evans wrote in his *Final Report* a decade before came to mind. Had we not found the way, or had we experienced calamity in trying, our project would have met a bureaucratic death, never to be resurrected. We were Evans's Lazarus. I named the enormous crevasse field we'd just breached The Shoals of Intractable Funding.

Susan sported a blue plastic tiara studded with multicolored gems of paste. She looked absolutely silly. Red and green bunting and flickering low-energy lights in plastic tubes draped our galley. Judy and John Penney whipped up a pancake breakfast, which we relished, served with maple syrup and real butter saved for the occasion. Outside the sky was as bright blue as it'd been each hour of the past twenty-four. Today was Christmas.

"John Wright has offered a thoughtful design for the best drag for our purposes," Susan declared. "On a scale of one to one hundred, what is your score for his design?"

My brainchild consisted of multiple rows of heavy gauge six-inch diameter pipes, linked by chains that could easily be disassembled or reassembled to any configuration that matched the snow conditions.

"Ninty-five," Russ offered, deferentially. Susan wrote forty-seven on the chart she'd drawn on the white board.

"Thirty-six," Brad called out. Susan wrote forty-four.

The gang piled on. Between Susan's scorekeeping and collusion with the crew, I headed toward ignominious loss.

Russ offered a huge rolling drum fitted to an axle and a draw bar. John Penny drew a broad inverted plate bearing chevron ribs that stirred the snow as it dragged along. At the final tally, Jim Lever's design, looking similar to mine but with the addition of plastic sheets loaded with fuel bladders, won resoundingly. I had to find $1,000,000.

Slipping outside the living module for a moment, I left the crew to judge whether or not I were a piker. But I reentered the galley, opened my wallet, and ceremoniously pulled out a $1,000,000 bill. With all the pomposity I could muster, I announced, "Jim Lever, according to our impartial judge in this rigged contest, you have won this prize. I freely give it."

Jim got his bill, and everyone else did, too. "This is your bonus, spend it wisely." The seven $1,000,000 bills I had purchased for seven dollars at a Colorado greeting card store.

We hung out for the day on the south side of the Shoals, waiting for a Twin Otter. When it landed that afternoon, one pair of our McMurdo eyes crawled out sporting a red Santa hat. George Blaisdell brought mail from home and digitized ASTER imagery on a disk. We saw for the first time in our galley what he'd been looking at. Plainly, when ASTER did see a crevasse, a crevasse was there. Equally plain, our camp lay at the southern limits of the satellite's coverage. ASTER would be of no further use from here south.

Outside, Brad and Judy refueled the Twin Otter. It'd battled headwinds most of the way out, though there was no wind at our location. The plane took on 351 gallons to assure its own trip back to McMurdo. That amounted to two tractors worth of fuel on a big day. As George reboarded for the return flight, he asked if there were anything else he could do for us.

"Thank you for that. You might look into flying supplemental fuel to us. I hope we get into the Leverett. But who knows what we'll find between here and there. If we do get there, I want to get to the top. I'd hate to turn back for lack of fuel."

"Will do," he agreed.

"George, if we make L-00, you'll know we are on the Leverett. We'll get serious about fuel then."

The day after Christmas, we slept in again, breakfasted late, and remained generally idle. We'd launch again the next day, and we had a few chores around camp to prepare for that. As long as our heavy tractors stood down, we burned little fuel. Our camp generators running around the clock consumed only a gallon and a half per hour.

Stretch and I prospected the next fifteen miles south. We stopped at a turning point where our new course would take us straight to L-00, another fifteen miles away. But looking straight at L-00, we couldn't tell what the glacier we sought was. There was no break in the mountains, or clear valley before us. All along the foot of the mountains, to our right and to our left, the Ice Shelf dipped into a low swale, and then rose gently up the other side to meet the coast of the continent.

In the mid-1990s Evans's team assessed the Leverett route over the Transantarctics leading onto the Polar Plateau. They airlifted onto the glacier, disembarked crew, snowmobiles, camp gear, and simple survey devices for a ground reconnaissance. They didn't have ground-based ground penetrating radar. However, a New Zealand helicopter that year brought Steve Arcone, Allan Delaney, and their radar out from the not too distant Shackleton Glacier Camp, a temporary science field camp. They flew an aerial radar survey of the Leverett. I inherited their information.

We, on the other hand, had ground-based ground penetrating radar. We'd see things Evans's team had not.

On December 27 our fleet approached L-00. That was the farthest down glacier our predecessors had reached. L-00 supposedly located the base of the Leverett where it converged with the floating Ross Ice Shelf. Our maps even plotted L-00 precisely on the continental shoreline buried beneath the ice. But, seven miles short of L-00, our tractors started laboring up a gentle grade. We were on Leverett ice for the first time and had left the Ice Shelf behind in the swale. L-00 did *not* mark the base of the glacier.

We'd emptied four out of eight three-thousand-gallon fuel tanks and were now drawing from a fifth. By straight measure, we were dipping into our return reserve, and the ground ahead was unknown to us.

"We have a deeply buried crevasse here, *Fritzy*," Susan's voice squawked over my radio. She ran a quarter mile ahead with John Penney and Jim Lever.

"Copy that," I answered. "Come back and give us a camp circle."

It was midday. We stopped the heavy fleet several miles short of L-00.

I joined the prospecting team after lunch, taking a seat behind Susan where I could see her radar screen. Then the four of us launched back toward L-00. The next two miles brought twenty more crevasses. The PistenBully broke through the thin bridge of the twenty-first. Susan and Jim lurched forward, thrown against the front of the cab. The radar slammed into the dashboard. I lay plastered against the front of the passenger compartment.

"Man, I hate this shit!" I swore.

"*You* hate it?" I heard Susan mutter.

"Aw! Aw, jeez!" That was Jim.

None of us was hurt, and for the moment the PistenBully seemed stable. But we had no idea what lay around us. Any move we might make gambled making a dangerous situation worse. Susan's side of the PistenBully had dropped in. She couldn't get out through her door. Jim's side, the left side, rode up. If he got out, that might be all it took to send us and the PistenBully into the void. Plus, he'd be leaving the driver's seat. If he got out, there'd be no one at the controls. I could get out on the left side, too, through a side door. But I'd no idea what I'd be stepping onto, or into, and I wasn't going to tie myself off to the PistenBully.

It had to be me. As we tipped over the edge, I crawled out to size up our situation.

John Penney came up behind on a snowmobile. I signaled him to stop, then I looked around. The antenna boom lay flat on the snow in front of us. The right track of the PistenBully had broken through a crevasse lid. A faint depression in the snow approached us at a low angle from behind and to our right. This was the sneaky one Russ had foreseen two years ago in the Shear Zone. Susan had been about to call halt for a crevasse that just appeared on her screen, an image of what lay twenty feet ahead. But our right track had already found it. Jim backed the PistenBully out, teetering for one heart-stopping moment before he found flat ground.

Our approach to L-00 had brought us up the eastern side of a broad out-flow fan of glacial ice. All the crevasses we'd just encountered lay over the edge of that fan, on its shoulder.

We'd talk over our second close encounter in the morning.

The following day we withdrew our camp to the foot of the glacier, down in the swale. From there the scouting team worked westerly around the base of the fan and located a looping, crevasse-free route to L-00. Elated by a quick solution for a change, we sidetracked three fuel tank sleds and two tractors at the base of the glacier. With the remaining fleet rigged for the climb, we started up, sailed past L-00, and made camp ten miles beyond it. December 29 was a good day for us.

Now firmly on the Leverett Glacier, we entered the Transantarctic's jag-ged, alpine mountains. Nunataks poked their stony tops through the glaciers that nearly buried them. Solid rock took on real colors of browns, reds, and blacks no longer washed out in the vague grays of distant horizons.

That night I sent "Report from the Field #6" to my bosses in McMurdo. Copies, as usual, went to Dave and George. Field reports described our doings in narrative detail not readily gleaned from daily reports. We were on the Leverett at last, but we had new terrain problems ahead. Our fuel supply allowed two more days of southern advance.

The next evening's check-in with Mac-Ops brought a hopeful message: my bosses requested an Iridium phone conference in the morning. I looked for good news of fuel coming our way.

"Good morning. What can I do for you both?" I greeted them when I phoned in at the designated hour.

"We don't understand your latest messages," they replied. "Are you using some kind of code?"

"No . . . I have no idea what you're talking about," I answered, nonplussed.

"Well, what, for example, do you mean by 'loo?'" They pronounced the word like the British word for a toilet. Possibly they referred to one of their higher-ups named Lou.

"Ummm . . . could you spell that, please?"

"El-oh-oh," they came back. "What are you trying to say here?"

"That's el-zero-zero. Outside your office, posted on your wall, is a map of our proposed route. The key turning points are all labeled. One of them is L-00. We have been trying to get to L-00, and have finally succeeded. It means we have crossed the Ross Ice Shelf. It means we are on the Leverett Glacier."

"Oh."

"Is there anything else?"

"No, we see. That's all."

"Wait a minute before you hang up . . . Can you advise any news of supplemental fuel?"

"Fuel is short everywhere." The curt reply ended the phone conference.

Later that morning we advanced the fleet fifteen miles up-glacier. The mountain walls slowly enclosed us. In the afternoon the prospecting team probed another fifteen miles forward. They returned to camp declaring the route segment crevasse-free and flagged.

"George, we're up here with three tractors and one tank sled half full. I left three tanks and two tractors at the bottom for the return trip. I believe we can get to the headwall, but I don't believe we can climb it with what little fuel we have," I explained over the Iridium phone. It was New Year's Eve. We were camped halfway up the glacier, waiting for another Twin Otter.

"An assessment of the headwall would still be good," George encouraged. "But I don't think we can get fuel to you at your location."

"I don't need fuel at this location. But if you can get me fuel on the Ross Ice Shelf sometime later I'll go back down-glacier and get those other tanks now. I'll use that fuel to get up this thing."

"I see. I believe the Air Guard will do that. Proceed as you describe, and try and make that assessment. But stay in touch in case something new comes up."

When the Twin Otter completed its resupply and mountaineer exchange we again refueled the plane from our own stores. That left just over a thousand gallons in our one tank sled. I'd been on the cusp of calling the turnaround that day, but the hope of receiving landed fuel on the Ross Ice Shelf changed all that. We had a chance for the top. I sent half the crew down-glacier to re-cover the depot.

On January 2 the reunited fleet camped just short of the headwall basin. Our next course bent around Mount Beazley's stony, beige buttress. Through the narrows, we stared up at the unbroken, snow-covered rim of the Polar Plateau. It encircled the entire headwall under a brilliant blue sky. Our task stood vertically before us.

Jim Lever and Allen O'Bannon, who'd replaced Susan at the Twin Otter put-in, made the camp circle for the evening. They cleared half the ground inside it and called the fleet forward. While the rest of us unhitched and refueled, Jim's voice broke onto *Fritzy*'s radio: "We'll be right with you . . . just as soon as we've crossed back over this crevasse we just found." Those were the exact words I'd used when Susan and I broke through the first time.

I muttered, looking out from behind our refueling station.

The two men were standing outside the PistenBully, a hundred yards away. The PistenBully was on its feet and running, not down in a hole. I called them back on the radio. They were okay, merely sizing up their situation. They did not want the D8R to come out and fill their hole with snow.

"Take some pictures," I radioed. "We'll talk about this one tomorrow morning, just like the others." They recrossed safely, but that was our third close encounter.

January 3 the crew split once again. Russ, Stretch, Judy, and Brad remained in camp. They greased bearings in the sleds' running gear, replaced turntable pins, and checked cables, turnbuckles, and shackles in the rigging. They left nothing to chance for the climb.

I joined John Penney's team scouting into the headwall basin itself. We followed the 1995 team's path. Our radar found many crevasses on a three-mile stretch where they'd climbed over a shoulder and onto a glacial "street."

"Streets" are elongated ridges of ice, aligned with the flow of the main glacier. They might be a hundred yards to a quarter mile wide, and they might stand ten to fifty feet high. We'd discovered street tops gave us crevasse-free surfaces here. And we'd followed street tops through all their bifurcations from L-00 to our present camp.

This street flowed right out of the basin. Our last two close encounters had found crevasses on street shoulders, just like our radar showed us now. The heavy fleet wouldn't attempt going over it. But getting into the headwall basin *was* our next job.

The PistenBully continued along the 1995 path into the basin. We entered an open snowfield at its bottom, a parade ground big enough to hold the Million Mom March. And we found no crevasses there. The Plateau rim now completely embraced our horizon. It lay seven miles away. And the headwall held the steepest slopes we'd face. My evening report to McMurdo contained this message: "Have prospected a course to *L-10* . . . *on your map*. Have found crevasses. Not insurmountable."

Under clear skies the next morning, January 4, the fleet advanced four miles, where it stopped and we made coffee.

The prospecting team departed at that point, retracing its path over the shoulder into the Parade Ground. Following up on our hunch, we located a looping crevasse-free detour out of the basin, around the point of the shoulder, and back down to the waiting fleet. With events unfolding rapidly in our favor, we didn't dwell long over coffee. The heavy fleet advanced along the detour. By midday it arrived at the Parade Grounds and made camp for lunch. The prospecting team set out again to scout a route to the top.

RADARSAT imagery had shown us thousands of crevasses in the basin ahead. Now that we were here, we could see they were not all hidden. Their open blue-ice maws ringed the entire headwall. Yet with uncommon luck, we flagged a crevasse-free path the first four miles to a level bench, halfway up to the rim. From there, we dodged side-slopes and open crevasses, and then we quickly found the last three miles to the top.

From the suddenly expansive panorama, the frigid, white world lay below us. A frozen cascade, as big as Niagara Falls, draped over the plateau's rim. Down in the valley, the Leverett Glacier flowed placidly around Mt. Beazley. Three years to get to this place, and now we *were* the horizon.

Enjoying lungs-full of cold Plateau air, we planted four green flags and called that point SPT-18.

"I wonder if the tractors can make these grades?" I mused to John Penney, Allen, and Jim. "On our way back down with the radar, let's offset our trail by a hundred feet. If we're lucky we'll prove a corridor that we can move in."

By 1800 hours, we rejoined the fleet waiting in the Parade Grounds below. The others were rested, ready, and eager. The clear, calm weather was a gift we wouldn't waste. I called it: "Break camp. We're going to the top tonight."

Stretch and his D8 bulldozer pulled out first with the camp modules, a 100,000-pound sled load. He made the summit to SPT-18, scratching his way up the steeper slopes but never losing all traction.

Russ and the *Elephant Man* followed, towing a support sled and the one tank which now held only 292 gallons.

Judy and tractor #283 pulled an empty tank sled, a spreader bar sled and a trail drag. She followed Russ up the slopes with ease.

Then I in *Fritzy* and Brad in *Quadzilla* started up. With our heavier loads, we both lost traction several times and wallowed in. John Penney patrolled between us on a snowmobile, helping rig our tow straps. Brad and I took turns towing each other to the top.

By 2130 hours, January 4, 2005, we claimed our foothold on the Polar Plateau.

We had hurled ourselves to the summit. Now we sat down to a late dinner in camp at SPT-18. The weather was still clear, but it was noticeably twenty degrees colder than the Parade Grounds below. We'd been sixty days on the trail. In the last seventy miles, we climbed from 400 feet above sea level at the Leverett base to 7,200 feet at its top.

Jim described the sight that played to the triumph now gripping each one of us: "Standing well back from the edge and watching a tractor top-out, I saw the roof of the tractor first, just below the rim. Maybe ten seconds later the whole tractor appeared. It really *was* a ponderous and stately event."

Before dinner, I sent a simple message to McMurdo:

> We have completed our assessment of the Leverett Glacier headwall region. In fact, we have ascended the Leverett headwall and are now camped squarely on the Polar Plateau. We request a phone conference tomorrow morning, January 05, regarding onward traverse.

"Report from the Field #8" to my bosses in McMurdo, with copies to Dave and George, followed after dinner:

> We are prepared to go farther south, and feel the only southern goal left for us this season is South Pole itself. The crew is unanimous in will to do this. We have sufficient fuel to make the remaining 298 miles to Pole, but not to complete the return. I prefer to take on fuel at South Pole Station to guarantee our return to McMurdo this season, rather than accept deep field refueling on the Ross Ice Shelf. I'd also like to deliver the D8 to Pole as cargo in satisfaction of one of the Proof-of-Concept requirements. Fuel in exchange for the prize of a D8 may be persuasive.

January 5 was Russ Magsig's birthday. We slept in, and I filed no report that day.

Several of us called home over the Iridium connection that morning. I managed one call to my family, who this time was visiting cousins in Christchurch, New Zealand. They'd dropped by the USAP offices, of all places, where the wonderful lady who worked there arranged the call. I knew the very room where they stood. It had a big map of Antarctica on the wall, and it thrilled me to have them point to the top of the Leverett, at the very edge of the Plateau where Daddy was, and feel our excitement being here.

Later, while we waited for an answer on fuel, Jim Lever awakened me from a nap. "I've been elected to go over some figures with you."

"What is this . . . a 'me and the boys have been talking' thing?" I sleepily asked from my bunk.

"Yeah," he laughed. "Me and the boys over in Boy's Town." Boy's Town was the bunkroom opposite the galley from the one I slept in. We had Judy on our side.

"Okay . . . what do you got?" I sat up, yawning on the edge of my bunk.

"You've asked for nine thousand gallons at Pole," Jim opened.

"That's right. It could be that much depending on how things go. We'll only know when we get there."

"Well, we've put the pencil to it and figure we could do it for less. We leave one tractor here, we go in with four, leave the D8, and come back here with three. I calculate three thousand gallons would do it."

"Any margin in that?" I asked, wary of engineer's sharp pencils.

"It works out right at three thousand gallons," Jim reasserted.

No margin. Amundsen always planned for margin . . . surplus against the unexpected. Scott planned right at the margin, and then pushed past it. Scott blew it.

Jim's three thousand gallons gave no allowance for unknown terrain. Should our radar fail or another crevasse field block our way, either one forcing a turnaround before Pole, we wouldn't have the fuel for that. A one-way trip was out of the question. Wintering the fleet at South Pole diverted precious station resources it couldn't afford. The proof-of-concept was in the round trip, anyway.

To satisfy the boys I sent an additional note to George. New calculations suggested the *range* of our fuel requirement was between three thousand gallons and the nine thousand gallons I'd originally asked for. All caveats I'd previously outlined for support were still in force. But we were in a pretty good place, and we knew it. Whether we went on to Pole or back to McMurdo, the will to complete in three years rested solely with NSF now.

The requested phone conference with my bosses in McMurdo did take place, though their opening line left me at a loss:

"What would you like to talk about?"

I repeated last night's message: "We are unanimous in our will to go on. We are warm. We have plenty of food. All our equipment is in good working order. We do need supplemental fuel. With that support, we believe we can get all the way to Pole and back to McMurdo and complete the proof-of-concept mission this year. What is your pleasure?"

George sat in the conference room with my bosses. He explained that deep field refueling by a landed LC-130 was no longer an option for the traverse. The Air National Guard crews had changed in the last few days. Its new commander was not willing to land on the Ross Ice Shelf.

"Well how about at Pole?" I asked. "Can we take on supplemental fuel there, brought on a regularly scheduled mission?"

The phone conference concluded with uncertainty. From our perch on the Polar Plateau, we waited for a decision.

The next day I conferred with George by a separate phone call. He asked straightforwardly, "What would you do if you were in my seat?"

"George," I spoke after a pause, for his was a big question, "I do not know what it is like to sit in the big chair in McMurdo, nor do I have access to all the information you do. But I've only one answer for you: If you cannot *fully support* us, then this is as far as we go. Less than full support won't get it."

At the beginning of it all Erick Chiang had declared, "The National Science Foundation announces its full support for the development of the South Pole Traverse."

The morning of January 7 we received Erick Chiang's decision. Dave Bresnahan, who was in Washington, D.C., at the time, relayed it:

We have . . . with all the input that has been received been able to balance the opportunities, risks, and impacts and have come to the conclusion that we should not push on but complete this phase of the year's efforts and have the traverse team return to McMurdo.

I know this will be a big disappointment to the members of the team, but it should in no way diminish this season's achievement.

We all wish the members of the traverse team a speedy and safe journey back to McMurdo.

That morning we rigged for descent. After lunch, after a group photo at SPT-18—our new farthest south—after caching three hundred flags we no longer needed, and after sixty days on the trail, we turned around. Eight heavy hearts, five heavy tractors and their trains, and one scout vehicle started back down, over the rim of the Polar Plateau, profoundly disappointed. But trotting down slope, our butts bouncing in our saddles like Plains Indians headed home from a raid, we had taken many scalps.

Bits of information suggested the USAP anticipated serious fuel shortages. We knew little more than that. From our camp in the Parade Grounds that evening, cynical utterances vented our disappointment:

"That was a million dollar decision," declared one hand.

"That's just about exactly right," I responded. "*If* NSF chooses to continue the project for another year, it'll cost right about one million dollars. But this was a three-year project. Who knows if NSF will pony up? Fathoming the mind of NSF is like contemplating infinity."

"How does NSF propose to solve this problem they have created for themselves?"

"You got to pay to play. Pay now or pay more later. You lose face if you quit. Look at what they'd be throwing away! Three years!"

"If they really wanted to support us, they could have."

"Apparently they couldn't support us."

"Did they fail to anticipate we would succeed?"

"NSF is unaccustomed to success. We took them by surprise."

They. None of us were part of *them.* We were seasonal contractor workers. And for us, NSF was a distant, inscrutable institution directing the program. But these facts remained: we struggled to reach the Polar Plateau, and we took that ground. From our farthest south, we put the ball back in *their* court. *They* refused us.

We descended the Leverett in two days, enshrouded in pea-soup fog and wet, blowing snow.

On our arrival at the Leverett base, we built a snow berm and parked the D8 for the winter. Leaving the D8 at the bottom had been part of my published operations plan, albeit a small part of the plan. The D8 was a slow moving fuel-hog. By stationing the D8 at the Leverett base, we'd conserve its return fuel for the rest of the fleet's use. And for the first time we'd test the unhampered speed and performance of the other tractors as we headed north.

We left the D8 on its berm with little fanfare. Not until two days later, and ninety miles farther north did I mention in the daily report that, according to plan, I *had* left it. It would be another day, and another fifty miles, before our McMurdo counterparts might reply. By that time, we wouldn't have enough fuel to retrieve the D8, even if so ordered. And leaving the $500,000 machine at the Leverett might give some leverage for winning a fourth year.

Our return to McMurdo slowed a day or two on account of blizzards, but we did post record days, picking up speed, heading for the barn. On January 15 we made sixty-six miles. The next day, eighty-two miles. And the next day, ninety-four miles. Running in high gear, and at 75 percent engine load, we flew across the Shelf on our road, unhampered by the slow D8.

On the morning of January 20 we pulled up to the Shear Zone. Allen O'Bannon and I radared the crossing and found it good to go. By 1100 hours, the main fleet rolled across. At 1430, we crossed the city limits into Williams Field. Along the way we passed a solitary laborer working in the air cargo yard. He'd witnessed our approach from the horizon.

As we drove by, he mounted a cargo pallet and waved two thumbs up, shouting, "Way to go!" Each of us acknowledged his salute as our fleet moved wearily into the Williams Field winter storage area.

We left our sleds there and drove our tractors towards McMurdo. In six more miles we drove onto dirt and stone. As we passed over the high road to town, my boss's boss drove past us in a pickup truck going the other way. He lifted his forearm a couple of inches off the steering wheel.

In town, we found the whole of the USAP caught up in a tempest of fuel woes.

Cargo and fuel flights to South Pole Station had been twenty flights ahead of schedule before we launched in November. Now they were forty flights behind. A protracted spate of foul weather in McMurdo had cancelled many missions. Even Pole's tractor, the one we'd hoped to drive to its new home, was still in McMurdo.

The B-15 iceberg that broke off the Ross Ice Shelf and corked McMurdo Sound two years before had disrupted the annual sea ice formation in the Sound. This year, the ice edge lay eighty miles off shore, where fifteen miles was normal for this time of year. The tanker ship bearing the USAP's annual fuel allotment stood off that ice edge, waiting for icebreakers to open the channel.

One Coast Guard icebreaker tied up at McMurdo, standing down for repairs. Its sister ship anchored stateside, refitting in dry-dock. A Russian icebreaker, standing by to assist the Coast Guard, delayed its arrival at McMurdo Sound. We heard it was in Singapore. Desperate plans had been laid to shut down McMurdo and South Pole to skeleton maintenance crews if the tanker could not deliver. Into the middle of this perfect storm waded the South Pole Traverse.

Two weeks before our return we'd begged for a few thousand gallons of fuel from the top of the Leverett Glacier. Six days after we returned, U.S. Coast Guard and Russian icebreakers escorted U.S. tanker ship *Paul Buck* to the pier in McMurdo. The *Paul Buck* offloaded 6,115,744 gallons of diesel fuel.

|10| Traverse to Williams Field

Erick Chiang, the headman from NSF, stopped by my lunch table in the Mc-
Murdo galley shortly after we returned from our third year. He wanted to see
the fleet with me that afternoon.

"Sure. Got a truck?"

"We'll take the Chalet's. Meet me there at 1:00?" he asked, though it was
more of a polite command.

The Chalet at McMurdo was the well-appointed office building that
housed the big chair, where the senior NSF representative sat. The Chalet
showed off polished wood floors, paneled walls, vaulted ceilings, ceremonial
flags of the Antarctic Treaty nations, and two plush offices among lesser offices.

I walked into the Chalet and caught Erick's eye in one of the better offices.
He was a handsome man, broad shouldered and muscled like an athlete, and
clean shaven with jet black hair. His face and the set of his eyes suggested an
Asian heritage. He stood a head shorter than me. He was always impeccably
clean, even in his Antarctic gear.

With a nod, I signaled I'd wait outside.

In the other offices sat the contractor's staff, among them my boss's boss.
While I grappled with how to do this job on the ground, they wrestled with
managing the cost-plus contract, and with pleasing NSF. They wouldn't be
happy to see me heading off with Erick.

I waited by the truck, alone with my racing thoughts, hoping for a glimpse
of our future. Surely NSF wouldn't throw away three years. There was that
bulldozer at the base of the Leverett. Nobody would leave it there forever. A

traverse sent to retrieve it may as well go the rest of the way. But maybe we were done.

Erick drove while I rode shotgun in the red NSF pickup truck. We left the stony ground and headed over the monotonous snow road to Williams Field.

"Tell me how it all went for you this year?" Erick asked.

Flag after flag zipped by our truck on the flat, white stretches of the Ice Shelf road to Willy. He knew how far we got. What did he want to know besides what he already knew?

"Erick, it went well. We solved all our mobility problems. Not one broken sled. Not one tractor broke down. No shuttling . . . everything worked." Did he understand *no shuttling*?

"Our surface across the Ice Shelf held up. Nobody got stuck." I continued. Did he understand when one tractor got stuck, the whole traverse stops?

"The biggest factor slowing our progress was that huge crevasse field at the far side of the Shelf. It took us weeks to figure a way across it. But once we did get through, the Leverett opened for us with welcome arms."

"A big crevasse field, huh?" Erick asked.

Erick would not have read our daily reports, but I had expected him to know about the crevasse field that damn near scrapped our whole project. That meant nobody told him. Until now.

"Yep. Bigger and more complicated than the Shear Zone. If we hadn't found a way across that, we'd be done now and shouting," I prophesied in hindsight.

We neared the winter yard at Williams Field where our sleds were parked. I pointed across the dash board toward the fleet: "That's our stuff over there. If you go around through those flags, you can drive right up to them."

Half the crew was running borrowed gear back to town, but Russ was still out there "dinking" with something or other to make things just right for winter. Bearded and rough-looking like the biker he was, his overalls and hands bore the grime of his habitual labors. Russ was well known to Erick. Familiar smiles passed between them when we pulled up to the generator module.

"Howdy, Erick," Russ welcomed him eagerly. "So you want to see your *stuff*?"

"Russ," I interjected, "I'm going walk Erick over to our sleds. Can you visit with us for a few minutes in the living module when we get back?"

"Shoor," he drawled. "Happy to."

Erick had seen nothing of our fleet yet. So I showed him all the design improvements we'd made with the supplemental funding won after Year Two: a ski's reshaped nose, a foot wider overall; longer benches that held sled skis astride the tractor tracks; spreader bar sleds that dragged whole pairs of fuel tank sleds outside the tractor tracks. If these did not translate to mobility gains for him, at least he got a visual on what the taxpayers' money had bought.

When we joined Russ in the galley of the living module, Russ immediately asked Erick the big question: "Are we going back to finish the job next year?"

"We'll see what you can do for us, first. I just wanted to see what all this traverse equipment looked like," Erick said.

Russ and I exchanged a questioning look.

"Well . . . has John shown you everything you want to see? Is there anything I can show you?" Russ's brimming enthusiasm could do us nothing but good.

"I have seen the sleds," Erick explained with a quick wave of his hand. And then looking around our well-kept living module, he commented, "It looks like you take good care of this place. You must be comfortable in here?"

Erick was a sporting yachtsman who appreciated ship-shape. That was all Russ needed.

"Well here, look at this." Russ opened a cabinet revealing a trash compactor we installed under the galley sink.

"You wouldn't believe what a fine thing this is. We only brought back three tri-walls of trash from this whole trip!"

Russ referred to triple-walled corrugated cardboard boxes used throughout the program. Our trash tri-walls measured four feet to a side. Did Erick connect reduced waste volume to space savings on a cargo traverse?

"And over here, look at that," Russ said, pointing to an industrial sized microwave oven on the countertop. "It's even got *four* magnetrons! Want to see the engine room?"

Erick checked his watch. "I've got to be back at the Chalet."

Russ and I, two on one, both wanted to know if NSF would fund another year. But Erick was probably tired of getting cornered in McMurdo by folks wanting something from him. Maybe that's why he came out to Willy. Now I heard his clear invitation to leave.

Driving back along the Williams Field road to McMurdo, Erick let me have it. "I would like you to run two traverses next year. I would like you to deliver as many LC-130 loads of cargo to South Pole as possible."

"Erick," I measured my words, "we are tooled up for a proof-of-concept project. We have yet to prove the concept. You are talking regular traverse operations. To do what you ask, you have to first pray that the ground will let us get there. Then we need to buy more sleds. We need to buy more tractors. And you need to send more money."

"Why do you need more tractors?"

What a simple question. What a complex answer.

"We are in the best position to deliver tractors. They could be here at McMurdo already, and we can drive them to South Pole. Next, we need fuel tank sleds. We don't have the capacity to get more than five tractors to Pole. And right now we are seeing that it takes four and a half tractors just to get ourselves there and back before we can deliver anything. We proved *that* in Year Two. Fuel tank sleds invest in future traverses, as well as next year's effort."

"Why can't you do it with what you already have?"

"With what? I just told you we have barely enough to get ourselves there. And you didn't want that D8 we tried to deliver last month."

"How many fuel tank sleds do you need?'

"At least sixteen. Four for each new tractor. We might burn two tanks worth for each tractor making the round trip. The rest of the fuel becomes deliverable cargo. LC-130's deliver a tank-full with each flight in their wing tanks, if that's all they're carrying. One tank sled, one flight."

"Well, how much does that cost?"

There it was . . . Would there be a next year?

"If you're committed to seeing the traverse project through, what does it matter how much it costs? You buy the fleet now, or you buy it later. The stuff you're asking about has to go out for bid, but you'd be looking at $4 to $5 million."

"It's a question of how much we money we have *now*," Erick said.

Meaning how much is left in this fiscal year?

"Erick, how would you run two traverses and get around the environmental documentation? All we're permitted now is to run the proof-of-concept. Three years. Do we amend the initial evaluation to extend another year? Call the first traverse the proof-of-concept, and the second one *regular operations?* As far as I know, the comprehensive evaluation covering regular operations is still in draft."

"The proof-of-concept is over," Erick declared flatly. "But I hadn't thought of the environmental business. You let me worry about that."

"The *concept* has not been proved!" I heard the edge to my voice. "And you can't pretend that it has just by saying so. We've still got three hundred miles to go. What's that like?"

"We are not spending any more money on the proof-of-concept project."

It was a budget category, a line item Erick just vetoed.

I did worry about the environmental business, though. Any screw up and the world's environmentalists would be on us like a curse. Many already thought we were building a superhighway over the pristine continent. That was a nutty impression born in an office and spread by errant pens. I worked in open collaboration with NSF's environmental consultants. We found common ground in safeguarding against fuel spills. It meant life or death for us. They looked at long-term environmental degradation. Our proximate interests were identical: no fuel losses.

And getting two traverses through next year when we hadn't got one through yet required the *full support* he'd once declared. Next month Erick would have to give me $4 to $5 million that he didn't have now to hustle tractors and sleds in time for airlift next August. If we waited any longer, build-slots at the tractor factories would be purchased by somebody else. The lead time to build sleds was nearly gone already. We'd lose two months or more at the get-go just to get the paperwork through the contractor's office.

"You need to be thinking in terms of two traverses next year," Erick declared again, adamantly.

We drove onto the dirt of Ross Island, thus completing our traverse of the McMurdo Ice Shelf to Williams Field and back, in a fat-tired pickup truck over a well-groomed, hard-packed snow road. Erick's reality lay in a fiscal land. Mine was on the snow somewhere between McMurdo and South Pole. I connected with Erick as well as he connected with me: not well.

Back at my McMurdo cubicle, in a building far removed from the Chalet, an e-mail awaited me from my boss's boss: "Next time you want to make an appointment with Erick Chiang, you need to clear it with me."

✧ ✧ ✧

My contract expired in May, after the write up of Year Three. If no money showed up by the end of March, the proof-of-concept project *was* over and I was gone.

My bosses remained indifferent to the project's future, yawning: "NSF will decide. There's only so much money to go around." They were right. It was the same cost-plus no matter where the money went. But as full timers, they enjoyed the luxury of waiting out their jobs to the end of the ten-year contract five or six years away. But I and my crew of seasonal workers were passionate to make this traverse a reality. We wanted a big win for the Antarctic Program. Fighting for our project's future also meant fighting for our jobs.

In late March, I convened our Second Over-Snow Mobility Workshop in a small meeting room of the Denver office. The room opened directly onto the sea of cubicles surrounding my desk. A long oval table dominated the room that was well equipped with computer links, projection equipment, whiteboards, and a dozen plush executive-style caster chairs. That was more than enough chairs for the five of us in conference.

Russell Magsig looked comfortable wearing slacks and a polo shirt, so different from the torn overalls he wore while peering into the inner workings of some tractor. After I promised Russ that we'd have showers, I asked him what role he'd like to play in the traverse future. He wanted a guiding hand in designing and selecting equipment for the future fleet. And he wanted to look after its readiness in the long term. I always involved Russ in key skull sessions like this one.

Two CRREL faces were in the room, including Russ Alger, the University of Michigan snow scientist who had joined us for short stints each of our three years. His work related regional snow quality to our mobility. He'd been on the Leverett with the Evans's team in 1995. His field notes and personal counsel diverted me from the prescribed line up the glacier to locate our own successful route.

Jim Lever, mobility engineer, had also joined us those years. He'd experienced our frustrations at the Shoals of Intractable Funding and our triumph on breaking through. He'd scrambled up the Leverett with us and shared our deep disappointment all the way back to McMurdo.

Both Alger and Lever were solid teammates in the field. Both lent technical credibility to whatever came of our workshop proceedings.

Finally, Dave Bresnahan joined us. Dave's passion for the traverse matched ours. His involvement went back well before Evans's project, and he, like Russ Magsig, had been around when *Linda* went down. Dave knew that when *terrain* came up, the topic was not casual. His presence certified NSF's interest in the outcome of our workshop. He could steer us toward the fiscally doable and prepare his own intramural arguments supporting our conclusions back in D.C.

Our agenda flashed onto the screen. My welcoming comments focused the next three days:

"We are here to see what we can do with *one* traverse. We are not here to dally with the impossible. We have unexplored terrain in front of us, and apparently limited funding, if any, behind us. We have limited *time* as well. Against our agenda, we have deafening background noise: NSF's wish to offset as many LC-130 loads as we can, and second . . . to run two traverses next year."

Each year, the program had accumulated cargo backlogs to Pole with shortfalls in planned airlifts. The traverse had not caused those problems. If anything, NSF's sporadic support for traverse development contributed to that backlog. *Time* now did not permit the matrixed analyses NSF demanded to justify its use of taxpayer money.

"We are going to set the background noise aside until the afternoon of Day Three," I looked squarely at Dave. "I have two reasons for doing this, against which there is no argument. The first is: we can only pull so much load. The number of LC-130s we could offset is a direct function of what our drawbars can pull. Right now, almost all we can pull is invested in getting *us* to Pole, not in delivering cargo. The second reason is simpler: any second traverse requires that the *first* traverse succeeds. Otherwise, the second traverse is not *second*. And we have not proved we can get the first traverse through."

Hypothetical futures that could not come to fruition in one month were off the agenda. Biscuits on the family table were at stake for two of us in the room. Turning our dream into reality in the near future was at stake for all of us.

"So this is what I need you all to help me with: let's see what we can do with *one* traverse. Everything else comes after that."

✧ ✧ ✧

Three weeks later, on April 19, Erick showed up in the Denver office. In a closed-door session, squeezed between his more important meetings, we met in my boss's boss's small office. Erick wore the neat gray suit, yellow shirt and blue tie he'd arrived in that morning. I wore jeans and a long-sleeved tattersall shirt. Both my bosses were present. Their boss was present, too. So was George Blaisdell. His engineering background could translate our mobility issues for Erick. George sat beside me.

"So you want to buy another Caterpillar MT865 tractor?" Erick opened. He sounded familiar with our workshop's concept of operations.

"Another tractor, yes . . . we've proven that need in each of Year Two and Year Three. But not an MT865. The procurement window for that option closed five weeks ago. It'll be another Case," I corrected him.

"But you're delivering South Pole's MT865. Why don't you just take that back to McMurdo, and run a second traverse with it?"

Erick must have been way out on a limb proclaiming two traverses. He was not *that* familiar with our Con-Ops.

"Erick, we're delivering tractors and sleds and a small amount of bulk material cargo. In one traverse, if we get through, we'll offset eleven flights. If we take those same tractors and run them back and forth a second time, not only does the total number of offset flights go down, but South Pole does not get to use the tractor. And we don't have the cargo decks to haul more than one plane-load worth on a second traverse."

Our most favorable scenario depended on delivering tractors, not on taking them back. Taking them back meant we had to take on fuel at South Pole, fuel LC-130s delivered. There'd be a net loss in offset flights. It was a complicated formula, and I knew Erick was smart enough to get it. But I think he had a simplistic vision that he just could not, or would not, shake. He passed over the subject.

"What are these red-sleds I see on your proposal?" he asked, still running the fiscal comb through my line items.

"We still need to haul more fuel with us to run this traverse," I explained. "The lead time window closed on our steel-tank options eight weeks ago. The red-sleds and bladders, and all the stuff in that group, are an idea we came up with in Year Two. They're the only things we can get in the time remaining *and* field a traverse this coming season. Note the cost of two of them is 20 percent the cost of one steel tank sled. Two red-sleds, with bladders on top, give us four thousand gallons. One steel tank gives us only three thousand."

Struggling across the snow swamp in Year Two, we'd dreamed of floating huge loads across the Shelf on hover barges pulled by tractors. That was experimental technology forbidden to us from the beginning. But those dreams spawned our last-ditch solution with the red-sleds today.

Immediately after that field season, I'd found a maker of flexible fuel transport bladders. These were large pillows of rubbery fabric filled with fuel. At eight feet wide and a variety of lengths, they were ideally sized for us. *And*, they were available off the shelf.

The recovery skis we put to good use that year inspired us to try large plastic sheets to carry the bladders. CRREL engineers gave us the final design work, and we found a plastics maker who could make the sheet-sleds to their specifications. The sheets, with the bladders on top, would lie directly on the snow.

"Think they'll work?" Erick asked.

"I don't know. But I want to try them across the Ross Ice Shelf. If we get out two hundred miles, I'll have emptied enough from the steel tanks to transfer the bladder contents into them. The risk is two hundred miles, not the whole route. I'll test them in McMurdo before we launch. If I have any doubts about their performance on the red-sleds, I'll put one bladder on a flatbed sled and haul only an extra two thousand gallons instead of four. If I do *that*, you lose one LC-130 load of bulk cargo."

Erick winced slightly. He didn't cotton to losing a planeload to an experiment.

"We have to amend the Initial Environmental Evaluation to try this," I persisted. "But it is in the spirit of proof-of-concept . . . what technology *will* work?"

He winced again, perhaps at the sound of "environmental," perhaps for the cost to prepare the amendment.

Or did he wince for something else?

Recently, the third and highest floor of the Denver office had seen auditors from the Defense Contracts Audits Agency in residence for a week. I'd no specific idea why they were there, but maybe it was no coincidence that relations between NSF and the support contractor lately seemed less than congenial.

Erick looked squarely at me. I looked squarely back. All other spectators faded into peripheral gray. Erick had been in my tunnel once at South Pole, just him and me then, just straight talk and respect. Perhaps he was judging whether he still heard straight talk, or carefully rendered company-man talk.

"Very well," he ended our meeting. "I will approve your $636,000 proposal, including the Case tractor and the red-sleds. And we will call it *proof-of-concept.*"

Erick's declaration hung in the air for a long moment. Then, with our eyes still fixed on one another's, I nodded slowly: "Thank you."

Nothing more needed saying. I left the cramped office and wandered back to my cubicle. At $636,000 now, and another $340,000 in fiscal year 2006 to run the show in the field, Stretch had been right. That was a million-dollar decision turning us back from SPT-18.

PART III.
YEAR FOUR: PROOF

11 | Return to Farthest South

The last of the breakfast crowd shuffled slowly out of the McMurdo galley, heading off to shops and meeting places to start their day's work. We gathered at our headquarters, an abandoned round table in the corner of the dining room, near the windows.

At round tables in earlier years, we took turns closing our morning briefing with a thought for the day: a poem, line or two of prose, a quote from memory. Spreading the inspirational message duty diluted the oratorical tendency of some and opened fascinating glimpses into the souls of others less prone to speak up. This morning I asked Russ to open our meeting.

"What was that quote you gave us a couple years ago from Jonas Salk?"

Russ had described seeing a girl in an iron lung once. Years later he spied a pile of iron lungs in a scrap heap. Now he leaned back in his chair, rolled his eyes, and searched out a memory residing in a far corner of his brainpan. "Polio gone forever. Lemme see . . . yes . . . I think it was . . ." Russ opened his eyes and leaned forward: "*You can only fail if you give up too soon.*"

That started our Year Four.

Around the table sat Russ, Stretch, and John Van Vlack, our new mechanic. They'd been on station since late August bringing our tractors and sleds out of hibernation. John V. had several years on the Ice working out of the McMurdo Heavy Shop. Clean shaven, sandy hair short to the point of bald, and deeply freckled, John V. was ready with a smile and pleasant to work with.

Judy Goldsberry rejoined us. And Brad Johnson finished his Greenland job in time to help us start this one again. Tom Lyman, our mountaineer from

Montana, brought back his curious mix of high-tech savvy and basic earth-sense. He'd been with us through the heart of the Shear Zone.

The young marine I met on the plane home that first year now joined us. Capt. Greg Feleppa had been called back to service in Iraq. I found him a year later working the parts window at the heavy shop.

Of the five of us who returned, Stretch was the most reluctant. Our exasperation on turning back was, for him, particularly acute. Many of us felt we weren't getting any younger. Maybe we'd not physically qualify for another year . . . if there were another year. We couldn't then penetrate the rationale that turned us back when we were so close to the Pole. We'd all felt robbed.

I cajoled Stretch last April, "If *you* had not left *your* bulldozer at the Leverett, we wouldn't have a Year Four. Are you going to let some other guy take your title: The Man who Drove the Bulldozer to South Pole?"

"I'll think about that," Stretch answered in an e-mail.

I later sent him our Con-Ops for Year Four and asked the straightforward question: "Are you in?"

His reply came back, simply worded. "I'm in."

Every one of us was "in" this October, gathered around the breakfast table. I looked across to Rick Campbell, our traverse coordinator. Rick was the skinny, ponytailed fellow who'd met me with a pile of reports my first day in Denver. He'd briefed Brian from the field support office in McMurdo before Brian took off in *Linda*. The only one of us employed full time, Rick was allotted half of that full time toward traverse support. His heart was 100 percent with us.

"Rick, tell us where we're at with our stuff coming in, please, sir."

"Happy to." Rick flipped open his stenographer's book and ran down the list.

A C-17 delivered our fourth fleet tractor: a new red Case Quadtrack. Counting the Pole's MT 865, our launch fleet now numbered five. We'd pick up a sixth, Stretch's D8R, at the Leverett. Then we'd deliver both the MT865 and the D8R to Pole.

The same plane brought our fuel bladder sleds. Environmental permission to use them came while we were at McMurdo, rigging for launch.

A few odds and ends were still missing, like 1,500 green flags on ten-foot bamboo poles. These would mark our new trail and restore markings on the old. Two weeks before launch they'd been put on a boat in California and sent to New Zealand. They wouldn't arrive on-Ice until mid-December.

"On a fucking boat?" I shot back at Rick, who had the unfortunate duty to inform me at my McMurdo cubicle.

We'd scheduled them for airlift to Christchurch, then airlift again to the Ice. Airlifting was a penalty we paid for late project funding. Meanwhile, NSF had been leaning on the contractor's logistics group for delinquent deliveries. The pressure filtered to the purchasing group which changed the *required on station* dates to reflect a new *on time* performance. The new on time for us would occur a month after we left McMurdo.

My boss was on the Ice occupying a closed-door office around the corner from my cubicle. "Did you know about the boat?" I asked him.

"No," he said, plainly surprised.

I, our whole project, needed all the time in the field nature would give us to get that one traverse through. My e-mail to the logistics group pleaded our need for the missing items, begging for any way possible to get them to us and not delay our launch. On the copy list I included my boss, my boss's boss back in Denver, and Dave Bresnahan, who was on the Ice. We were all in the loop.

Forty-eight hours later a return e-mail from my boss's boss chastised me for including Dave on my original, breaking the chain of command. The scolding recalled a desperate scene from a familiar movie where all the Zulus in the world were busy wrecking a British square. A frantic soldier in the center tried smashing open an ammunition crate with his rifle butt. The supply sergeant threatened courts-martial, insisting the crate be opened according to regulations: by twisting the screws out with a screwdriver.

Dave was the top of the chain, and he'd told me to keep him informed in that first phone call I made from Denver. I promised if I took the job, I would. Dave could order our stuff delivered with priority, if he felt it was a priority. I returned an e-mail to my boss's boss in Denver, asking simply, "Did you know about the boat?"

"Yes."

✧ ✧ ✧

Eight at the breakfast round table would be heading out soon. Rick would see us off, then head home for the States.

"So we're going to have to come up with work-arounds," I said, managing a calm tone. "Let's start with flags. Rick, how many green flags do we have coming?"

"One thousand, five hundred." Rick's spreadsheet mind dipped into his archive. I couldn't ask for a more meticulous coordinator.

"And they're ten-footers, right?"

"Right."

"How many can Science Support spare us?" I asked.

"Six hundred and fifty," he said, right back at me. "But they're only eight-footers. Air Field Management will give us 950, also eight-footers."

Our flags were durable, quality-made items on poles stout enough to withstand gales and tall enough to remain visible after years of snow accumulation. We depended on those flags. Others would depend on them for years to come.

"And both Science and Air Field will send us off with theirs, and accept our ten-footers in a month or so?"

"Yes."

"Good. Rick, take Greg and Judy. Get the flags down to the staging area on the sea ice this morning. We'll load them up this afternoon. What else you got?" I asked, expecting news of other missing items on the boat.

"Air Field asks who's going to pay for the labor to cut two feet off our ten-footers?" Rick reported.

I sighed. "Cut me two feet off of one of the eight-footers, would you please? Make it the top two feet with the green banner still on it. I'll see if they really want a two-foot flag."

That drew a laugh around the table. The rest did not. Corporate Safety had issued a new rule prohibiting anyone from lifting over forty pounds, or working above four feet without tying off. The forty and four rule. Safety required an elaborate, written justification for any variance.

"Over the next few days, be careful who's watching. Let's get out of town before paper work grinds us to a halt."

The day was gray, the same color as the sea ice we stood on at our staging area just off-shore from town. There was no wind. Air Field's spindly flag poles, each as big as my little finger, lay on the ice strapped down to a pallet. I pulled one out of the bundle and the bamboo stick snapped in two.

Stretch lay down on the ice, working on one sled's running gear. When he finished his job, he crawled out and joined me by the milvan, which was a standard shipping container that served as our parts supply sled.

"You wanted to see me?" Stretch asked, business-like. At six feet, five inches he stood a good two inches taller than me, and now close enough to me that I could speak softly.

Stretch had served on the Defense Early Warning, or DEW, line project in the Canadian Arctic years ago. He later became a sergeant in the combat infantry in Vietnam, though he'd wanted helicopters. He returned from that war to Wisconsin for farming, and he raised a beautiful daughter who'd since grown into a sharp, professional woman in the information technology world.

Stretch was a deep thinker. When he acted, he acted deliberately. Give him the information he needed, and he'd bring any mission to a successful conclusion. Yet he shunned the madness of crowds. His current reading interests included biographies of Benjamin Franklin and Thomas Jefferson. I'd brought a book or two with me this year, specifically to share with Stretch.

"Stretch, two new guys this year have asked who takes charge if I'm unable to carry on. I haven't answered them yet, but I'm about to. And I want your buy-in. If something happens to me on the trail, I want you to take charge. Whether that means go forward or come back, that'll be for you to decide."

Stretch's eyes bored into mine. "I am surprised. And I'm flattered you have such faith in me."

"I always have, Stretch. From the days we first ran the radar out to GAW. Just you and me. And ever since then. You studied the maps, and ran your own GPS. You, of all, have a better idea of where we are at any time. The rest of the job is a gimme. You know the machines. Folks respect you. What say you?"

"Very well, I will," he consented.

I didn't intend to announce my choice, exactly. Teasing on the trail, such as might arise from my announcement, we could do without. But I told Stretch that he was my designate last year, too. Stretch's eyebrows rose at this new knowledge. The question didn't come up then, so I hadn't mentioned it. I simply placed his name in an envelope stored in the cubby by my bunk. Another of the crew would unseal that envelope if it was necessary.

This season, with the subject in the open, I advised my boss of my plans. But he declared the decision as to my replacement would be his and his boss's. "You're not hearing me," I hurled back. This was not about job-title changes and paperwork and approvals and policies and procedures and human resources and other irrelevancies. "I'm talking about a bad situation in the field that requires an instant leader and change of command."

Eight of us had just enough room to shuffle around our own galley. Some sat on the bench mounted along the wall, behind the narrow board that was our dining table. Others sat on stools, and some leaned against the kitchen counter. With nine of us today, the ninth being Rick, somebody had to stand back in one of the bunkrooms to hear.

"Tom and Greg have both asked, 'Who's in charge if something should happen to you?' A legitimate question, it deserves an answer."

Tom, at sixty-four, was the oldest of our crew. Greg, at thirty-three, was the youngest. We joked that I hired Greg because I hired Tom . . . to bring down the average age of the whole crew, or *they* would not let us go. All of us together averaged 51½ years old.

Small group dynamics in remote field settings were a natural concern of Tom's. But he understood the traverse business was not solely a mountaineering proposition. He also understood we were dealing with big machines on an industrial scale.

Independently, Greg asked the same question. Greg, however, was totally new to our group. I'd sought advice on his marine background from my friends who were marines. One Desert Storm veteran observed from Greg's resume that he'd been given command of an amphibious assault vehicle company, as a second lieutenant.

"That's rare, and speaks well for him. Company commands usually go to captains," my friend explained. "The other stuff tells me the Marines invested pretty high-power training in him. They don't do that for everybody." He referred to Greg's training in Anti-Terrorism tactics and command. Greg's question came natural for a marine.

I cleared my throat. "Among our combined talent, we've got all we need to deal with any situation. At this stage, I'm not particularly important . . .

except I've a better feel than any of us for the ground ahead. But down the trail, my incapacity for any reason could happen." Thinking of Brian in *Linda*, Bwana Kim in the Shear Zone, and the three close encounters last year, I began with the ultimate "incapacity." "If I die, my first wish is that my body be left where it is. My wife understands that. Although at the time, we were thinking of letting the coyotes have at my bones . . ."

That raised a smile or two.

"But if you must move my dead body for whatever reason, know that my second wish is that I be cremated."

More smiles linked the dying wish of Robert Service's poem "The Cremation of Sam McGee."

"That's out of the way . . . In the event of my incapacity, a marked envelope in my cubby contains my instructions for succession. I want one person to open that envelope and read it at the appropriate time. Stretch, you be that one who opens the envelope. Call McMurdo after that, if you want."

Stretch nodded. The one word penned on the paper sealed inside that envelope read: "S-T-R-E-T-C-H."

If they had to turn back for whatever reason, flags planted every quarter mile pointed the way home. Tom, Greg, and John V. had not been on that trail. They couldn't visualize that elegant simplicity stretching 738 miles from McMurdo. I pointed to maps and distance charts posted on our galley walls. All anyone needed to know about getting back to McMurdo from the top of the Leverett was there. If they wanted more, route notes and operations reports stored in the cabinet above the comms desk would give it.

None of us knew what the ground beyond our farthest south was like. Part of our job was to find out. But all my research on those last three hundred miles traveled with us, and I'd brief them on the ground ahead at appropriate times on the trail. Now I showed them where that information resided on our computer's desktop. Anyone was free to access it, without a password, at any time.

"As a final note," I explained, "in the event of my incapacity, the best of us to interpret those digital maps and coordinate lists is Tom Lyman." I hadn't spoken of that to Stretch, but he just learned he'd not be alone.

"This afternoon we'll start staging sled trains to Williams Field along the Pegasus Snow Road. We're going to launch from Willy sooner that you think."

✧ ✧ ✧

All our tractors and sleds lined up head-to-tail on the Williams Field road at the "city limits." The fleet weighed in at 933,000 pounds, our heaviest launch weight ever. For now we parked, with engines idling. It was picture time.

Dave Bresnahan showed up. After we'd won our funding in April, I extended Dave my formal offer to join us. We'd discussed the possibility for over a year. NSF stood to win, for it did not have anybody within its walls that knew traversing by experience. How unlike the French program that was. It had Patrice Godon. On the other hand, we'd get to pick Dave's brain in the field and fathom the bureaucratic mysteries that propelled us. A few days before my deadline, Dave opted out for the very good reason of other needs of his family. I immediately phoned Greg Feleppa: "You're hired."

Dave generously threw us a party two evenings before in McMurdo, dates and friends only. The intimate affair at the comfortable NSF quarters brought Ice stories out of all of us.

Ann Hawthorne, an NSF grantee photographer, also showed up. We'd become close friends, and she held the respected position in my family of "honorary auntie" to my two children. The striking gray-haired woman, half-hillbilly and half–southern belle, once remarked that she and I were fraternal twins, separated by birth.

Ann took the pictures that morning. The long line of tractors and sleds defined her horizon. In her foreground, our disorderly crew bore smiling, hopeful faces. A warm sun lit her subjects under a bright blue sky on the chill November day.

After we stood for the picture, I walked across the snow to my waiting tractor, smiling at a message George Blaisdell sent me that morning: "Take the big scalp this time." George and Dave fought the intramural battles for us at NSF that sent us out to the field to fight for ourselves. Now, looking forward to the unknown future, I felt pretty good. There was nothing more we could do to be ready. I climbed into *Fritzy*'s cab, repeating to myself once again, "There is no other job. This is the job."

A cesium clock on board a Navstar satellite overhead signaled my GPS the time was precisely 1100 hours local.

"Mac-Ops, Mac-Ops . . . South Pole traverse."

"Go ahead, South Pole Traverse, this is Mac-Ops."

"Mac-Ops, South Pole Traverse is departing McMurdo at 1100 hours on the eleventh day of the eleventh month for the South Pole, with all souls, tractors, and sleds as previously noted. Estimated time of return . . . sometime in January or February 2006."

"Copy all, Traverse. Good luck. Mac-Ops clear."

"Traverse clear."

Switching to our own frequency, I called Greg at the head of the line: "Take us out!"

The PistenBully crawled forward slowly, pulling a long rope tether tied to two snowmobiles on red plastic sleds. Greg captained our radar and flagging team this year. We'd recently named his vehicle *Wrong Way*.

Brad pulled in behind Greg, running the new Case tractor. We named that one *Red Rider*. Brad pulled the living and energy module sleds. Behind those, he towed a steel tank sled. And behind that, he pulled a single CRREL spreader bar sled hitched to the two bladder sleds. Each bladder rode on its own red plastic sheet. All together, Brad pulled seven thousand gallons of fuel in addition to the modules.

Judy rolled out next in the *Elephant Man*. John V. rode with her as passenger for the time being. The *Elephant Man* pulled our food van and another steel fuel tank sled.

I swung into line with *Fritzy* and its rear-mounted crane, pulling our spare parts van and two steel fuel tank sleds.

Stretch followed in Pole's MT865, which hadn't been flown to Pole last year after all. He pulled a flatbed sled loaded with a skid-steer tractor and its accessories. Hitched behind the flatbed sled was a ninety-cubic yard capacity belly-dump trailer on tracks specially designed for hauling snow at South Pole Station. It weighed sixty-two thousand pounds, cleared eight feet high when empty, and ran thirty feet long assembled. Since it was painted all white, we called the trailer *Snow White*, or sometimes *Black Beauty*. Everything in Stretch's train, including his tractor, was deliverable cargo.

Russ brought up the rear with *Quadzilla*, our first Case tractor. He pulled a CRREL spreader bar sled, which in turn pulled four steel fuel tank sleds, paired two by two on either side of the spreader.

Ann's pictures show that right after we rounded the post marking BI-SP, less than a quarter mile off the Willy Road, the weather sat down on us.

✧ ✧ ✧

Greg lay a track to the right of the green flag line that took us out to the Shear Zone. He looked for flags in front of him, but through the blowing snow they appeared and disappeared. The rest of us had tractors to look at. It had to be quite a storm before we lost sight of a whole tractor a hundred yards ahead. It wasn't that kind of storm yet, but the light was flat enough that I couldn't make out the *Elephant Man*'s tracks. I focused instead on Judy's tank sled, closed the distance, and readied to stop in case she did. Then I settled back in my seat, and breathed a heavy sigh, happy to be underway.

I put Judy in the *Elephant Man* this year deliberately. She'd be running the *Elephant Man* back from our farthest south. If that happened to be South Pole, she'd be hauling back one or more passengers. Because of the calming effect Judy had on us, we were nicer to each other. Her presence in that outsized cab would dampen the grumbling that could infect the group when some rode as idle passengers.

To hedge my bets, one morning two weeks ago at our breakfast table back in McMurdo I called the meeting to order: "We will have only one cynic this year."

It was pretty easy to read everyone's face: What the hell is he rattling on about now?

"Any cynicism shown by anyone else will not be allowed," I spoke sternly. "Captain Feleppa?"

"Yes, sir."

"Captain Feleppa, you are our designated cynic."

Greg's eyes widened. Before he could say, "but, but, but . . ." I continued. "This is an important job. We can't every one of us be cynics. But every group needs one good one, so long as he's on our side. We didn't have any good cynics last year. A good cynic is invaluable. He's the one that catches us in the middle of some harebrained idea we're about to go off on and reminds us: 'What makes you think you can get that part you need in time?' You'll do this job for all of us."

Greg fought to keep the corners of his mouth from curling. How I kept a straight face, I'll never know.

"From time to time, I'll call on our designated cynic for his input. Do we all understand?" The group returned bewildered nods all around. "Okay. The team cynic is Captain Feleppa."

After we broke up, Greg approached me rising from the table. "Boss, I don't think I can do this job very well. I'm more of a positive, straight-ahead guy," he said, seriously concerned.

"You mean you can't do that job, marine?"

"No sir, I don't mean that. I just think somebody else could do a better job for you."

The galley was completely empty now, but for him and me. "Greg, look. I had a bunch of real sourpusses last year when we came back. Any of us, including me, might make a mistake or get confused. We lost all humor about it. I don't want that to happen this year. It's better to laugh. By officially designating you as cynic, you who are nothing if not positive and straight ahead, then I've officially said nobody else can have that role. Now, can you do that job for me or not?"

Greg looked at me sideways. "I'll try," he said. "It'll take practice."

"Don't worry about that. You've already done most of it by innocently sitting there. When I need the cynic, you'll know it. It'll be when somebody else tries to take your job away from you. I'll need you to step up and reclaim it."

That conversation was two weeks old, but I thought about those things once I was alone in my cab: Judy and Greg, and keeping the crew's spirits in good shape.

We pulled into the Shear Zone camp at GAW with enough visibility to see its perimeter flags and set up camp.

I'd been here a month ago with CRREL's Steve Arcone to inspect the crossing. Back in McMurdo, we combed over the printed radar record and then compared it to last year's. Several crevasses had widened, their walls separating from our fill plugs. Unusual sagging in the surface layers appeared above our fill plugs. But overall, I judged the crossing safe for this year.

We could still work the crossing in this weather, and we had three hours left in our day. Keeping our momentum outbound felt right. So I assigned tasks to different folks, then Brad and I took *Fritzy* across the Shear Zone first.

We stopped at a two-inch-by-four-inch board standing upright and showing only two feet above the snow. Carved into both sides of this signpost was its name: HFS 3+8. It marked eight flags past the third milepost due east from

GAW. At HFS 3+8, our route turned hard right then headed south to the Pole. When we made that turn we *knew* we were looking south.

I turned *Fritzy* around, then Brad and I stepped out onto the snow to do a job we'd done before. While I unfolded the crane, Brad grabbed a light cargo chain and walked over to the signpost. I positioned the crane hook a few inches above it. Brad wrapped the chain around the board and looped it over the hook. I raised the boom, tensioning the chain. When the icy grip of snow released it, the eight-foot-long board popped straight up. Then I lowered the crane, and Brad re-stood the post in its same hole, this time showing six feet.

Folding the crane back up, I nodded to Brad, "That ought to be good for another two years."

We climbed back in *Fritzy*, moved up the line towards GAW, and stopped at HFS. The old milepost now showed four feet above the snow. Ten feet showed when we'd first planted it three years ago. After we bolted an extension to it, it stood ten foot tall again. I said, to myself as much as to Brad, "And *that* might be good for five years. Who knows when we'll come back this way again?"

Brad dryly added, "I think we'll be back here in January."

I enjoyed working with Brad. He once flattered me when I was driving the tunnel at Pole by asking my advice on a blasting problem he faced in McMurdo. Brad was a more accomplished blaster than me. He'd worked on the Crazy Horse Memorial in South Dakota, an entire mountain sculpture. I, on the other hand, merely extended my mining skills to blasting problems in Antarctica. However, I became very good at blasting snow and ice. More than once Brad and I approached each other as colleagues. Today we worked as partners.

We were raising the signpost at Crevasse 20—Snap—when we gave way to Stretch in the MT pulling the flatbed sled and *Snow White* toward HFS. Behind him Russ and *Quadzilla*, with John V. riding in the cab, pulled a spreader bar sled across.

This spreader bar was a triangular frame made of six-inch iron pipe. Its apex, or point, hitched directly to the rear of a tractor. Four-foot-long skis at its rear corners supported its eighteen-foot-wide span. Hitch points welded above each ski held a sled train apiece. Since the whole assembly, sled trains and all, was too wide for our twenty-foot crossing, Russ brought the spreader bar sled across first.

Brad and I had worked back to the Miracle Mile signpost when Russ and Stretch passed us going back to GAW, this time with just their tractors. We'd worked our way to Personal Space when they passed us again, each pulling two steel tank sleds headed toward HFS. Given the traffic, it felt like we were working in a railroad switching yard.

Near Crevasse 6, where we'd once stuck a bulldozer, Judy, Tom, and Greg passed us going the other way too. They were reflagging the strain grid. They should've passed us long ago, but here they were, still working in the first mile of the crossing. Tom did not look happy.

"John," he said, "These flags are snapping in two, or even splitting when we try to push the bamboo into the snow. They're toothpicks! We have to poke holes with a shovel handle before we can plant them."

Our sturdy ten-footers sailed somewhere on the Pacific Ocean. Jeff Scanniello would come out to the Shear Zone in a few days to resurvey the grid. The grid flags were getting low enough in the snow that they'd be buried in another year. I'd told Tom to plant the new flags with the banners plenty high.

"Tom, Greg, Judy . . . these are all we've got to work with. Maybe when we get back to McMurdo in January or February our good flags will be on station. Meanwhile, we need to do this here for Scanniello. Do your best." It could've been worse. Roald Amundsen forgot shovels. But he faced his shortcoming with a self-deprecating humor I found unattainable in our circumstances.

Back at camp we put an end to a good day, while the weather turned nasty with blowing snow.

That evening, I phoned in our first daily report to an after-hours answering machine in McMurdo. Tomorrow morning Rebecca Hooper would transcribe the report and distribute it through the e-mail system. Personality entered the process in the outgoing voice messages she directed our way. Rebecca was a bright, pretty young lady, eager to act as our official point-of-contact with the world. From time to time she would leave a cheerful message for me, or a flirtatious message for one of our bachelors. A new message from Becky always made the rounds in camp.

I didn't expect any messages this first day on the trail, so I was surprised to get one from Rick: "John, your flags arrived today on a C-17. Your instructions?"

Dave must have stamped his feet and made something move!

"Judy," I hailed from our comms desk. "How far did you guys get with your flagging today?"

"About halfway. We'll finish it up tomorrow," she answered.

"I've got a new job for you three. Take the *Elephant Man* back to Mc-Murdo. Return those flags we got from Air Field. Return the Science flags, too. Our ten-footers arrived today. Load them all up on the *Elephant*'s deck and bring them back here. Rick will be expecting you. Bring back anything else of ours that may have arrived."

"You want that tomorrow?"

"Yes I do. Fuel up in McMurdo before you come back, please."

Stretch woke ahead of me and had already started into his huge bowl of oatmeal. Outside our galley window, the weather had turned to blizzard. The flags would have to wait. Quietly, I whispered into each bunkroom: "Sleep in. We're not going anywhere."

When I called a "sleep in," I usually gave a new time for up-and-at-'em. Normally, we tried to get rolling by 0730. This morning, I sat down at the breakfast table and stared off into space, thinking of things we could do. Then I made a pot of coffee for me and those who would be trickling out of their bunks soon.

"Stretch, hasn't this happened to us every year?" I whispered. "Our first day out of town, we get stuck with a blizzard at the Shear Zone?"

"I believe you're right," he played back his memories. "Mm-hmm. Every year."

The blizzard didn't let up the entire day. Later in the morning Tom gave an hour-long class on mountaineering knots. In the afternoon I lectured on our route across the Ross Ice Shelf. Three of our group had never been on the Shelf. The others needed the reminder. Using the big map on the galley wall and detailed maps stored on our laptop, we reviewed the terrain features and crevasse areas ahead. I announced four planned stops where our mechanics could schedule maintenance. On those days others would search for crevasses, or tend to chores we'd save for the occasion. When I finished the briefing, Greg's prospecting team lingered.

"John V., when we get our good flags back here, we want to re-flag the next hundred miles to SOUTH. That's as far as we got at the end of Year One. Those flags were getting wind-whipped and threadbare when we last saw them. This year there's not much left but the poles.

"Greg, you and Tom run the radar all the way. Even though we've been over this ground before, it'll be good practice. And Tom, you're going to see flat stratigraphy for a long time, but you'll have a complete radar perspective of the whole Shelf."

Realizing I'd stepped on Greg, I corrected myself. "You are captain of the prospecting team. Switch your team's roles around as you wish. But I'm interested in everybody learning each other's job. Okay?"

"Copy that, Boss," Greg said.

"My name's *John*," I reminded him.

"Now another word about flags," I continued. "We run our flag lines straight. It means everything when visibility is low. If you can spot two flags ahead of you, you can line on those two to find the next one. If your flag line is crooked, you don't know where to look, and you'll get off the proven road. On this next hundred miles, put a new flag twenty feet down the line from the old one. Put it exactly in line with all the ones you'll be looking back at. You can do that by eyeball. Do *not* put a new one right next to an old one. Can you tell me why?"

Greg spoke up, "Because two flags planted close together mark your old campsites."

Good. Greg's studied the route notes.

I planted the camp flags myself, usually a red flag right next to a green one. That's where I took our GPS position for the daily reports. Even though the banners might get completely worn off the bamboo, two sticks standing next to each other marked a ghost town. We may have peed there, and I didn't want that snow getting into our snow melter.

That ended the briefing. With the blizzard still rocking our quarters atop its sled, each of us worked out our own solution for the day's remains. I went to my bunk and took up H. G. Wells's *A Short History of the World*. I wanted background on the Middle East business. Wells gave me a Victorian's eye view.

✧ ✧ ✧

In workable morning weather, Judy, Tom, and Greg departed for Mc-Murdo. Brad and I completed re-flagging the strain grid using some of the better Science flags we held back. Then the five of us who remained in camp finished shuttling sleds across the Shear Zone. By afternoon, the dregs of the storm blew out. A blue sky broke sunny and clear.

By 1700 hours we reassembled on the Ross Ice Shelf side of the Shear Zone, pointed south. I kicked back inside the galley with Stretch, thinking about starting the evening meal. Brad, Russ, and John V. puttered around outside, soaking up the sun on a fine afternoon in Antarctica.

The comms desk radio squawked: "South Pole Traverse . . . *Elephant Man.*"

Due west, out the window over the galley sink, a dark dot moved over the snow near GAW.

"Go ahead *Elephant*," I answered.

"Can we come across?" Judy asked.

"You bet. How'd you do?"

"We have presents."

A halfhour later the *Elephant* pulled up to its slot and plugged in. Beautiful bundles of ten-foot flags, all 1,500 of them, were securely lashed to the tractor's deck. Judy also brought electric heating pads for the tractors' oil sumps, a spare data link for our iridium phone, and a vacuum cleaner . . . not everything we had coming, but all good stuff. They'd made a long trip into town and back, and I thanked them.

"Boy, were they surprised to see us!" Judy laughed. "They all thought something horrible had gone wrong!"

With a sense of piracy this morning, I'd reminded Judy they would arrive in McMurdo in time for Sunday brunch. This evening we enjoyed her loot: fresh fruit and cheese and pastries for dessert.

We awoke to a beautiful, clear day. The Ross Ice Shelf before us stretched south to infinity. To the east, its vast reaches led to places we would not go. The stony ground of White Island, Black Island, and Minna Bluff formed our western horizon. In a few days they'd fall away as we lost all sight of land. Behind us steamed Mount Erebus, the mighty volcano that made Ross Island. Erebus would be the last to disappear. Perhaps in a week we'd catch our first glimpse of the rising Transantarctics.

In *Fritzy*'s cab, sunlight streamed through the window glass and warmed my mechanical environment. Our tractors and sled trains were so big that I couldn't see around any of them. Nor could I see any single person, either in their own cab or outside of it. The mere thought of running over someone walking around a sled train when its tractor started moving brought shudders. At 0730 I started the radio check.

"*Wrong Way*, you got three aboard?"

"Two aboard, one on a snowmobile," Greg called back. *That's three.*

"Brad, are you ready?"

"*Red Rider*'s ready."

Four.

"*Elephant* . . . Judy. You ready?" Judy and Brad would run in front of me today.

"*Elephant*'s ready."

"Stretch?" Stretch was behind me.

"R-ready."

"Russ? How's the caboose?" Russ ran behind Stretch.

"*Quadzilla*'s ready." *Six and seven, and I make eight.*

"Okay, Greg. Take off."

The clang of drawbars clapping steel hitches rippled through the fleet as we pulled into formation, one tractor at a time. The PistenBully swung in front, towing two snowmobiles. John V., bundled up, rode one of them with fifty flags at the ready. Brad rolled out next. Behind him one, two, three, and finally four sleds started sliding forward. Then Judy and the *Elephant Man*: one, two sleds. Then me in *Fritzy*. I felt my train lurch: one, two, three sleds.

A few seconds passed. Stretch radioed, "I'm rolling."

Finally Russ: "*Quadzilla*'s rolling."

The Ross Ice Shelf is for crossing, and this morning our sails unfurled. Our best daily distance made good for the loaded, outbound traverse last year logged 50½ miles. This year, once we passed the dorniks and sailed past SOUTH, we made fifty-five. The next day we made sixty. And the day after that we made seventy. The paper traverse to Pole worked if we averaged only fifty miles a day.

Our sixty-mile day might have been better, but for an unusual interruption. I told the crew that morning, "Expect a Twin Otter sometime today. If we're moving, close up ranks and stop in line on the trail. He'll land beside us. We won't make camp."

New digital data had come into McMurdo a couple days before. Our Iridium link didn't have the capacity to receive it in the field. Dave copied it to disc and tried to chopper it out to us, but McMurdo weather had grounded him. We'd since passed out of helicopter range. Today Dave was going to try it with a Twin Otter.

"What is it?" Brad asked.

"I expect it will be a map of some sort."

A map of the breach through The Shoals of Intractable Funding, I hoped. The measurements at our monument posts last year predicted the ice moved fast in that region. Our flag line could've drifted toward some shoal we didn't know about. The breach might not be open this year, and I didn't want to spend another month looking for a new one.

"It comes from the National Geospatial-Intelligence Agency." That sounded impressive. "They call themselves NGA, and they're wrapped up some way with the National Reconnaissance Office. They were looking at the Shoals last month. It's spook stuff, and I don't understand all I know about it."

Eyebrows raised around the galley. We had an event coming.

My desire for a reliable map of hidden crevasses found expression before I'd ever seen the Shear Zone. And though we'd tried airborne infrared and airborne radar in the field that first year, we had little success making that map.

After the year of our miserable slog across the Ross Ice Shelf, I attended a USAP Planning Conference in Syracuse. This was near the New York Air National Guard's base at Schenectady. As always, the Guard was well represented. And they were friends of the traverse. They saw the traverse not replacing air missions to Pole but offering them mission options to different locations around the continent.

Colonel Dunbar was one of those friends. He caught me at the snack table, in the hotel hallway between conference sessions. He was probably a little bit older than me, but like all the clean-shaven guardsmen, he had a boyish face. Wherever I ran into him, whether on the Ice, at the contractor's office, or at these conferences, he was upbeat about the Guard's mission.

"There're some people here I want to introduce you to. They're with the National Geospatial-Intelligence Agency, and I think they've got something you can use. They want to meet you."

"The National what?"

"The National Geospatial-Intelligence Agency. They run the satellites that look down on you and read what brand of cigarettes you're smoking."

"Well, I don't smoke. Can they read that?" I laughed. Colonel Dunbar laughed, too. I licked the pastry remains off my fingertips, grabbed a napkin to finish the job, and wondered how reading cigarette labels in Antarctica from an orbiting satellite was going to help the traverse.

Colonel Dunbar led me to an unused room off the hallway. Turning through the door, he beckoned to a couple other men standing among others mingling in the hall.

"John, this is Colonel Bright," he said, indicating the one who wore an air force uniform, another boyish looking man. Then, gesturing to the other gentleman dressed in business-like civilian clothes, he said, "And this is Pete Ofstedal with the NGA."

Pete wore glasses and was balding. He was a fit man who displayed perfect posture.

"Howdy, fellas," I greeted them, shaking hands.

"Colonel Bright and Pete Ofstedal are working on analyzing deep field landing sites in Antarctica. You might be facing some of the same problems they're looking at."

I could imagine their concerns with deep field landings. A picture at my desk showed one of their LC-130s with its ski slumped in a crevasse. That happened two years ago. I picked it up from there: "You want to know where the hidden crevasses are? And something about the surface roughness of a prospective landing site?"

Pete nodded, "Precisely."

"And you're using satellites to look down and see what you can see?"

"They are among our 'National Assets,'" Pete confirmed, using an oblique reference to "secret satellites."

"Colonel Dunbar here says you can read the label off a cigarette pack at one hundred miles. Can you see through snow and find a hidden crevasse?"

"That's what we'd like to know. We have a multispectral capability."

Meaning not just the visible spectrum that reads cigarette labels, I thought. "Are you talking infrared?"

"That's classified," Pete said.

Nobody had ever said that to me seriously before. Always it came in the form of a joke, followed by "If I told you, I'd have to kill you."

"Could you could produce a flat map that showed hidden crevasses?"

"That's *exactly* what we'd like to do," he said.

"Me, too. How can we help each other?"

Other folks peeked into the room, and, seeing the four of us quietly talking, they ducked back out. Movements in the hallway suggested another conference session was getting started. The four of us, however, were content to stay where we were.

"I understand you know where some hidden crevasses are?" Pete asked. He'd seen my presentation earlier. It included pictures of the Shear Zone.

"And you want to do some ground-truthing?" I asked. My eyes narrowed, looking sideways at Pete.

"That would be ideal."

"How close can you get? If you can read a cigarette label, you are talking pretty close?"

"How close we can get, as you say, is also classified. But we can produce geo-referenced imagery, and each pixel has a tag."

Geo-referenced meant latitude and longitude fixes. The question was: how big were their pixels? I already had access to twenty-five-meter pixel imagery on RADARSAT. They were too large to show all but the biggest crevasses.

"I'd like to know something about your wavelengths *and* your resolutions."

"You need a security clearance for that. Do you have one?"

"No, but I'll get one. I don't know how to do that yet, but I will," I told him. "But how about an image itself?"

I told them about a fellow at NSF who once sent me a "derived" image of ground we crossed on the way to the Shear Zone. Colonels Dunbar and Bright were both familiar with that ground. It was the White Out Landing Area downwind from Williams Field. The derived image showed lines and color-shaded areas, but the fellow who gave it to me couldn't, or wouldn't, identify its classified sources. The image was of no use since I didn't know what the symbols meant.

"We could probably work around that," Pete encouraged me.

"Great. So, I need to give you something *you* can use."

Our road across the Shear Zone crossed a lot of crevasses. We blew up their bridges and filled them. All our work was now covered under new snow, but I'd marked every crevasse with signposts and flags. Because the markers, and in fact the whole road, moved, Jeff Scanniello surveyed the markers annually. He used highly accurate, differential GPS.

"The crossing is three miles long. Suppose I gave you the coordinates of the endpoints of that line, and simply told you 'between these two endpoints are many crevasses,' but I didn't tell you where they were. Could you then take that information and have a look at the ground along the road?"

"Yes," Pete said. "That is exactly the kind of information we can work with. And you would be able to tell us afterwards how our work compares to what you know?"

"Certainly. But I'd want to see your product, not just send you the answer sheet."

"With a *secret* level clearance you can do that," Pete explained.

I was quite satisfied with the way our conversation was going. Pete and the two colonels were, too.

"What does all this stuff cost, by the way? I don't manage a huge budget."

Pete answered, full of gravity, "We do not charge for the use of our National Assets. The National Science Foundation has no cost exposure in what we are discussing today. I'm due to make a presentation about it tomorrow. I hope you'll attend?"

Looking squarely into each other's eyes, we shook hands in agreement. The four of us then ambled down the hallway to rejoin the conference underway in the big room.

Back in Denver, I began the entangled process to win my clearance. Meanwhile, I provided NGA with the information it required to run its test on the Shear Zone crossing. NGA conducted that test near the start of our third year in the field.

My clearance came through after that field season. In June 2005 I visited the NGA office at Scott Air Force Base. It was full summer in Illinois, and the middle of the long winter's dark on the Ross Ice Shelf

Pete, along with NGA analyst Steve Wheat, escorted me to the second floor of a windowless, brick building. Steve stopped me just short of their own sea of cubicles while he went ahead. His voice sounded over the cubicle walls: "There's a *secret level clearance* on the floor."

I swelled at having my presence heralded with such formality for I was proud of my clearance, proud to be participating in the high-level government world of classified knowledge. Steve came back to get me and led me past those same cubicles. Every computer screen I passed had been blanked out or turned off completely. Steve had been warning folks that I had *only* a secret level clearance, not nearly as high grade as the top-secret field around me.

Laughing, I followed Steve into a secure conference room in the center of that office floor. Inside was a long table, surrounded by plush, comfortable swivel chairs. An assortment of air force officers, Colonel Bright among them, and National Reconnaissance Office personnel joined us. In that room, we viewed the classified imagery.

I was astonished. The numbers of crevasses they saw, their locations and orientations in the field, all agreed precisely with my ground truth.

When the meeting broke up, Pete and Steve drove me across the green, tree-lined campus in Pete's compact sedan.

"Pete," I said, "I'll have to submit a trip report describing what I've found, so I want to know what I *can* say. I don't want to spoil our collaboration by saying or doing something clumsy."

Pete discussed his guidance with me at length. Then he asked, "Having seen what you have today, and confirming the accuracy of our work, wouldn't you say there is a high potential here for science in Antarctica?"

"You mean because National Science Foundation runs the show? Of course. But I could care less about science, Pete. What I'm talking here is mission safety assurance. I'm talking about saving the lives of my crew."

Pete smiled, nodding deeply, signaling our convergence. "The assurance of public safety is the prime component of our mission."

"Well, Pete, I don't know how many people constitute 'public.' But I've shown you pictures of *Linda*. Two people went down with her, and by rights they should both be dead. I don't want any Lindas. Those two people, and the ones that may follow me . . . is that public enough?"

"No more *Lindas*," Pete repeated.

"Hey, can you guys look at something else for me before this next Ice season starts?"

A motorized roar crawled up my backbone and passed overhead. Inside *Fritzy's* cab, I ducked. The red-and-white Twin Otter, then its shadow, buzzed low over the length of our caravan.

At 115 miles past SOUTH, our trains closed up and halted. The light ski plane circled overhead. Wherever they might find us today, the probability of crevasses alongside us was nil. When the plane taxied up to the side of the living module, a tall, bewhiskered Irishman stepped out and walked right up to me. These days he was our project's greatest ally.

"I believe you wanted this," said Dave Bresnahan.

"You bet I want it. We'll be there in a few days. Thank you."

Dave placed the fruits of space-age technology in my hand. Less than a century ago the likes of Shackleton and Scott strained in their traces across this same stretch of Ice Shelf, man-hauling sleds for weeks.

"I also brought you these. Today was cookie day in McMurdo."

The others had dismounted their idling tractors and tentatively approached us across the snow. I hollered, "Come on over, gang. Cookies!"

As they gathered around, I explained to Dave, "We'd like to invite you in for coffee, but we're rigged for running and on a record pace."

Dave graciously bowed. "I'm not one to stand in the way of a record." But then as an afterthought he added, "Some of your folks in the Chalet gave me these . . . they said you need to sign them."

Dave pulled a small sheaf of folded papers from his hip pocket, and handed them to me. The papers spelled out rules for use of the McMurdo information systems. There were three forms, one each for Stretch, Russ, and John V., who had all arrived on Ice in August. They'd signed the forms then. And then the form changed. The crew that arrived in October signed the new form. The other three had signed the old form. They needed to sign the new form. Today's forms came from an intermediate boss that my boss's boss had recently installed between him and my boss. And they came with a threat from the new intermediate boss: "Anyone who does not sign I will happily send home on the next plane north."

My folks? The southwestern horizon showed no mountaintops yet. That's where we'd see them first. Here, the flat white sameness surrounded us.

"What could they possibly be thinking. . . ?" I muttered.

Dave grabbed the papers, and gestured as though he were wiping his butt with them. He handed them back, smiling, and said, "That's what the papers are good for. Just sign 'em." Dave was getting good at tempering my frustration with the bureaucracy.

We snapped a photograph of the signing: Dave looking on, Stretch signing the papers using my back for a desk, the Twin Otter in the background . . . at 82 degrees South latitude on the Ross Ice Shelf.

On November 20 we took a long lunch under a warm sun at the 180 degree meridian. The Transantarctic Mountains had just reappeared on our southwestern horizon when we crossed into the western hemisphere.

The next day we passed the monument post at RIS-1, still on good pace. I stopped there only long enough to capture the post position on GPS and to record the snow level. The others showed their respect to our old farthest south by driving right past it. The snow swamps of Year Two had become nothing but a bad, bad memory.

But our idyllic passage broke up toward the end of shift when Stretch radioed, "I got smoke!"

"Traverse, halt! Wait for further," I grabbed my mike. "Russ, go up and take a look, tell me what you need. Acknowledge, PistenBully."

"*Wrong Way* copies," said Greg's voice.

We stretched out over a mile. The PistenBully ranged farther. Russ, whether he heard me or not, would close up on Stretch and look it over. Nobody would get in front of Greg.

Shortly Russ's voice came over the radio, "*Fritzy*, I need the long-handled torque wrench and the 1¾-inch socket."

"Copy that. Do we need to make camp there?"

"We may just tighten the hub bolts. But it may be something inside."

When *Wrong Way* moved out again, we had two hours left in our day. But before two miles had passed Stretch radioed, "I've got smoke again! I'm stopping."

"Traverse halt! Make camp."

Wrong Way approached from the south to make the camp circle around Brad. Judy circled Brad, parking the *Elephant Man*'s train on his left. I pulled up right of him, unhitched *Fritzy*, and then ran a mile back.

Stretch and Russ stood outside of their tractors, looking over the left rear drive wheel of Stretch's machine. Blistered black paint on its hub exposed rusty, brown metal flakes. Raisin-sized black bits clung to the hub, and lay scattered on the bottom of the track belt. There was no smoke now, no steam, no melting snow. No oil on the snow. The drive wheel was dry as a bone. But it had been hot, and probably was still hot.

"I used the fire extinguisher," Stretch explained as I walked up to them. I didn't spot residue, but I smelled grease and oil. Not rubber. It was something inside.

"Russ, I take it you don't think we should risk driving this to camp?" I asked.

"Right."

"Okay. We'll drag it. Plan on tomorrow to work on this." A day to figure out our situation took pressure off Russ. He'd enjoyed our southern momentum as much as I did, but now he'd feel responsible. I didn't want him to assume that burden.

We unhitched Stretch from his train. When Brad and Greg arrived in *Red Rider* with a pair of the plastic recovery skis, Stretch drove his crippled tractor onto the skis. I listened for metal grinding around his hub, but didn't hear it.

After *Red Rider* towed him away, Russ and I stood alone on the snow. It was a rare moment on the trail when I could pick Russ's brain without an audience. It was the sort of moment I treasured, though the present circumstances were not joyous.

"Russ, you know we're carrying all the spare parts South Pole ordered for that machine?" I opened.

Russ half-laughed. "Yeah, but there's nothing in that small box that'll help us. This is major. It needs parts we don't have, and a shop too." Russ thought any attempt at a field fix would risk more damage.

The MT865 was deliverable cargo. In our medium of exchange, it represented three flights to Pole. We counted on driving it there and pulling a load with it.

"Run your diagnostics, Russ. Tell me what's wrong and what we need to fix it. I'm going to think about dragging it to Pole and all the stuff that comes of that. Right now I'm casting a larcenous eye on those big plastic sheets under the fuel bladders."

"I'm thinking the same thing," Russ said and grinned.

I grinned back. "All right, then. Pull your load up to camp, I'll have Brad come back and retrieve Stretch's. *Fritzy* can't pull it."

In this last-chance year, the loss of a tractor could mean failure two-thirds of the way across the Ross Ice Shelf. Whether we went forward to Pole or retreated to McMurdo, the remaining tractors would share Stretch's load *and* pull his disabled tractor. We didn't have the drawbar strength to do that without shuttling.

But nobody wanted failure. Eight assessments of our situation brought as many, or more, solutions and partial solutions. That was all good energy for going south. At dinner I made it clear.

"We're not going anywhere right away. We'll stay here tomorrow, relax, and figure out what we *can* do. We can *do* that . . ." I looked first at Greg, then to the others, and repeated, "We can *do* that because nobody's shooting at us. We've also got a big friend waiting two hundred miles ahead at the base of the Leverett. I'd rather struggle two hundred miles forward than 450 miles back."

The ultimate solution was as much an enigma to me as to the crew. But they now knew I leaned south.

Russ and John V. reported the Pole tractor had "suffered a bearing failure on the left side drive wheel, induced by a failure of the oil seals and resulting loss of lubrication oil—by burning." The spare parts we needed were not on the continent.

The choice was simple: either leave the tractor beside the trail and drag it back to McMurdo on our return trip, or drag the deadweight to its new home at Pole.

We'd not tried towing it yet, except on the recovery skis. That was no way to tow it the remaining six hundred miles. Our best chance lay with the twin plastic sheets under the fuel bladders.

Brad tended our fuel inventory this year. He said we now had enough empty capacity in our steel fuel tank sleds to hold the bladder fuel. Greg had rigged the bladder sleds in the first place. He and Brad saw to transferring their contents. The others helped fold and bind the empty bladders and used *Fritzy*'s crane to lift them in *Snow White*'s hold.

Russ and Stretch secured the MT on top of the plastic sheets, chaining the tractor to the spreader bar sled that pulled them. The rig worked nicely in trials around camp. But in a sudden stop, the MT and the plastic sheets slid forward, colliding with the spreader bar. We could live with that if we remembered to stop slowly.

To get a leg up, we sidetracked two steel fuel tank sleds, one empty and one full, for our return traverse. Then we redistributed the remaining sleds among our four working tractors. One or two of them would be overloaded. When we logged fifty-four miles the next day, even after rescuing stuck tractors, my damage report went in to Rebecca.

Thanksgiving Day brought a blizzard of heavy, wet snow. We hunkered down, feasted, and sent holiday e-mails around the world. The day after Thanksgiving Russ closed our morning briefing: "Yippee! We get to make a *turn* today!"

Since departing the Shear Zone we'd run a straight course for four hundred miles. When the Transantarctics finally appeared on our southern horizon, they grew ever larger as we approached their fixed panorama. Now we turned left at FORK, striking a parallel course to the mountain fronts, skirting just north of the Shoals at their feet.

We motored past the mouths of deeply carved valleys, some cutting back into the Plateau for two hundred miles. Blue-ice glaciers filled the valley bottoms. Orange and yellow sunlight reflected off their mirrored surfaces with startling beauty.

Greg and Tom prospected ahead in the PistenBully. From what I could see at a distance, they'd got out of their vehicle and were examining the ground ahead of them. My heart sank. Last year, somewhere near here, we'd crossed a quarter-inch-wide crack and traced it for over a mile, but it behaved more like a thin tidal crack than a rip-snorting crevasse.

"John, I think you ought to take a look at this," Tom radioed.

The fleet pulled up, and we all got out of our tractors to inspect. In front of the PistenBully a long, trough-like track, eight inches wide, crossed our trail. Knife-like gashes marked the snow on both sides of it. Three-point dots, close together, skipped along the left and the right sides of the trough. The track looked like a giant zipper running across the snow.

Penguin tracks. Adélie penguin by the looks of it. Belly sliding.

How a penguin could have wandered this far "inland" over the ice shelf, let alone survive, mystified us. We were five hundred miles from the nearest open water. Yet here were these tracks headed straight for the Axel Heiberg Glacier.

In 1911 Norwegian Roald Amundsen, whom I regarded as the greatest polar explorer of them all, selected that glacier for his ascent to the Polar Plateau. He became the first man to reach the South Pole. His modern-day countryman Børge Ousland chose the same glacier in 1997 for his descent from the Pole onto the Ross Ice Shelf. When Ousland skied into McMurdo, he became the first man to cross Antarctica alone and unsupported.

I mused aloud, "Amundsen's Ghost. Let's take this as a good omen."

In fact, we made two turns that day. Our evening brought us to CAMP 20. We turned right at the post and settled down a half-mile past it. Now we pointed directly into the breach of The Shoals of Intractable Funding.

A storm again stalled our advance from CAMP 20. All day driving, wet flakes plastered our tractors and sleds. We made four miles then hunkered down once more. The foot of the Leverett Glacier was only two days away.

We waited impatiently. We had enough visibility to slog it out, flag to flag. But seventeen miles ahead lay the breach. It may or may not be open this year. I wanted all the visibility we could get if we ran into crevasses.

At 1000 hours we crowded into our galley, looking at ASTER imagery of the Shoals on our laptop. Pointing to CAMP 20 on the map, I began pompously: "We are heah." Then pointing to ASTER 2: "And they are theah."

Our course cut across the ice flow as it approached the breach. At ASTER 2 our course turned left and headed upstream. Downstream from the turning point lay a shoal of crevasses. ASTER 2 was drifting right for it. I didn't know if the crevasses were moving, too, or if new ones were forming there just waiting for our drifting trail to drop into them.

"This ice is moving two and a half to three feet per day. I think."

Last year did not allow enough time between measurements to get a reliable figure. We had only proved a hundred-foot-wide swath along the flag line. And the ASTER imagery was now three years old.

"Let's look at what NGA sent."

The NGA showed us a heavy black line representing our route. It started at CAMP 20, turned left at ASTER 2, ran through the other ASTER points, and terminated at ASTER 6. A light gray field covered both sides of the route to a width of a mile. Steve Wheat had drawn dark blue lines within that gray field wherever he saw a crevasse. A couple of dark blue lines plotted closely downstream from ASTER 2, but they did not yet encroach on our route.

"The analyst was looking at original imagery. We have here only his representation of that. But it looks to me like the passage is still open."

The laptop made the rounds so everybody could get a good look. When it got back to me, I pointed to the crevasses between ASTER 2 and ASTER 3.

"These we know about. We drilled them and crossed them last year. Hopefully they'll be safe again this year."

Then I pointed to a dense cluster of blue lines just south of CAMP 20. "I have no idea what this is. We didn't see anything there last year. But we only look down twelve and a half meters with our radar. So I don't know what the analyst was looking at."

I finished. "Now you know everything I know about this place. Any questions?"

None.

"Right. When the weather lets us, I want to check out the breach with Greg and Tom in the PistenBully. We'll take an Iridium phone and call you on the hours. If we get to ASTER 2 and everything looks okay, we'll call you forward. I don't intend to come back here unless we have to."

The skies broke clear the morning of November 27. The PistenBully headed out.

Our radar didn't pick up anything to tell us what NGA saw south of camp with that first cluster of blue lines. It all looked like plain, unbroken ice on our screen. That was good news.

Farther down the line, ice movement at ASTER 2 and ASTER 3 measured much slower than I'd predicted. That was more good news.

We looked over the crevasses we already knew about and saw no change in their radar signature. By all appearances, the passage was good to go.

I called the waiting fleet forward. We threaded the needle's eye, made forty-six miles, and left The Shoals of Intractable Funding behind us.

The next day, we reached the foot of the Leverett Glacier. From five miles out, I spotted a black dot down in the ice valley below it. Our big friend waited for us.

We ran down the gentle slope over crumbly ice, its glazed surface preserving the tracks we'd made a year ago. We followed them right to the D8 where it sat proudly atop its berm, basking in the warm sun. Russ and John V. would wake the bulldozer from its sleep tomorrow. Others would reconfigure sled trains for five tractors now.

I was more interested in checking the route up the foot of the glacier. If the ice had moved as much as I anticipated then we might be locating an entirely new route. But the post nearest our camp had only moved an incredible fifty-three feet since last year. While that made me hopeful, I kept such thoughts to myself because so many things were about to change.

In 640 miles we'd barely left sea level. Over the next seventy miles we'd climb seven thousand feet. Some of those pitches were steep enough that tractors would be towing tractors.

Five tractors for the climb were good. Sidetracking another pair of fuel tank sleds would lighten our overall load, too. All but one tractor would drag two sleds upgrade. *Quadzilla* would pull three. On the Plateau we might reconfigure: four tractors, three sleds each, and use *Fritzy* as a flagging tractor for the new route. It'd be cold up there. The flagger would welcome a warm cab to follow the PistenBully. Meanwhile, we were still at the bottom.

The next morning Greg, Tom, and I prepared to scout the old route. I solemnly approached Greg. "You understand that up to now you have been traveling across the Ross Ice Shelf?"

"Right, Boss," he said.

"It's John. And you understand that the Ross Ice Shelf is afloat?"

"Right."

"And up to now, you have never been on the continent of Antarctica before?"

"Yes."

"Unfurl your Marine Corps flag. Fly it behind the PistenBully. Somewhere in the next five miles we're going to cross onto the continent. The U.S. Marines will lead us onto that shore and take the beach."

Some beach. A cartographer had drawn the inferred continental shore line on our maps. We crossed his shoreline somewhere that morning on snow and ice. Fourteen miles later and two thousand feet higher, we turned around, looking down on the Ice Shelf no longer in front of us but below us. We'd found not one crevasse. The old flag line had hardly moved since last year. If that held and our path was crevasse-free last year, it ought to be crevasse-free now.

In camp at the foot of the Leverett, a fuel burning heater thawed the ice out of the D8's engine compartment. By mid-afternoon, Russ and John V. had the bulldozer running and hitched to the module sleds. That would be Stretch's load the rest of the way to Pole. The other sled trains were coupled and ready.

At day's end, everybody's news was good. We'd be at SPT-18 in a couple days, and I didn't plan on stopping there.

Greg and Tom led with *Wrong Way*, working westerly around the foot of the glacier. Stretch and the D8 pulled out with the red modules. Brad in *Red Rider* went next with the flatbed sled and *Snow White*, Stretch's original loads. Judy and John V. followed in the *Elephant Man* pulling the reefer van and a fuel tank sled. I came next in *Fritzy* pulling the spare parts sled and another tank sled. Russ ran caboose with *Quadzilla* pulling two tank sleds, and the crippled Pole tractor. This day was November 30.

In three and a half miles, we turned left and started upgrade. *Fritzy* and I hadn't rounded the corner when Stretch radioed, "I'm overheating. I'm stopping."

Where was everybody? John V. was ahead with Judy; Russ was behind.

"John V., can you get up there with Stretch and check it out?" I radioed.

We all stopped, waiting on the sunny slopes at the toe of the glacier. John V. radioed back, more to Russ than to me, "I think we've got some cross over at the transmission oil cooler. It's pulled some glycol from the cooling system into the transmission."

Russ radioed back, "How low is the glycol?"

They decided to top it up and keep an eye on it. I had all the oils and fluids with me in the spare parts van. When John V. showed up on a snowmobile to get a five-gallon can off me, I hailed him out of my cab door, "We've got seven miles of climb, on slopes like what you're on now. Then we're looking at a flatter stretch for forty or fifty miles."

"Copy that. Good to know. We'll get the D8 going again shortly."

Fritzy idled seventy miles from our farthest south. The bright sun streamed through my window glass. I waited. I worried. I played what-if games. We'd brought every bit of deliverable cargo here. We'd shed tank sleds and fuel along the trail to pull that Pole tractor. If the D8 went down, no way we could drag that beast to Pole. If we abandoned it, we'd lose four LC-130s worth of cargo. Abandon cargo altogether, just prove the route?

"Okay, we're ready to go again," John V. radioed.

Stretch had gone over a rise before his engine overheated. I couldn't see him, but I saw Brad in *Red Rider* start up the slope, then the *Elephant Man*. Finally, I turned the corner and started up the grade. Russell to my left was rolling now, too. Not much chatter on the radio from any of us.

Halfway up the glacier, we made camp on the long, gentle grade. Mount Beazley appeared fifteen miles farther up. Our course doglegged right around that mountain and led through the narrows into the headwall basin. A mile to our right, the spectacular jagged Gould Peak shouldered its way out of surrounding ice. To our left, rocky tops of nearly buried foothills dotted the rolling glacier-covered country.

The D8 gave us no more trouble that day. While I plugged in *Fritzy* outside the living module, Russ shuffled over the snow toward me. He'd just plugged in *Quadzilla*. His shoulders drooped. He looked weary.

"You okay, Russ?"

"We're screwed." *Quadzilla* had blown an idler wheel bearing at the end of shift. Another tractor down. "And we don't have the parts to repair it," Russ said.

"We can't move it?"

"Right."

"Then all we can do is stay here until we find out what we *can* do about it. How's the D8?"

"We need to work on that, too."

"Okay, Russ. Get your mind around being here a couple of days. Identify the parts we need. If we can find them on continent, maybe we can get them air-dropped to us. If we can figure out how to do this thing with four tractors, maybe we can get the parts flown to Pole and repair *Quadzilla* on the way back. I don't know what we're going to do yet, because I don't know what we *can* do."

Russ already knew that, but he needed to hear me say it. I needed to hear myself say it. But Russ's eyes still said we were screwed.

"I'll tell the others we'll be here for a while," I sighed.

Two days of Iridium phone calls to parts supply in McMurdo and to dealers in the United States. Two days of odd jobs around camp. John V., Stretch, and Judy changed out the D8's transmission oil. Greg helped Russ tear down *Quadzilla*. Brad and Tom snowmobiled back down the trail searching for missing parts off Russ's tractor.

Some of the parts we needed were in McMurdo. The rest were back in the States. An air drop wouldn't help us. One choice remained: leave *Quadzilla*, while spare parts expedited from the States flew to Pole. If we got to Pole, we'd bring them back with us. And if we returned with only three tractors, we'd be officially screwed if one of them went down.

Today, my brilliant plan for reconfiguring the fleet went right out the window. We still had all our cargo. But with four healthy tractors pulling uphill, instead of five, each would pull three sleds. Pulling heavier going south worked exactly backwards from anybody's plan. And once we got to the top, we were still looking at three hundred miles of what?

The briefing on December 3 started upbeat. "We get to make a *turn* today!" Brad quipped, "We get to *move* today!"

Russ groaned, mourning the loss of his tractor. He'd ride in the *Elephant Man* with Judy.

"We were planning on shuttling up the headwall anyway," I continued. "If we shuttle on the Plateau 'cause we're too heavy . . . well, we do have enough fuel to get us to Pole."

I looked at Stretch, "And that's all I have to say about that."

Stretch started up off his stool.

"But . . ." I timed it just right. Stretch scowled and sat back down. "I do have something else to say, and I've been holding it until this moment."

Everyone was impatient to move out.

"Two years ago, Dave Bresnahan and I started this . . . now it's official. Just around the corner past Mount Beazley, look off to your left. You're going to see a rocky outcrop, about four hundred meters high. It forms a buttress on the west flank of the Stanford Plateau. That's the east flank of the entrance to the Leverett headwall basin. That buttress has a name . . . the *Magsig Rampart!*"

Gasps rose from everybody. Russ had wanted a place on the continent named for him. Not some far-off place, but a place he could see. A place he had been to. His history with the program went back to stations and winters forgotten or never heard of by most. We'd officially registered Russ's rampart with the U.S. Geological Survey's Advisory Committee on Antarctic Names. That name was officially accepted just before we launched this year. I read from the text of the application:

"Reason for choice: To honor a mechanic whose decades of service to the USAP over far-flung outposts of the continent of Antarctica now culminate in his key role enabling the success of the USAP's pioneering South Pole Traverse Project."

The stunned crew cheered, wildly applauding the honor.

"Now . . . shall we go see that rampart?"

Stools scudded across the floor. Cabinets slammed shut. We scrambled out the door to our warming tractors.

Over the wind-swept, flatter section of the glacier we drove over tracks we'd put down last year, still visible on the crust. That surprised me, for I remembered snowy surfaces back then.

Ahead, Mount Beazley stood in full sun. Whirling sprites of snow-dust danced around its rocky summit. We rounded the dogleg corner and pulled abreast of the Magsig Rampart. Russ would stop and take a picture, but I was keener to see the headwall that had just come in view. Up there huge curls of wind-blown snow poured off the Plateau and spilled into the basin.

We left our icy tracks behind and started onto new drift snow. The trail steepened. *Fritzy,* the *Elephant Man,* and *Red Rider* stuck many times. Tom and Greg ran ahead into the Parade Grounds to sweep the camp circle. Tom felt the frigid blast pouring over the rim when he stepped out of the PistenBully. "It's dangerously cold up here. Be prepared," he radioed to us still below. Tom had climbed Dhaulagiri in the Himalayas. He knew cold.

By the time *Fritzy* and I struggled into the Parade Grounds the wind had died down. We'd made thirty miles for the day. From the comfort of my warm cab I spied the route flags planted last year. We'd left eight feet of pole above the surface then. Now they were half buried. Our packed trail would be too deep to do us any good this year.

A fierce ground blizzard whistled through our camp when we woke. With only seven miles to the top, no one slept in. Our fingers drummed, waiting to seize a break in the visibility.

The monument posts up the glacier had moved little in a year, two hundred feet at the most. That was great news for the future traverse business. It meant the Leverett route was stable. But that puzzled me. The Leverett was the shortest glacier that drained from the Plateau into the Ice Shelf. The Scott Glacier west of us and the Reedy Glacier to our east were both a couple hundred miles long. And they cut down through the same elevations. In only seventy miles from top to bottom, the Leverett had the steepest gradient of them all.

"It ought to be roaring through here like a freight train. But it's hardly moving. Now let's look at an image of the headwall cirque."

A RADARSAT image flashed onto our laptop. Others had seen it, but Tom, Greg, and John V. had not. The 1997 image showed the basin ringed by myriad white gashes against a dark background, each gash a crevasse. A thin red line superimposed our route onto the image. The red line strayed close to many of those gashes.

"Wo-oww," John V. exclaimed. Tom studied the image. Greg remained silent, serious.

"Some of you have seen these crevasses. You'll remember many are open. When I flew over here a couple years ago, I looked down on them in living color. It looked just like on this image, jillions of them. But if our route's not moving much, it ought to be like we remember it from last year."

While they took turns studying the image again, the wind abated with a crash of calm. The basin brimmed with still, cold air under a clear blue sky.

"Greg, you and Tom in the PistenBully. Lay us a track right down the old flag line, if you can find the flags. Most of them will have been whipped to death in these winds. There might not be any standing at all."

Greg acknowledged.

"Stretch, ride with me in *Fritzy*. We'll re-flag the track."

"Want to take a load up, as long as we're taking *Fritzy*?" Stretch suggested.

"Good idea. Let's drag the MT. The rest of you think about going up later this afternoon. Do whatever you have to do to get us ready for that. Judy, you're on comms. I think we'll do fine by radio, but we'll take an Iridium just in case."

Wrong Way started up the first grade, climbing onto a stair step bench of snow. *Fritzy* followed its tracks. A quarter mile along Stretch asked, "You going to put in a flag here?"

"What?" I stopped.

"You're right next to it," he said.

Stretch sat on my left. I leaned across him and looked down through the glass door. A bamboo nub with a green rag wrapped around it poked out of the snow no more than three inches. "Now how do you suppose Greg saw that?"

"Young eyes." Stretch got out of the cab to plant a new flag beside the remnant.

"And eight feet of snow since last year."

"Worst I've ever seen it," Stretch laughed.

We planted new flags all the way to the top. Though some of last year's stuck out as much as two feet, it all seemed oddly familiar. When *Fritzy* broke over the rim, the PistenBully was lining on a dark object on the snow a mile ahead. Our cache at farthest south: three hundred flags stood like a bamboo menhir at SPT-18.

I half-expected the cache would've moved over the plateau rim into the headwall basin, yet, when we pulled up to SPT-18, my GPS said I was six feet off of last year's position. Out *Fritzy*'s window to my right, the bundles of upright flags stood six feet away. I showed Stretch the GPS. "SPT-18 hasn't moved."

Our old route up the stair step pitches was still good. In seven miles up from the Parade Grounds, Tom hadn't seen a single crevasse on his radar. Stretch and I unhitched the Pole tractor then followed the PistenBully back down the headwall. Greg and Tom ran a hundred feet offset from their out-bound track, and again found no crevasses.

Halfway down the slopes, I radioed to camp, "Warm up the tractors. I'll just want a few minutes with everybody in the galley when we get down."

"Copy that." Judy's voice sounded pure delight.

A skiff of snow scudded no higher than our ankles. *Red Rider*, the D8, and the *Elephant Man* idled, hitched to their loads. I climbed the stairs into the galley.

"Last year's route is still good. To your left, you've got all new flags next to the old ones. To your right, you've got the tracks we made coming down. Stay between them. Neither track found any crevasses under it, but you'll pass by some open ones. There's a lot of drift snow. You're not going to find any road under you. We'll make camp at SPT-18 where we camped last year. There's enough new snow up there we can use the top two feet safely for our snow-melter." Seeing no questions, I shook my head with disbelief. "SPT-18 did not move at all."

Stretch had made it last year pulling the modules without any help. "Did you see anything today that makes you think you couldn't do it again?" I asked.

"Nnnope. I think we'll do just fine."

Judy thought she'd get stuck right away and wisely asked for a tow. "Hell, it's only seven miles to camp."

"I'll leave my load here then, and pull you with *Fritzy*," I volunteered. "Brad, see what you can do with *Red Rider*. If you get stuck, I'll come back after Judy's on top."

Brad nodded.

"Greg and Tom, hang back with the heavy tractors. If any of them get in trouble near the sidelines, you may have to do some prospecting out of bounds."

"Right, Boss."

"It's John. Okay. Let's go."

Cupboards slammed, kitchenware clattered in the sink, and boots shuffled out the door.

Judy and I followed Stretch onto a long, flat bench two miles above the Parade Grounds. Brad radioed, "I'm stuck. Halfway up the first grade." He couldn't see us over the rise.

Judy had judged right. The *Elephant Man* would've stuck several times without *Fritzy*'s help. As soon as we topped the rim, I cut her loose. John V. dismounted to help.

"It's pretty neat up here. And cold, too!" He approached me cheerfully.

"Welcome to the Polar Plateau, John. You're on top of the world now." I spoke in haste, but with a smile. He'd take his own time with the views after I split off. Stretch was up ahead with our warm camp at SPT-18. Judy had a mile to go on flatter ground. Brad and his load, and my load, were still below. The sky started graying-over.

John V. coiled my heavy tow strap and secured it to my side deck. I spun *Fritzy* around and started back down.

Brad hadn't made it far. My load in camp sat just four flags below him. When I backed up to Brad's wallow on the slope, we got out of our tractors and met halfway. Brad took an end of my tow strap. The air was calm down here, but above us snow dust started curling over the rim again.

"It's cold up there, Brad. And the wind's picking up. Hey, Brad," I asked in a moment's realization, "haven't we been here before?"

Brad smiled. Last year he and I had been the last to top out. We took turns even then towing each other. When the last of our loads reached the top, we stopped on the rim and unhitched. Brad had looked back over the Ross Ice Shelf below us and beamed, surprising me with an exuberant embrace. I remembered that, now. Brad and me. Last to top out again this year, we shared a warm handshake now and finished hitching our tractors together.

Topping the first stairstep onto the bench, we called out RPMs, gears, and speeds to each other on the radio, adjusting to each other's performance. We set an all-traverse speed record for climbing the headwall.

Just over the top with a mile to go, we unhitched and turned immediately back down. The wind rose. Our visibility was dropping. The growing overcast would flatten our light.

Brad reached the Parade Grounds with a half-mile lead, and hitched *Red Rider* to my load. I caught up, spun right around, and backed up to him. He already had his tow strap waiting for me. I watched out my rear window. Brad fit the tow strap around *Fritzy*'s hitch pin then signed thumbs up. I nodded. He climbed back aboard *Red Rider* and we started up the headwall again.

Along the gentle bench in the midsection of our climb, we passed below open crevasses tens of feet to our left. I'd spotted them a couple years ago from the office with our GIS lady, Kelly Brunt, on her computer. We plotted a course correction there in Denver. Above me now were those same gashes; it was strange that they did not fill up with all that snow curling over the rim.

Today Kelly's point bore a post scribed SPT-16. We turned left there and started up the last, steep grade. Two miles farther, we topped out with ease. I took *Fritzy* to the other load where we'd left it, and stepped out of my cab for a word with Brad at the back of my tractor.

Wind blew bitterly against our faces. We had everything on top, all souls intact, and all deliverable cargo. Three hundred miles of unknown ground before we saw Pole. Yet Pole was only halfway for us. I shook Brad's hand once again, and said what I had to say: "Thank you."

Brad ran that last mile ahead of me. The light completely flattened and the ground blizzard swelled to cab height. The events that brought us to this place exactly eleven months ago replayed themselves. Three years culminating in profound disappointment. Another year getting back, despite two crippled tractors. The place still had a "high" feeling to it. But, it didn't bring the same breathtaking accomplishment we'd felt when we first established our foothold here.

Now I wanted only to get off of the spot.

|12| Sastrugi

Somewhere on the Polar Plateau lurked sastrugi of mythical proportions. I'd never heard of sastrugi before I came to Antarctica, yet old Ice hands spoke respectfully of them as "bad" sastrugi or "big" sastrugi.

"What's a sastrugi?"

One old-timer, exasperated with my newness, offered this terse explanation: "They're these weird wind-carved forms in the snow. They make a rough surface."

"Is that a sastrugi?" I asked, pointing to a four-inch-tall ridge of snow running across the flat sea ice near McMurdo.

"Sure, but that's nothing. Sastrugi get huge . . . six feet high, maybe more."

I stepped on the little ridge and crushed it. "Do you ever see any big ones around here?"

"No."

"Have *you* ever seen big ones?"

"No. But I've heard stories about them."

I never saw official sastrugi around McMurdo. I never saw them at Central West Antarctica. I never saw them at Shackleton Base Camp, around Oliver Bluffs, or the Beardmore Glacier.

I saw my first official sastrugi when I got to South Pole on the tunnel job. Long walks took me outside the station's inhabited perimeter, onto the virgin snows, away from tractors, heavy equipment, airplanes, skiways, and the groomed surfaces of the station campus. I found acres without end of fantastically wind-sculpted snow. Mesmerizing, beautiful in fact, they were not at all intimidating. They looked like free-form stairsteps, wind-carved into graceful curves and risers a foot and a half high. Their undercut snouts pointed directly upwind—useful to know if one came into a new area on a dead calm day.

I stepped onto the edges of these risers and they again collapsed under my weight. *What is the big deal with sastrugi?*

The *Dictionary of Geological Terms* published by the American Geological Institute offers this definition:

(Russian) Plural form of sastruga. 1) The minor inequalities of the snow surface as determined by the wind blowing over the inland ice have been mentioned more or less persistently by all Arctic travelers, since upon the character of this surface depends the celerity of movement in sledge journeys. All minor hummocks and ridges of this nature are included under the general term sastrugi. 2) Irregularities or wave formations caused by persistent winds on a snow surface. They vary in size according to the force and duration of the wind and the state of the snow surface in which they are formed.

Mobility, ease of travel, speed over the land . . . all are affected by surface roughness. Potholes on a paved road, washboards on a dirt road: these reduce the celerity of movement. Smooth the roughness and maintain it, mobility improves. Sastrugi at South Pole made a rough-looking surface, but they yielded easily underfoot or to a passing tractor.

Adventurers Liv Arnesen and Ann Bancroft skied into Pole one year, crossing the continent from near the Weddell Sea coast of Antarctica. They met enthusiastic reception from the station inhabitants.

I'd just got the night shift started on the tunnel and drifted back to the old station galley for hot cocoa before turning in. Inside, I spotted the two women seated at the far end of the room with station manager Katy Jensen. A dozen of the station's female workers crowded their table. They sought autographs, listened to adventure stories, and admired the great ladies holding forth. The two skiers radiated health and vitality, irresistibly attracting all souls.

They attracted *my* attention. But seeing the exercised patience with which they took time to speak to each of their admirers, I reckoned they did not need one more body hovering around them. I took my cocoa to the other side of the room.

Katy approached me to ask about taking the skiers through the tunnel. "Need to get them away from the crowd?"

Katy nodded.

Touring the tunnel turned out to be sheer play for all of us. Arnesen and Bancroft enjoyed watching the tunnel-boring machine at work. Then, leaving the crew to their shift, we walked down another long reach of tunnel into the darkness. The ladies thrilled to touch the tunnel walls, to feel the harder, denser snow lying well below the softer surfaces they skied upon.

When we reached the end of the dark tunnel, I asked them, "Where under the station do you think we are now?"

Arnesen answered in accents of Norway: "Well, I have no idea."

"Then shall we find out?" I suggested, taking our sole mine light to the bottom of a wooden ladder.

The ladder ran improbably up from the tunnel floor into the darkness of a perfectly round, three-foot-diameter hole. One by one, we climbed the fifty-foot ladder, gathering together again in a small, dark plywood shelter built around the ladder's top. I opened an overhead hatch in the chamber roof, and invited them to have a look outside. Dazzling sunlight flooded through the hatch as they climbed out the shelter, three feet above the snows of the South Pole antenna field, nearly a half mile from the old station where we started.

Katy, Liv, and Ann found footing on the snow. With half of me still in the plywood shelter, the other half sticking out of the hatch, I announced, "This is where I leave you."

"You want to join us?" Katy asked.

"I'd love to. But I need to go back and let the crew know you're out of the tunnel." I looked both to Liv and Ann: "I wish you both the best on the rest of your journey." Then I disappeared from their sight, and they from mine, as I lowered myself back into the darkness.

Arnesen and Bancroft started north from the Pole a few days later. From the top of a pile of snow bulldozed up near the tunnel entrance, I watched them go. Huge blue sails unfurled in the wind, pulling them along on their skis. The skiers in turn pulled modern one-man cargo sleds behind them.

They left a videodisc with Katy. One evening we watched moving pictures of the first part of Arnesen's and Bancroft's journey.

"Freeze that picture, Katy. Please!" I interjected.

Katy paused the video. "What do you see?"

"Look at that," I pointed to a still image of Ann Bancroft lurching her sled over rough ground. Sastrugi . . . three, four feet high . . . The chaotic terrain was full of them. Bancroft's skis bridged the tops of two, barely marking the sastrugi. Her skis flexed deeply under her weight across the span in air. I marveled they did not break.

That was my first good look at bad sastrugi.

Crossing the Ross Ice Shelf and topping out on the Leverett, we never encountered sastrugi like those. In the first hundred miles after crossing the Shear Zone, we ran into something we called dorniks. But dorniks didn't have wind-scoured ridges, or deeply carved risers. They looked more like smooth-skinned, icy whalebacks breaking a flat surface. Mostly they hid, shallowly submerged under soft snow.

Near the close of Year Two, George Blaisdell and I recorded our observations of sastrugi fields on the Plateau from the air. Likening them to waves, we estimated their wave lengths crest-to-crest, their angle across our proposed track, and even their height. Since we flew between two thousand and four thousand feet over the Plateau, our height estimates were suspect. But it was a clear day. We had shadows to go on. And we relied on the pilots' estimates, figuring they had more experience judging sastrugi heights from the air. Our notes recorded "bumpy" terrain over the first 174 miles from Pole. We thought the sastrugi might be two to three feet high and perhaps fifty feet crest-to-crest. Over the next thirty-six miles we noted "moderate" sastrugi with wavelengths from two to four hundred feet. The pilots thought they might be three to five feet high. The next fifty-two miles showed "moderate to light" sastrugi, four hundred feet apart, two to four feet high. From there, to the top of the Leverett, we noted "knobbly" sastrugi, light by comparison to all we'd just flown over.

Sastrugi covered the entire Plateau section of the route. If legendary giants lurked there, they were in that thirty-six mile stretch. From the air we spied no smooth passage through or around the sastrugi anywhere. Avoiding them was out of the question. We would have to deal with them. That meant bulldozer blades and some form of road building.

✧ ✧ ✧

At the start of Year Four, I ran into Anne Dal Vera in Christchurch, New Zealand. We were drawing our cold weather gear at the U.S. Antarctic Center. Anne was another intrepid adventure skier whom I respected enormously. I didn't know her well, though she lived fifty miles south of me in Colorado. I knew her work and reputation in McMurdo. The husky woman was soft-spoken, sensitive, and a good listener. I asked would she mind giving me a minute of her time.

"Not at all. What's on your mind, John?"

"It's sastrugi, Anne. I'm thinking about giants I've heard about but never seen. I've heard tales of some six and eight feet high. Have you run across any of those?"

"Well, six feet, yes."

"On the Plateau?"

"Yes."

We walked to the large map of Antarctica hanging on the foyer wall of the Clothing Distribution Center. It was the same map my children looked at last year. The map showed South Pole positioned in the center, surrounded by the circular form of the continent. Mapping conventions for Antarctic projections typically hold the zeroth meridian from the Pole pointing toward the top of the map. The 180th meridian points toward the bottom. Anne's finger traced the line she'd skied to the Pole from ten o'clock on the coast. Her line ran close to Sir Vivian Fuchs's route. Fuchs led the British Commonwealth Transantarctic Expedition in 1957–1958.

"Where did you run into the big sastrugi on the Plateau?"

She studied the map before pointing to the 86th parallel. "Somewhere between 86 and 87, maybe farther south."

Our route converged on Pole from seven o'clock on the same map. But between 86 and 87, her route and ours were close enough to Pole that if Anne's giant sastrugi existed as a region, that region could easily extend into our territory.

"And then you came out of them?"

"The big ones, yes. Are you thinking about those for your traverse?"

"I am. I'm thinking of Fuchs's book, *The Crossing of Antarctica*. He was forever breaking drawbars and sled hitches in that ground. It must be rough, but I have no feel for that kind of terrain."

"It *was* rough."

"My hat's off to you, Anne. I guess I have some more thinking to do about it."

"Crossing the Plateau ought to be a piece of cake, don't you think?" Dave Bresnahan quizzed me over the phone while I was in the Denver office during the planning season before our team deployed for Year Four.

He hoped to co-opt my assent to an easy, speedy crossing of the Polar Plateau. From time to time he asked questions like that, and I never knew what was behind them. Something in his office in D.C. Maybe he or somebody else was deciding where to put NSF money. Maybe he'd gone out on a limb and needed some back up. I could never dole out a swaggering, incautious answer like: "Sure, Dave, no problem."

Questions like his put me on guard. I always answered honestly. Today I answered, "Sure, Dave. About as easy as crossing the Ross Ice Shelf."

Dave cleared his throat on the other end, as if to say "Smart ass!"

"Dave, you know we don't know what's under the red line on the map. There're sastrugi up there. Big ones from what I can tell. But I haven't crossed sastrugi, and you haven't either. The USAP doesn't have a whole lot of experience with them. But Fuchs did. He had a lot of trouble with them. There're crevasses up there too. I haven't even started looking into them. Who knows what else is up there? Not me. I haven't been there yet."

"Yeah, yeah, yeah." Dave countered in kind, which made our exchanges fun. We were both thick-skinned enough to deal with hard banter. "How're you going to deal with the sastrugi?"

"Blades, and bulldozers or tractors to doze them with, is a good starting point. Make the rough places plain. Build that thing we're not supposed to say what it is. I don't know how we'll do it until we get there, and *see* what we're looking at."

"You confident you can do it?"

"Pretty confident. There's one thing I'm *not* confident of, though." I waited until Dave cleared his throat.

"And that is?"

"The PistenBully."

The PistenBully wouldn't have a road in front of it. It had to face those sastrugi without any help. The rest of us could follow the D8, and the D8 could drop its blade and do us some good. But the D8 couldn't go except where the PistenBully went because the PistenBully would be looking for crevasses.

"Suppose the PistenBully can't look for crevasses in that rough stuff? The whole project comes to a crashing halt. We don't want the D8 ahead of the radar. "

The specter of *Linda* in the blue depths of a monster crevasse rose silently between us.

"I hear you. Anything I can do to help?" Dave asked.

"Yeah. Hustle George to follow up on my questions to those glaciologists."

|13| Farther South

Another night of three hours sleep. I awoke ahead of my alarm clock set at 0515, shut it off anyway, stretched out in my sleeping bag, and listened. The blizzard outside screamed soprano. Our living module rocked in the gale. The good folks in Alberta had built such strength into our shelter that it never split open under these winds to leave us cold and naked on the Polar Plateau.

The whirring microwave in the kitchen stopped with the timer's high-pitched whine, announcing Stretch's oatmeal was done. A soft clomping crossed the galley floor. The muffled oven door opened and shut.

With just my long johns on, I rolled my feet off the bunk and slipped on wool socks and fleece booties. Greg's bunk across from me, Brad's above his, and Judy's above mine still had curtains drawn. I stepped quietly through the bunkroom door.

"Morning, Stretch." Stretch sat with his huge bowl in his customary place, way across the three-foot expanse of the comms booth and the great plains of the twelve-foot-long galley.

"Morning, John," Stretch whispered.

Taking my parka off its hook in the vestibule, I poked my face briefly outside the refrigerator door of our shelter. Fine-grained pellets of wind-blasted snow filled my eyes. I retreated. "Jeesh."

Shuffling past Stretch to his bunkroom, I opened the door and whispered, "Sleep, fellas. At least a couple more hours. Gather at 0900," then back across to my own bunkroom: "Sleep. See you at 0900."

Zipping up then, I headed for the energy module. Wind grabbed the heavy door as I stepped outside, slamming it shut behind me like an explosion. *Damn!* I'd been quiet until now.

Against the swirling blizzard, I picked my way between the modules and the tractors. All the heater cords were still plugged in, their slack lines buried under snow, weighted down under the drifts.

Thirty feet down the line, I gripped a hand rail, climbed the energy module stairs, and fought the wind for the vestibule door at the top. Inside, all the windows, doors, and skylights were still shut. *Fine.* I opened the generator room doors. The gen-sets howled back. *Fine in here, too. Warm, and no snow.*

I stared into the mirror over the lavatory sink. *What are you going to do this morning . . . besides stay put?*

Ten minutes later, back through the blizzard and back in the galley, Stretch was still the only one up. I wrote a note in red marker on the white board hanging outside the comms booth. "Briefing @ 1000—The Route Ahead."

The crew dressed in sweats, t-shirts, and slippers. They'd already coffee-ed and breakfasted. The laptop sat on the galley table.

"They told me nothing." I recalled that Brian had snarled when he said those words back at the True Grit Café.

That will not happen here.

"Brace yourselves. This is going to be a lecture. For the record, how many of you have been to South Pole before?"

All but Greg and Tom raised their hands.

Pole sat in the middle of the Polar Plateau. From Pole, the plateau stretched out in all directions, nothing but snow, flat as a pancake to the horizon. We were on the Plateau now, at elevation 7,400 feet. Elevation at Pole was 9,300 feet. We had a climb. Over three hundred miles, that was not much, but it was not a steady climb. Our route had two summits. The highest one might be 10,000 feet. Russ would be thinking about engine performance at that altitude.

"We'll be coming downhill into South Pole. Slightly. Before I show you where those summits are, look at our route map for the Plateau section ahead."

The map appeared on our laptop. Judy passed it around the room. It was an older map, based on aerial photography, and it traced three alternate route lines. All lines started at our present position, and all converged on a point fifty miles away. Two long, glacial valleys flanked both sides of the route lines: the Scott Glacier to the west, and the Reedy Glacier to the east. I grabbed a cup of coffee while the map made its rounds.

"We'll get to the route lines in a minute. But, let me make this first point: we are not on the Plateau proper. Not like some of you are familiar with at South Pole. We are on a peninsula, or a promontory off the edge of that plateau. The headwaters, so to speak, of the Scott and the Reedy capture all these little tributary glaciers. The headwalls of those form escarpments on the flanks of our peninsula."

A route that strayed too close to the edge risked wandering into crevasses in the headwall cirques. Since the ice on our peninsula shed off on both sides, we needed to pick our way along the top of the ice divide between the Scott and the Reedy.

Tom asked, "Where does the Plateau open up into what you've called the plateau proper?"

"Excellent. Just off the edge of the map, at a point on the blue line labeled Pc. That's 130 miles from here."

I looked to Stretch, and then to Tom. "Okay. Now the route lines"

There were three of them, each different colors. The green one, an older one, we would not follow. It led over the crevasses George Blaisdell and I spotted from the reconnaissance flight. The green line also turned at a point plotted off an inaccurate coordinate location, an inherited mistake that would have taken us into one of those tributary glaciers I'd just cautioned about.

"The best chance for us to dance down this divide and get away with it is to link the points this way: start here, at SPT-18, follow the blue line about thirty miles to T-1. That should be where we see our first summit. It's a thousand-foot rise from here. Then turn southerly on the yellow line to T-2. We have a downhill somewhere in there. At T-3, we join the blue line again and work our way south from there."

The crew's faces registered facts taken in, but not necessarily appreciation for how they were gathered.

"Two more things on this map," I said. Eyes turned again to the laptop. "Twenty miles south of T-3, on the blue line, we come to Pb. That's an old point, common to all three routes. From Pb to Pc, another thirty miles, we have this . . ."

Zooming on the painted map enlarged a feature halfway between the two points. The blue line split a "saddle" between two painted areas plotting crevasse fields. The cartographer who made the map had looked at air photos, saw crevasses there, and labeled them. George and I didn't see these crevasses when we flew the route, but whoever made the map saw them. And if he saw crevasses, then they were *open* crevasses. That probably meant there were *hidden* crevasses near them. The distance between those two crevasse fields was only five miles.

"I'm glad I didn't tell my wife about that!" John V. spoke up.

"John, you haven't been with us since the beginning. But we've got pretty darn good at picking our way through crevasse fields with radar. I'm okay with it, as long as we're careful."

I looked particularly at Stretch and said, "This little place here, where we thread the needle, may very well be the place where we turn around. Mother Nature may say *no* to us. Right there."

I took a deep breath, buying time. The sound of my own voice bothered me.

"All right, here's the last thing I need to tell you. At Pc, we turn and follow the 132 degree West meridian straight to Pole for another 170 miles. Somewhere in that stretch we'll find our second summit."

I also thought our probability of crevasse hazard from Pc onward was very small, but I didn't entirely trust my judgement on that. So I'd asked George to get in touch with the glaciologists he officially contacted and refer my question on crevasse hazard probability from Pc onward to them. That was back in August.

"And?" Tom asked.

"I haven't heard back," I replied flatly. It was December 5.

"Now I'm finished. Does anybody have any questions?" I asked, relieved that I'd reached the end of my lecture.

"Yeah . . . what about sastrugi? Where are they?" Brad asked.

"I forgot about them," I sighed, tracing the findings from our recon flight across the same map. "The worst of them were about half way from here to Pole. My notes also say we saw no clear way around them."

Brad grimaced.

"Brad, that's why we have a blade on *Red Rider*, and we have that big blade on Stretch's D8. We'll find sastrugi out there somewhere, and we'll just have to figure what we *can* do with them then."

I needed a break. In ten minutes I'd speak to the radar team separately. Greg joined me outside where the blizzard still raged. We took our fresh air through polar fleece mufflers.

"Greg, look behind us and tell me how many flags you can see," I asked, thinking of that three-inch stub of bamboo he spotted yesterday.

"I can't see any of them," Greg said apologetically.

"Me neither. From now on you're my eyes. You will determine our official visibility. We won't proceed unless you can see at least two flags behind you. Those of us trailing you won't have any trouble seeing your red PistenBully, but you need to see at least two flags. If you can't, you must stop. And we'll all stop. Do you understand me?"

"Yes."

Greg went back inside while I walked around in the blizzard, patrolling our camp and clearing my mind for the next lecture. Even with my back to the storm, peering out of the deep tunnel of my parka's cowl, frigid blasts of icy pellets still found my face. Snowdrifts had begun to bury our sled skis and spin up in the lee of our tractors. We'd have to move them soon.

Russ came outside and passed me on his way to the generators. We said nothing. His mind was on something else. Russ dinked around to get away from a crowd.

I stepped back into the galley after stamping my feet in the vestibule, the last of the snow falling off my boots and pants. Greg, Tom, and John V. were waiting. Stretch had gone back to his bunk to read. Judy sat at the laptop in the comms booth writing a letter to her twin sister. Brad lay back on his bunk playing some hand-held electronic game.

Stretch's stool offered a change in perspective. I took his seat, and rested my back against the galley wall. "Fellas, tomorrow your job changes. Six miles ahead we run out of flags."

Last year's prospecting team had started our new line in case NSF said go. Beyond their last flag lay what we'd just talked about. On top of looking for crevasses, Greg's team would be laying new flag line. They knew this was coming. I'd hoped to free *Fritzy* as a flagging vehicle for them, but now I needed *Fritzy* to pull sleds.

"You'll use a snowmobile, instead. Your flagger won't have a warm cab. So Greg, I don't know how you want to do this, but I expect you'll rotate your crew. I do, however, want you to obey this one simple rule: *Nobody gets cold.*"

My old tunnel rule would serve well on the Plateau. We had all the extreme cold weather gear we could ask for, and we had heated cabs in every tractor. But on an exposed snowmobile, a flagger might push too hard and get dangerously cold.

"If any one of you gets cold, you must immediately tell Greg. And Greg, you must take immediate steps to get that person warm. Even if it stops everything everybody else is doing. If *you* are the one who is cold, you must warm yourself. Remember, we are only eight here."

Greg looked straight back at me with no expression. I couldn't read him.

"Acknowledge."

"Acknowledged."

"Okay, now let's talk about how to lay out a straight flag line."

For an hour we discussed savvy won from three years on the trail, an improbable combination finessed from grounded experience and intelligence from orbiting satellites. They'd still make a crooked line to start with, until they figured it out. But the flags told us where the radar went, crooked line or not.

"The three of you are leading the rest of us. We've got to know we're following you into safe ground. If all else fails, we can follow the flags behind us to McMurdo because we know that's safe."

Silence.

"All right. Tom knows the radar. If Tom goes down, Stretch and I can read it, too. Just so you know."

Silence, again.

"Fellas, thanks for your time. That's a lot to unload on you. But I can't think of a better way to spend a morning in a blizzard. I'm done talking now."

"Thanks for *your* time," Greg said. Tom and John V. added their "yeahs" to Greg's polite remark.

The blizzard still raged next morning. For sport, Greg called Weather Forecaster Bill—"Wx" Bill—in McMurdo over the Iridium phone. The weather office might have something to say about this particular storm. Several of us eavesdropped from the galley.

"Bill, this is Feleppa with South Pole Traverse. We're on the Plateau at the top of the Leverett. We've been in a blizzard for the past twenty-four hours and want to know how long this system might be with us. Can you help us out?" Greg spoke from the caster chair at the comms booth.

"Yeah, steady thirty to forty knots, blowing snow," Greg reported.

Greg's eyes rolled back over his shoulder. "Bill says we got wind."

"No, we're right at the edge of the Polar Plateau . . . here's our lat-lon." Greg read our coordinates.

"Visibility maybe two hundred feet," Greg added after a pause. Then he smiled. "Bill says we're in a system, and we have low visibility, and it might be this way for a while."

"Ask him to study up on our situation . . . now that he knows where we are," I laughed. "Brad, can you be ready with your show after a while?"

Digging out of drifts consumed the rest of our morning. We advanced our camp one hundred feet upwind. Then we hunkered down once more.

I'd asked several folks to bring along a slide show, or prepare a lecture for days like this one. After lunch, Brad entertained us with pictures on living and working at Greenland's Summit Camp.

After Greenland, I kicked back on the galley bench. "Greg, you know that military alphabet for calling out letters . . . Alpha, Bravo, Charlie, Delta?"

Greg leaned back against the kitchen counter, his arms folded over his muscular chest. "Sure."

"Steve Wheat at the NGA was working on an alternative alphabet. He had things like *M* as in *mnemonic*, and *P* as in *pneumatic* or *phone*. Had us all in stitches, acting out some hapless dispatcher taking dictation over the radio. Imagine yourself under fire in Iraq, calling in an air strike: 'No you idiot, that's *A* as in *aisle*!'"

Greg got it. We giggled.

The alphabet on our white board filled up quickly: *C* as in *cue*, *E* as in *ewe*, *S* as in *sea*, and *W* as in *wye*. Others letters came more slowly, but Greg scored big with *O* as in *ouija*. Our alphabet stayed on the board several days. From time to time, others added their own contributions.

At 1430, I asked Greg to place another call to Wx Bill. "Before you do that, tell me how many flags you can see."

Greg was only outside a moment. "Four flags, Boss. Got some fog and light ground bliz. Three flags for sure."

Boots hit the floors in both bunkrooms. "Let's get off this damned spot!"

Within three miles the blizzard sat down on us again. We crept flag to flag. Our fleet speed was now limited to the D8's best. At this altitude we managed three miles per hour, beating down tracks in virgin snow. But *Fritzy* wallowed in once and *Red Rider* twice.

Brad's jaw clenched tight when I met him with my tow strap. The tank sled, the flatbed sled, and *Snow White* were too much for *Red Rider*. Up ahead, Stretch pulled the modules and a tank sled. Both pulled the same gross weight, but the D8 fared better.

"I'm glad we're only going six miles today," Brad sighed, teetering in the soft snow.

In camp, the mood was more upbeat. We'd moved off the bad luck spot the moment the weather loosened its grip. And we found a message waiting for us at the end of the flag line. Written in duct tape and bamboo poles planted upright in the snow, it spelled: "HI."

"Welcome to the new farthest south," I offered encouragingly. "In twenty-two more miles we'll hit that first summit. Stretch, count on this . . . when we empty that tank you're carrying, we'll drop it and you'll pick up the one Brad's got. Judy, how'd you do today?"

"Oh . . ." her voiced quavered. "We slipped our tracks a lot. But we didn't go down. Just lucky."

✧ ✧ ✧

The ground blizzard still clobbered us the next morning. If it didn't kick snow too high, we could see over the top of it through a tractor's cab. But this morning's blizzard wasn't benign. Snow struck the top of our modules. Though we saw blue sky overhead, we couldn't see one green flag behind us.

By early afternoon Greg could see well enough, and he champed at the bit to get his flagging party going. "Call us when you've made a mile," I told him.

Twenty minutes later he radioed back, "Four flags set." Already in our tractors, we started after him.

In a few miles, the blizzard swelled again and stopped us. We waited in our cabs, engines idling for an hour and a half. Then shortly after our second spurt, Brad radioed "And that's all it took."

We'd just started up the slow rise to the first summit when Brad stuck down hard.

Thanks to that inconstant blizzard and the slight grade, we didn't arrive at the summit until noon of the next day. *Red Rider* and *Fritzy* wallowed several times. Brad finally split his train and shuttled his loads forward. Shuttling so soon alerted me to watch our fuel consumption.

The downhill was short lived. We dropped only four hundred feet in four miles. But Brad could pull his full load, and none of us got stuck. We leveled out on hard dorniks, like those past the Shear Zone and just as rough. Every tractor rocked and jarred its way over each one of them, jerking and slamming us around in our cabs.

After dinner, I penned "23 miles" in my logbook. I'd just written such descriptive terms as "dornikville" and "bad ju-ju," when Greg squeezed by my chair at the comms booth. He and Tom felt the worst of the rough ground in their dual-track PistenBully.

Judy spotted Greg sliding into our bunkroom. She read the fatigue written all over him. "Do you want to borrow my vibrator?"

Hoots erupted through both bunkrooms.

Judy referred to her electric vibrating hot-pad, a cushioned backrest that extended down to mid-thigh. They were popular among long-haul truckers. When Judy lay down on her bunk above mine and turned on her "vibrator," my bunk thrummed like she was rocketing to outer space.

"Some other time, Judy. Thank you," Greg said appreciatively. Then to me, "I think we ought to call that place the *dornikle forest*."

"Spell *dornikal*."

"Djibouti, ouija . . ."

Ground blizzards halted Greg's team intermittently for several days. Under better circumstances, they might range four miles ahead of the lumbering fleet, so long as they maintained radio contact and two-flags visibility. To gain against the ground blizzards they reduced their flagging intervals to one-fifth of a mile.

Meanwhile, the ground got rougher and our daily mileage shorter. I stopped counting immobilizations and recorded them merely as "many." So much for Dave's prediction that the Polar Plateau would be a piece of cake; we now measured progress in small victories.

Sidetracking Stretch's emptied fuel tank, lightening our load by twelve thousand pounds of steel, was one such victory.

Then, on December 11, we entered sastrugi of legendary size.

Six-foot-tall giants ran out in long ridges of wondrously fluted, wind-sculpted snow. Carved into windy arroyos and coulees, they called to mind the Badlands of South Dakota. Whole armies of Sioux warriors, draped in white camouflage, could be hiding among them not more than a hundred feet away. I'd never see them from the warmth of *Fritzy*'s jolting cab, behind my sheltering glass.

And they were hard. They'd bend a shovel. In places the D8's steel tracks barely left a cleat mark on the trail. The flagging crew augered holes before they could plant a flag. Yet, oddly, little drift snow accumulated among them despite the high winds.

Stretch's big blade took down the tops of some. Our other tractors lined up directly behind him. No need to track-pack a wide road base here. The surface was hard enough already. All the while, the rough ground took an aching toll on each of us and our machinery. It broke lock-downs on our container sleds. It broke *Snow White*'s axles. When something broke, we all stopped. Pole seemed very far away.

On December 12 we celebrated another victory in passing 87 degrees South, a whole degree since the top of the Leverett. That particular degree-made-good meant we'd successfully sidestepped the crevasse field spotted on the aerial reconnaissance. At the end of this day, I found Greg outside the modules, plugging in his PistenBully. He and his crew had yet another rough one.

"How you doing?" I asked cautiously.

"We ought to name this place Sastrugi National Park," he declared, offering a more noble handle than Dornikal Forrest.

"Greg, how would *you* move a platoon of marines over this ground?"

Greg stared thoughtfully across the icy rills, moving imaginary troops.

"Helicopters," he said finally. "What's on your mind?"

"That'd be the ticket." I laughed. I'd expected some twist on amphibious assault vehicles.

But a lot was on my mind. We were getting beat up. What if we needed a medevac? There were no helicopters at Pole. If one of us went down, a Twin Otter wouldn't have a prayer for a safe landing here. We'd have to retreat a long way to better ground. If we retreated, what more damage might we bring on a victim or the fleet? And there was no telling how far ahead these badlands stretched.

"Greg, until we can get back here with big blades and smooth the rough places in earnest, we'll have trouble moving ourselves. Right now we don't have the fuel to spend on grading. We dropped one of four fuel tank sleds. We're tapping into the second, and we haven't made it halfway from the Leverett to Pole. I'm thinking *fuel* for one thing."

Russ walked up then, his gait shuffling sideways, his shoulders drooping. We were all weary but Russ the more so because he worried about our machines. Even so, Russ mustered a laughing smile. "Whew! This is *rough*!"

"Yeah it is," I agreed. "Just get me the next thirty miles to Pc. Can you do that?" That gave Russ a target within reach. Something he could take on.

"Thirty miles, huh? Pc?" Russ walked away, mumbling, "Thirty miles . . ."

Each of my hands and feet operated different controls in *Fritzy*'s wildly pitching cab. The small of my back mapped every jolt. While my eyes sought to untangle the chaotic ground, my ears listened keenly to the radio for word from Tom or Greg.

Somewhere during the last two days our single-file line of heavy tractors had shot the five-mile-wide gap. We did it over the roughest ground we'd yet encountered. The radar never found a crevasse. And Russ got us to Pc.

We spent the morning just past Pc repairing things: adjusting the D8's track tension and fixing our radar antenna. Greg's team again got the worst of it. They broke their brake line, their steering controller, their antenna boom, and finally the antenna itself. Jostling over the rough ground had broken a wire inside the antenna box.

Once underway, the radar team moved out ahead of the fleet. For an hour and a half we advanced over the sastrugi when Greg radioed, "We've broken the antenna boom again and are returning to your position to make repairs."

Jeez-sus, what next? Two miles! "Copy that," I acknowledged. "Crew, close up and plug 'em in. I need everybody in the galley at 1100."

"Our situation is this," I explained. "One of our radar antennas is broken beyond our ability to repair. We're using our only spare, and we've a good chance that it, too, will break in this ground. We could easily find ourselves without ground penetrating radar."

We'd passed the last known crevasses between us and South Pole. Crevasses we didn't know about were, of course, the greater danger. While I felt we had a low probability of crevasses over the next 170 miles, I'd sought the additional opinion of experts on exactly that question. As of today, I had no response.

We were beat up, yet we yearned to move forward. But my issue was not how anyone felt. One of our charges had been to go over every inch between McMurdo and Pole with ground penetrating radar. Now we questioned whether the PistenBully itself, let alone the radar equipment, could hold up in these sastrugi.

"Like it or not, we may lose our ability to detect crevasses. Our choice would be grim: we turn around and go back to McMurdo . . . over the route we *have* proved safe."

Every face displayed abhorrence for that. I was willing to go the remaining distance without radar. But I wasn't the only one that mattered.

"If we completely lose it, I don't want to wait for a decision from NSF like we did last year, waiting for no fuel. I'm going to explain our situation to my boss and apprise Dave and George at NSF. Before I do that, I put this question to you because there is risk. Each of you has the right to your say: Are you willing to proceed to Pole without ground penetrating radar?"

No one wished to discuss it. I gave a scrap of paper to each, asking them to mark their answer with a *Y* for *yes* or an *N* for *no*.

"Take your time. We're not going anywhere else today. I'll look these over a bit later."

The crew placed their scraps into a bowl without hesitation. Then they left the galley to attend to camp chores and to repair the antenna boom once again.

Stepping back into the comms booth, I raised my boss back in McMurdo via Iridium phone. He'd been on the Ice when *Linda* went down, and the subject of crevasse detection had been particularly sensitive between us. Now, he was vague in his recollections of our agreement. He didn't object, however, to waiving the radar requirement at my discretion. And I didn't tell him of our poll, nor of the results, because I had not yet looked.

Next, I wrote an e-mail to Dave and George, informing them of our situation. I begged for one more effort at securing the glaciologists' opinions. It was another note in a bottle.

Seated in the comms booth, I leaned back in the caster chair with my hands clasped behind my head, gazing at the ceiling, and drew a deep breath. Finally I sagged forward, rocked to my feet, and reached for the bowl. This was my decision: if one paper said "no," we turned around.

Unfolding seven papers, I found seven *Y*s and smiled. Then I stepped outside to let the crew know, and to give each my thanks.

With sastrugi everywhere, we might lose radar at any time. But when we got underway the next day, nature seemed to approve of our decision. She gave us a daylong display of sundogs and haloes: otherworldly wonders of the polar atmosphere in geometric patterns of rainbow-like arcs surrounding the sun, filling the sky. A burning sun pillar appeared first on our eastern horizon, circled with the sun north behind us, then finally due west to our right.

At day's end, Tom approached me as I was plugging in my tractor. "About two miles out this afternoon, just after we got going, the ground got a lot smoother. It was actually pretty benign on the radar. Maybe it'll stay like this."

The evening's e-mail brought a response from glaciologist Gordon Hamilton, forwarded by George: "It is about as safe as you can get . . ."

December 16 was the day I mark in hindsight that we came out of Sastrugi National Park, which had delighted our eyes, wrecked our equipment, and rattled our bones.

This was also the day we started counting down the miles to Pole: 149 miles to go.

While watching the snowy surface for signs of more sastrugi from *Fritzy*'s cab, I mused over the origin of that field of monsters. All of a sudden, I felt a sinking in my tractor seat. I looked right, then left. My tracks spun faster than the snow went by me. My slip gauge registered 30 percent. Too much. *Fritzy* sank, slip at 100 percent. I shifted to neutral, cursed, throttled back to idle, and then grabbed the radio.

"Brad . . ." One word did it.

"I see you. Coming up on your right."

My feet sank sideways into the soft stuff when I got to the bottom of the ladder, and I fell. Through a face full of snow, I saw exactly what I expected: *Fritzy*, down on her belly pan, wallowed in.

In a too-familiar drill, I rolled to my chest, shoved my mittened hands down, worked my knees under me, staggered up in the soft snow, and grabbed my shovel and tow strap. Up front, I got down on my knees again and dug out the big shackle attached to *Fritzy*'s undercarriage. *One loop through the shackle, stand up. Unroll the strap. Wait for Brad.*

Brad stopped on my right, got out, unhitched *Red Rider*, got back in, pulled ahead, then backed up to me. I slipped the free loop around his hitch pin, stumbled back to *Fritzy*, and climbed in. Brad pulled ahead again, taking slack, and looked back through his windshield. We nodded "ready." He raised three fingers on his left hand. Two. One.

The strap stretched, *Fritzy* spun her tracks, and lurched forward. We arced up, out, leveled, and ran forward under tow until we footed on firm snow. Resurrected, we finished the drill. *Stop the tractor. Get out of the cab. Stagger around the snow. Unhook the tow strap, coil it, exchange a few words, climb back in cab, and try again.*

I always felt apologetic to my rescuer. But sooner or later, everybody helped everyone else. Coiling my tow strap, I met Brad between tractors, and said simply, "Thank you."

"No worries," he shrugged. "You suppose we're out of those sastrugi?"

"I wouldn't know. Flying over this country, I saw s'trugi everywhere."

There was no wind. A piercing blue sky overhead held a thin gray mist of floating ice crystals, like dust motes, stretching out to that brilliant, burning sun pillar. It was a fiery, biblical apparition dropping straight down from the sun to the land. A rainbow halo encircled the whole show. Looking back to Brad, and then at our two tractors, I remarked, "The CRREL boys call this an *im-mo-bi-li-za-tion*."

Mine was only the first immobilization of the day. I stuck many times. So did *Red Rider*, and so did *Elephant Man*. Only the D8R remained immune. Our immobilizations came so frequently that Brad and I split our loads five miles out from the evening camp. We shuttled them the rest of the day. That added thirty extra tractor-miles to reach twenty-one made-good.

When Tom told me the surface was better for the PistenBully and the radar, I thanked him, but mentally filed his report OBE—Overcome By Events. Maybe we'd left sastrugi behind, but now we had two tractors shuttling. If that got worse, we'd be seriously tapping our fuel supply.

The next day, *Fritzy* and the *Elephant Man* wallowed many times, but curiously *Red Rider* didn't. Why? I don't know, but I was happy for Brad. We posted twenty-eight miles without shuttling. The day after, *Elephant Man* and *Red Rider* saw all the immobilizations. *Fritzy* got off scot-free.

During the afternoon, Greg's team planted a tall post along the trail, scribed P-100. That meant one hundred miles to Pole. Somewhere within the last twenty miles, we'd topped our second summit. My GPS altimeter showed a high at 9,640 feet. But the surface everywhere around was flat to the horizon. Only our green flag line gave us any hint of direction.

Russ's voice broke my musings: "*Fritzy*, can you come back here and give us a tow?"

Russ rode in the *Elephant Man* with Judy. I looked over my shoulder and spotted their black dot on my northern horizon. They'd be about five miles back. *Red Rider* was still rolling halfway between us.

A mile north of the post, I passed Brad and waved. He waved back. Just as he did, *Red Rider* sank.

"I'll come back for you."

"Copy."

When things went well, replies came in the form of "copy that." Just "copy" meant we were tired.

Russ waited with tow strap at the ready beside the *Elephant Man*. I wheeled around, and backed up *Fritzy*. Automatically, Russ dropped my hitch pin through his strap loop, then climbed back aboard Judy's tractor. I took tension.

"Ready?" I called back to Judy.

"Ready."

Snatch. Jerk. *Fritzy* sank. I throttled down and looked back at the *Elephant Man*. It hadn't budged. Backing over my tracks, I turned slightly onto fresh snow, and took tension again. "Ready?"

"Ready."

Snatch, slip, grip, lurch. We crawled forward inching the *Elephant Man* out of its wallow. Then we were up on surface again.

"I'll pull you to the hundred-mile post, since I'm going there anyway. I'll cut you loose there."

"Fine. Just fine. Really. It's fine," Judy came back. She was tired, too.

"Camp will be five miles past that. Do what you can with what you got. Shuttle if you have to."

"Fine."

After turning loose of the *Elephant Man*, I ran a mile back to Brad. Like the *Elephant Man*, *Red Rider* had mired to its belly. I got out of *Fritzy* this time, stretching my back and arms, while Brad hitched the strap.

"You hear all that?"

"You mean 'five miles' past the post? Yeah. I've already unhitched *Snow White*. I'll start my shuttle from here."

We now had three tractors shuttling in this melee. But at five miles south of the hundred-mile post, we finally camped in two-digit country. That, at least, was another small victory.

"You guys, look at this!" John V. hollered at refueling time.

John stood a ten-foot-long bamboo flagpole on the snow, grasping it as high on the pole as he could. He drove it down six feet into the snow, with one hand, effortlessly.

"John," I addressed him with mock formality, "One measure of soft snow may be taken as its resistance, or the lack thereof, to penetration. Your flag-penetrometer has sealed the issue. We are in *another* snow swamp!"

I'd never expected a snow swamp on the Plateau. And now, with two tractors lost, we all ran heavy.

When Brad finished fueling us, he stuffed fuel in the generator tank, in the refrigerated food van's tank, and in any other place he could find. That left only 120 gallons, 840 pounds, in the tank sled.

"There's no need to drag twelve thousand pounds of nearly empty steel tank another day. Let's sidetrack it," Brad urged.

"Right you are. Thank you. Unhitch it from Stretch's train. We'll pull out of here tomorrow without it." I appreciated Brad's good thinking, for I had other horrors storming around in my mind.

Another rule of engagement laid on the proof-of-concept project was: "Rely on support from McMurdo only." Who would declare a draw on South Pole fuel as proof of failure? But shuttling three-miles-for-one from here would drain our fuel . . . and psyche us out.

Our camp sat ninety-five miles from Pole. Last year we made that distance one long day on the Ross Ice Shelf, on a road. If we dropped our loads now, we could get to Pole in a day with the fuel in our tractors alone. But we were tracking *with* loads on virgin snow. There was no reason to think the snow was going to change. That evening after dinner I wrote to Dave Bresnahan, now back in the United States:

> Dave, we have a situation. We are a hundred miles from Pole, and we find we're in another snow swamp. We got all our cargo with us, but we're going to have to shuttle it the rest of the way. To go forward, we will be drawing on our return reserve fuel. Understand, we're going in no matter what, but whether we turn around and head back to McMurdo, or winter the fleet at Pole, will depend on whether we can take on supplemental fuel at Pole. I have no idea what the fuel situation is in the USAP this season. But I am thinking that if it is anything like last year, my request for fuel will not be welcome. Can you advise?

In a surprisingly fast return that evening—it must have been morning wherever Dave was—he wrote back:

> I cannot make the call from here. You must make your case to the NSF Representative-Antarctica in McMurdo. Explain exactly your situation. He will decide.

Al Sutherland occupied the big chair now. He was a good egg whose management area was Marine Science Operations. Before I wrote him, I sent a note to the contractor's South Pole area manager advising her of my intent to request supplemental fuel from the station's supply. I'd created a predictor for Pole's winter fuel consumption some years before. The area manager would greet my request as a threat to next October's reserve when they would be sucking fumes. But, as Dave said, the NSF would decide.

I also advised her of our probable arrival date: sometime during their two-day Christmas holiday. We'd need a two-day turnaround ourselves for cargo off-loading and rigging for our return traverse. I offered to slow our arrival until after the holiday when the station was back at work.

Then I wrote Al:

> The amount of supplemental fuel we will need can only be determined
> when we get there, but my present estimate is between 1,500 and 2,500
> gallons. Alternative choices to fuel re-supply are: 1) We can winter the fleet
> at Pole, and not return to McMurdo. That risks mission failure in that a
> round trip traverse is an essential mission component; 2) We can drop our
> cargo here, one hundred miles from Pole, turn around and get back to
> McMurdo with what fuel we have. In doing that we will abandon one
> disabled tractor, presently stationed halfway up the Leverett. This alternative
> risks total mission failure not only in winning the total distance to Pole, but
> also in cargo delivery.
>
> Be advised, we are coming in. Can you advise status and permission to take
> on supplemental fuel?

The Big Chair was always busy with a crisis. Ours was just another. This time, however, I'd not wait in place for an answer. I'd take that answer on the move, headed south.

We might not be welcome at South Pole in the middle of its Christmas holiday. Visitors were not generally welcome. Any use of its over-allocated resources met with something akin to hostility. I explained this to the crew.

Russ took angry exception: "Any time somebody comes to visit, you treat them right. We're bringing them a whole lot of stuff they need and want. The least any human being should do is show some hospitality."

"You're right, Russ," I answered. "But I'm thinking of last year when we got turned around. Pole couldn't support us with fuel, or stand the possibility that we might winter-over our fleet. This past off-season Pole wanted projections on our expected draw of its resources. They were sensitive about use of their Heavy Shop for fleet repairs. We've already taken some of their cargo space on the LC-130s with spare parts. They measure that to the pound."

"Well, that's not the way people should be. I don't care . . . you're coming in from a long way and a hard trip. You ought to be welcome."

"Russ, I have to ask them. We don't know what the situation at Pole might be. I offered as much turnaround time as they needed between their mechanics and ours. But we have to give them the opportunity to say 'welcome.' That'll be enough on this subject." I closed the conversation, leaving it badly between us.

By the next morning's briefing, Al Sutherland had not responded. No matter what, we'd slog across the swamp. We'd plan on shuttling, and we'd tap deep into our return fuel to do that.

"Stretch, dropping that tank behind you lowers your gross towed weight to 100,000 pounds. What kind of speed do you think you can make?"

"Maybe two and a half miles an hour. I'm not hard hitched anymore. I'm pulling with the winch cable. If I slip my tracks, I pay out the cable to get me out of the hole. Then I winch the load forward to catch up. So, it's not steady. Maybe only two miles an hour."

"Got it." I addressed everyone next: "We'll build our shuttle plan around what Stretch can do. Stretch, lunch today will be twelve miles ahead. When you get there, stop. Greg, go ahead and mark the spot. *Fritzy, Elephant Man,* and *Red Rider* will be right behind you. We'll drop whatever loads we got there, then turn around and come back for what we left."

Flashing back to Year Two, I didn't like getting in front of the module sleds. If something broke on them, we wouldn't see it to warn Stretch. But our sled modifications were working for us now. Stretch would see a lot of us today. We'd check on his sleds when we passed him. With any luck, we'd be running three times his speed. With more luck, we'd all get to the lunch spot at the same time.

"I don't know what we'll do after lunch. Greg, get started. Call us when you're four flags out."

Greg, Tom, and John V. were first out the door. The rest of us battened down the galley.

Fritzy and I had no trouble pulling two fuel tank sleds and the refrigerated food van. I enjoyed running at seven miles an hour. Ahead, the PistenBully made a dark dot on that crisp line where polar blue sky met white snow.

Judy, in the *Elephant Man* behind me, radioed, "*Fritzy,* I can't pull both the Milvan *and* the MT865. I'm going to have to split them."

"Yeah," this was Brad's voice calling from *Red Rider*. "And I can't pull both the flat rack and *Snow White*. Going to split them up, too."

Send two tractors back to shuttle, before lunch? Can Fritzy make it all the way, and go back and get one load? We'd have to wait for the other tractor. Timing's off.

My trail thoughts drifted back to a difference of opinion with Jim Lever last year on the trail. Jim wanted to load up a tractor to the maximum it could pull without wallowing-in. That was one side of the equation. Given the expense of redesigning our sled fleet, and the unlikelihood of NSF funding a wholesale redesign, I looked on the other side. I fought uphill for a fifth tractor, just to carry what sleds we did have. My gut spoke for me: "For the money, give me another tractor, any day." "Not me," Jim said. But he had never shuttled through a swamp. With two tractors down, that alone begged for another tractor, any day.

What was it Patrice Godon did on the French traverse? "Wait! Hey Brad, you there?"

"Yeah, go ahead, John."

"Try something. If it don't work, it don't work. Judy, drop the MT865, and rig a tow strap from the back of your milvan sled to *Red Rider*. Brad, see if Judy can pull you without you having to break your load." If it worked, we'd eliminate one shuttle and save twenty-four miles worth of one tractor's fuel.

"Interesting. Copy all," Brad acknowledged.

When I pulled up to the lunch spot, John V. came to the back of my tractor to unhitch me. The routine was wordless, but I did holler out the cab door, "Which of you guys wants to go back with me?"

Greg scrambled aboard, taking the jump seat to my left. Out the back window, John V. gave me thumbs up. *Fritzy* pulled ahead, wheeled around, then started back north, tracking just outside the flag line. Stretch would be coming along right next to the flags, and I didn't want to chew up the snow in front of him.

Greg and I stopped beside a green flag two miles back down the trail, and watched. The boxy *Elephant Man* churned on by us, nose-high. Behind her came the milvan, and behind that, two long straps linked by a shackle bounced up and down on the snow. At the end of the tow strap came *Red Rider*. A beaming Brad flashed his pearly whites through the tinted window. Behind him came the loaded flat rack sled *and Snow White*, together.

"Hot damn! The mojo's working! We've got one up of the swamp, Greg. Let's go get that MT!"

"Plenty good, Boss," Greg grinned.

"Jeez-us, Greg, it's John."

Halfway to the MT we passed Stretch heading south with just enough time for a wave back and forth and a quick scan of his rig. He carried his blade high, watching the snow under it. Twenty feet of winch cable inchwormed the module sleds behind him. The sleds looked fine. Stretch hadn't been stuck yet.

In another mile, we spied the dot on our northern horizon that was the MT865. In forty minutes we were there. Greg bailed out, I backed into the hitch, and then we switched seats and headed south.

Stretch had been at the lunch spot ten minutes by the time we got there. The generators were fired up and a hot lunch was in the microwave.

"Pretty good for the morning," I said to no one in particular, enjoying the vegetable soup. The wall clock showed 1300 hrs. "Let's see if we can get ten more this afternoon. Can you give us that, Stretch, if we get out of here by 1400?"

"Oh, probably. It'll be a long afternoon," Stretch said, agreeably enough, though he looked tired. Of all of us, he saw the least action in slow motion, yet required the most concentration.

"Anybody check e-mail yet?" I asked.

"You had one from NSF-REP," Tom said.

"That was quick. Beats three days at the top of the Leverett." I called up the message on the laptop in the comms booth, and cried, "Thank you, Al! Go! Go man go! Listen to this: *We are not going to hold up the completion of your mission for a few gallons of fuel. Be safe. Godspeed.*"

Russ brightened first: "Well, all right!"

Judy was next: "All righ-tee, then."

Smiling faces and nodding heads ran all around the galley. The swamp wasn't our fault, and every one of us wanted to complete the roundtrip. We'd worked hard to bring all our cargo. We didn't want to pay a penalty for that.

We made the extra ten miles, posting twenty-two for the day. *Fritzy* covered sixty-seven miles to do that. We camped at Pole minus 73 on December 19.

That evening we received another e-mail, this one from the assistant South Pole station manager, Liesl Schernthanner. I read it aloud before we turned in.

We'd be welcome, Liesl said, whenever we got there. If that happened to fall on their holidays, so much the better. We'd be welcome to share their two days off and join their festivities, like cousins coming for Christmas.

"That settles it. I'm glad we asked."

We slept well that night, prepared to slog on.

The deeper we got into the swamp, the worse it treated us. Any tractor and load combination that worked for us one day did not necessarily work the next. We still reunited when Stretch reached the lunch mark. And depending on the time that actually happened, I set the distance goal for the remains of the day.

December 20 Judy and the *Elephant Man*, with the milvan in tow, could no longer pull *Red Rider* and its full load. So Brad split his train. *Fritzy* got off free again. And Brad finished his day towing Stretch into camp at Pole minus 51. We'd won twenty-two miles at a high cost.

While the others refueled, I sat at the comms desk readying our daily report. Heavy footsteps climbed the deck to the living module, and then tromped into the vestibule. Stretch entered the galley, staggering across the floor toward his bunkroom. Thinking better of it, he flopped down with a deep sigh onto the padded bench behind our long dinner table. His haggard expression bespoke absolute exhaustion. I'd never seen such a display.

"Oh, man!" he sighed again, involuntarily.

"Stretch, you look whupped."

"John, I *am* whupped." Stretch's eyes widened. "This snow is getting worse. I just watch the snow . . . watch the snow . . . watch the snow . . ."

To make our miles today, we ran a couple hours over. And I'd exhausted one man doing it, bringing him to the edge.

"I get the message, Stretch. I saw Brad pulling you. And I never thought I'd see that. Maybe we need to shut down for a day and just build road so that you can get up on it and go."

"Oh, that would be nice," Stretch nodded deeply. "Anything but this."

Stretch needed rest. Lots of it. I couldn't ask him for another day like today. Building road might not be the best idea. We all needed a good meal. At dinner, I'd ask everyone to think about ways of getting Stretch down the trail.

Camp sat in the middle of a perfectly smooth white dish. Its edges curled up slightly around all our horizons. The air was dead calm. Flags hung limp. This morning, brilliant sunny skies stretched to all points.

And Stretch looked rested.

I began the briefing. "Just 'cause there's only fifty-one miles to go doesn't mean we're going lunging through this last bit of swamp. Our job today is do whatever we can to help Stretch . . . without exhausting any of us. Period. Listening to you guys last night, and adding some of my own thoughts, we have three alternatives."

Greg interrupted. "What makes you think any one of them will work?"

Silence crashed over the galley. Greg scowled at me. Then his lips quivered, ever so slightly.

"Oh, our designated cynic has spoken . . . a fair effort, too."

Greg buckled, breaking into an embarrassed smile. "You've exposed me, Boss. I was only trying to do my job."

Brad broke in: "Do any of your three alternatives include the one where we just leave Stretch behind and let him come in whenever he pretty-pleases?"

"Whoa now, Bradley," Stretch admonished him in patronizing tones. "We know you've got a girlfriend waiting for you there. She can wait a little longer."

"Hee-hee. I'm just trying to make life easy for you old folks," Brad grinned. Stretch was fifty-nine this year. Brad was in his early forties.

"Ahem. Can I get in here?" I cleared my throat.

"Oh all right," Brad drawled.

"As I was saying," I started slowly. Brad whispered "tee-hee" back at Stretch.

"Three alternatives. The first is build a road out thirty miles, with three tractors, and shuttling half-loads forward. Stretch and the D8 stay here for the day, we come back with *Fritzy*, *Red Rider*, and the *Elephant Man*. We leave the PistenBully up ahead for the night, bring the flagging crew back with us. Tomorrow we all go forward with Stretch and the last of the shuttle loads on a packed road. What do you think?"

"What? Give the old man a full day off?" Brad yipped at the big dog.

Stretch shook his head. He was okay. He wanted to move.

"The second: We get a three-tractor shuttle going. Brad and *Red Rider* pull Stretch all day long. Judy and I shuttle all day. We don't get a lot of advantage in speed, but we might make twenty-five or thirty miles."

"Oh, poor old Stretch."

"Bradley, you leave poor old Stretch alone. You're as bad as McCabe," I cautioned, with mock concern.

"Brad," Stretch challenged him. "You just don't want me to get there ahead of you and see your girlfriend first."

"Oh, brother!" Judy voiced deep exasperation.

"That's right, Stretch," Brad grinned. "I'm really worried about that."

Russ said, "But then you'd still have one or two loads back here, and you'd have to come get them. You'd still be two days getting thirty miles."

"Right, no advantage time-wise over the first plan," I saw Russ's point as long as Stretch was good to go. I continued: "And the third one: a three-tractor shuttle, moving out in front of Stretch. Track pack what we can and see how Stretch manages on that. That's pretty much what we did yesterday."

"Let's just not make it such a long day," Stretch added.

"That one snuck up on me. Greg, give us a twelve-mile lunch stop. We'll see what we can do afterwards." I was already thinking less mileage. But this morning's banter told me if we were going to get twelve, we'd better do it while they were full of vinegar.

"Lunch at Pole minus 39?" Greg asked.

"Yes. Dropping two decades from the fifties to the thirties has a nice ring to it."

The D8R lumbered south while the other three tractors ran ahead pulling half-loads. Turning back from the lunch spot, we ran back to retrieve the other half. Three times that morning we passed Stretch, coming and going. Stretch got tired of waving. Brad flipped the occasional gesture in deference to his maturity.

During the lunch rendezvous, I set a day's-end target eight miles forward: camp at Pole minus 31. While the D8R advanced, the three other tractors ran half-loads past camp to Pole minus 27, following Greg's flags.

As we approached his team at the end of the line, John V.'s voice broke over our radios: "Hey guys, check that out!"

I looked straight ahead. John V. was two miles up there, and probably he was pointing at something, but he was only a speck to me. "Check what out?"

"Look out your windows to your right," he radioed back.

Then I saw it, too: low contrails in the sky off to our right.

Since we'd left the backside of the Transantarctic Mountains, the mo-
notony of shuttling and rescuing tractors had merged with our unchanging
horizon. We worked through our days in a collective torpor. Counting down
miles was a navigational statistic that did not assure us South Pole Station laid
ahead. The contrails were real sign.

I called back, "You think those LC-130s know where they're going?"

We dropped half-loads at the twenty-seven mile flag, then tracked back to
Pole minus 31. Passing camp, we returned to our old lunch spot at Pole minus
39, and brought up remaining loads for the end of shift. The day closed with
twenty miles made good. A four-mile stretch of track-packed road ran out in
front for the next day's start. It might set up overnight, and Stretch might see
better traction the next morning. Possibly he'd coax another half-mile an hour
out of the D8.

"Doing all right?" I asked Stretch privately at refueling time.

"Yeah, I'm fine. I'm tired, but I'm fine."

"Good. Glad we stopped at twenty today. Did you catch those contrails?"

"No, I didn't see anything," he shrugged, not remotely interested in the
news. "I got to watch the snow. I can't let it get away from me."

Our four-mile road worked. The next morning Stretch covered it in one
hour and twenty minutes, but the next eight miles over untracked swamp were
worse than ever for him. While the other tractors shuttled monotonously, a
bug-eyed Stretch alternately dragged and winched his load forward.

We made our twelve miles in time for yet another late lunch. There, at Pole
minus 19, I sat once again at the comms desk. Stretch reclined on the padded
bench alongside the galley table. He stared through closed eyelids into unpleasant prospects for the rest of the day. The others remained outside, basking
under the high sun on a brilliant afternoon.

I looked over Stretch's spent form and wondered if he was done. He'd
gone through his own private hell for days, but I had to know. The afternoon's
moves, like chess pieces, positioned us for tomorrow. It all depended on what
Stretch could do . . . and *would* do.

Bracing myself, I broke our silence: "Stretch, can you give us another six
today?"

Instantly his eyes opened. The indignant look he shot back spoke: "How dare you!"

We stared hard, eye-to-eye. He could say "no" and that would be fine. But his pride might not allow that. Unmistakable malice showed on his face. He never said a word. He never took his steeled eyes off me. Finally came his slow nod.

"Pole minus 13 is a bit over a half day out of Pole," I explained. "It'll take us the other half day to get settled in there. The next day is their holiday . . . and ours, too, now that we're invited, so I want to get to Pole minus 13 tonight."

I was just noise to Stretch. His unblinking eyes stared back.

"Stretch, that four miles of track-packed road set up good for you. From here, take as long as you need to get yourself rested. You do not have to leave right away. Hell, take a nap!"

Stretch blinked.

"I mean it. Take a nap. Russ and Judy will shuttle what they can from here, and from what's behind us, up to Pole minus 13. Brad and I and Greg's party will take loads forward to two miles out from Pole. We're going to build you a *road* all the way to Pole today. Tomorrow you will lead the heavy fleet in."

|14| Going In with Airplanes

Closing on Pole should have been exciting for all of us. But its proximity had become irrelevant to making just the next mile. For Stretch closing on Pole was an endless bummer. For me, Pole was only a halfway point, oddly receding over our unchanging horizon.

The day the airplane came . . . *then* we got excited.

We'd just finished refueling the D8 after lunch at Pole minus 19. Since it had an eight-hour tank, we topped it up every mid-shift and at the end of each day. The operation required three or four of us. I was on top of the tank sled disconnecting the suction hose when a deafening roar overhead dropped me to my knees. I grasped for the ladder. The low-flying LC-130 passed close enough I could count every rivet on its massive airframe.

The others stood on the snow, just as surprised as me. All eyes followed its flight.

The northbound plane had come right out of Pole. Its flight path back to McMurdo should've taken it well off to our right. This one had diverted to fly over us.

And it didn't stop with one flyover. Just over our tracks behind us, the plane climbed gently through a broad left-banking turn and came at us again, this time from the west. We ducked for the second time. East of our track, still low, it banked once more, hard. Its left wing tip cleared the snow by inches, showing us its entire topside. Then it crossed over us for the last time, climbing back onto its McMurdo course, shrinking in the clear blue sky, then vanishing altogether.

Forget the contrails, Stretch; you got the whole airplane!
Dismounting the tank sled, I crossed paths with Greg. He approved,
"That was impressive . . . even for the air force."

Greg's team started south. Brad followed in *Red Rider* pulling *Snow White*.
I followed with *Fritzy* pulling the flat rack. We took care to stay well to the
right of the green flag line. For today, that gap of virgin snow offered Stretch
a small measure of better traction than the cold, dry stuff our tractors churned
into granular fluff. Our tractors *did* compact the snow, but it took time to
sinter and form a pavement. Processed snow at Pole would set up "overnight."

When we came abreast of the camp flag Greg planted at Pole minus 13,
Brad swerved into the flag line. Now he laid his tracks just a foot to their right.
I swung over to stagger my tracks right of his. That'd be just right for Stretch's
road tomorrow.

The moment Brad swerved, the PistenBully appeared ahead as the familiar
black dot. I wondered what their horizon looked like now. At Pole minus 13,
we may as well have been at Pole minus 100. Unobstructed flat white stretched
to the curve of the earth, and we tracked a straight line through the middle of
it. But for the LC-130s appearance, we owned our horizons.

Amundsen owned his, too. All the way here, and forever. Scott owned his hori-
zons until he spotted Amundsen's abandoned tent.

By Pole minus 9 a bright white *something* appeared on our horizon, to the
right of our track. By Pole minus 8, it'd grown larger and shifted almost im-
perceptibly farther to our right.

By Pole minus 7, the white object resolved into a perfectly round ball,
like a small moon rising. A structure appeared underneath it. The ball became
a spherical dome covering the thirty-foot Marisat dish antenna. I was driving tunnel when the antenna had been erected. Back then the exposed dish
perched on a square platform supported by four enormous steel pedestals. The
protective dome was new.

The rest of South Pole Station slowly materialized from the snows ahead.
New black dots appeared both right and left of our track: outbuildings of the
station. All the time I'd worked at Pole, I'd never wandered this far away from
it and looked back. Mental maps now told me which buildings they were.

Stretch might've made three miles already. Judy and Russ might be going for their second load.

"Target acquired!" Greg squawked over the radio.

Greg stood erect on the snow, marine-like, with binoculars in hand peering stealthily over a horizon.

He'd spotted five black panels planted on the 132 W meridian. The South Pole surveyor had placed them two years ago. The panels marked the hold-back line, two miles short of 90 degrees South. By agreement, we'd stop there and request permission to come into the station. Since we'd have no idea of air traffic activity, we'd hold back until the station cleared us to cross the runway's extended centerline. A stuck tractor on the centerline could force an aircraft to abort.

But all of that we'd do tomorrow. Today, the hold-back line was our goal. I'd told Greg to abandon GPS navigation when he spotted the panels and set a visual course directly for them. Given ice movement and the convergence of meridians, the panels might not be on the 132 W meridian now.

"Excellent," I radioed back. "When you get to the panels, tell me what you see."

"Roger, Boss."

Jeesh . . .

By Pole minus 6, the full sweep of station structures stretched well left and right of us. The towering elevated station dominated them all. That new station had been the focus of all construction activity for the past several years. Now it neared completion. Presently it resembled a collection of two-story plywood shoeboxes elevated on massive pedestals.

Our horizon collides with the Station's. But we're still outside the city limits, in wild country.

At Pole minus 4, my radio squawked again: "*Fritzy*, this is Feleppa. We're at the hold-back line and have planted the last flag. There're a couple of folks on snowmobiles who've come to greet us. A PistenBully's headed our way from across the skiway."

"Well done, you guys!" I smiled, imagining a thousand miles of flags leading to this spot. "I'm going to contact South Pole Comms. Switch to 143.00

MHz. South Pole Comms, South Pole Comms . . . this is South Pole Traverse on 143.00 MHz . . . how copy?"

After thirty seconds, hearing no reply, I resent. Another thirty seconds passed, and still no reply. "Brad, Greg, you guys get anything from South Pole?"

"Negative," Brad confirmed. We were a mile from the hold-back line, still headed south.

"Negative," Greg responded, adding: "There's a guy here from South Pole with a radio that hears you. And he hears South Pole Comms acknowledge your hail with *clear copy.*"

"South Pole Comms, South Pole Comms . . . this is South Pole Traverse . . . we have negative copy on your reply. Be advised our intentions to drop our loads at the hold-back line and return to our camp over your horizon. We will be coming in tomorrow. Traverse clear."

Moments later Brad stopped at the panels. Moments after that, *Fritzy* and I pulled up alongside Brad.

The structures of South Pole Station loomed enormous. Directly right, one quarter mile away, stood the Marisat dome. Half a dozen Polies had come to meet us. But I strode purposefully toward the five black panels where Greg, Tom, and John V. beamed beside our PistenBully. The last green flag stood right in the middle of the five black panels. I congratulated them.

"Thanks, Boss," Greg said, grinning.

I rolled my eyes, giving up on it.

"Tom, I assume you've stowed the radar?"

"With great pleasure and finality!" Tom smiled. Tom's achievement in keeping our radar working to the end fulfilled a vital mission. I deeply appreciated his vigilance.

Brad had already found his girlfriend. She was a pretty brunette, svelte even in her overstuffed parka. Brad had introduced us back in McMurdo. Keen intelligence looked back at me then through her big, round, dark eyes. Now, I just smiled and waved at both of them. Brad grinned and waved back.

Turning to see who from Pole might've come out to meet us, I awkwardly looked over new faces after seven weeks on the trail. The boss of the South Pole cargo crew stood back a bit. I was fond of her. Soon we'd deliver her cargo, but for the moment, she stepped forward and we heartily embraced.

A guy with an enormous, shoulder-mounted camera hung back at the fringe. This was the *National Geographic* stringer who wanted footage of our arrival. We were not "arrived" yet.

Standing close by was a writer-photographer for the *Antarctic Sun Times*, an NSF-sponsored weekly of USAP doings. I knew that guy. I liked his work, though at present all I had for him was "Hello."

A tow-headed, clean-shaven fellow walked up. I'd met Jason Medley eight years earlier at Palmer Station when I'd wintered there. He had inherited a construction job, and despite a lack of materials that season, he rallied his crew and got a lot of good work done. I admired him for that. Jason now served as South Pole operations manager and would be my point of contact. I offered my hand.

"Jason, we have some radio difficulties. You're aware that we are *not* coming in today?"

"We weren't certain when we spotted you coming over the horizon. But I understand tomorrow's the day. We do have some papers for you to sign."

"Whatever that is, it can wait," I laughed. "Are those tracks coming out from Marisat the path we'll take into the station tomorrow?"

Jason had no objection to us parking our loads there, so I pulled forward on the new line. Brad pulled alongside to my left. His lady friend rode with him.

I was kneeling in the snow pulling my hitch pin, when a voice close at my back announced, "Jerry Marty wants to speak to you."

Jerry Marty was NSF's station representative. His enthusiasm for all activity at Pole was infectious. I liked him a lot. But I fretted over Stretch, Judy, and Russ. Jerry was not among the crowd, and I didn't want to go into the station for a parley. Without turning, I hollered over my shoulder:

"I'm working here! I haven't got time to talk to Jerry Marty!"

Moments later I had the pin out, swung the draw bar to the side, and freed my tractor from its sled. Straightening slowly, I turned and looked right into Jason's slack-jawed face. He'd been holding his walkie-talkie to my back, keyed to transmit. Jerry, wherever he was, and everyone else at South Pole Station, heard every word I'd just grumbled.

"Aw, shit. Jason, please tell Jerry we'll be in tomorrow at 1300. We're getting out of here." Jerry, I hoped, would understand.

We had a road to pack. I climbed back in *Fritzy* and radioed to Greg to start back for camp. Brad had already unhitched from *Snow White*, but was still standing on the snow in passionate embrace with his sweetheart. I hollered at him out the open door of my cab, jerking my head in the direction of the trail behind us.

He said he'd be along momentarily, but it looked as though it might take a pry bar.

Sometime later, *Red Rider* appeared in my mirror. That made three of us headed north: Greg's mob, me, and Brad, stretched out over two miles of trail.

Our passage back to Pole minus 13 was uneventful, save that I and the others marveled with each green flag we passed. Here, at last, lay a well-marked, safe trail linking McMurdo at one end to Pole at the other.

The D8 and its train had been at Pole minus 13 for some time. The flap on the generator's exhaust stack clapped up and down over the pipe poking through the energy module's roof. The food van parked in its usual position, its foot ramps down on the snow. The *Elephant Man* was plugged in. Two shuttle loads were in camp. Pole's tractor remained back at Pole minus 19.

Russ met me while I refueled. "Ah . . . it was getting late, so we left one back there," he apologized.

"Not to worry, Russ," I said. "I'll get it tomorrow morning. All else okay?"

"Just fine," he allowed. And *that* was good news.

The evening meal was nearly ready. In the galley, Stretch looked rested, and glad of it. I mouthed my thanks to him. He nodded and smiled back. "Errr, uhhh, perhaps you'd better look at this, John."

Stretch had been at Pole minus 13 long enough to field the incoming e-mails through our communal laptop. He called up one forwarded by his wife, Carol, who was back in McMurdo. The e-mail originated a few hours earlier, just as we turned around from the hold-back line. It was an all-stations, all-hands, all-facilities announcement originated in Denver from the contractor's Chief of Staff: "Only minutes ago, the South Pole Traverse arrived at South Pole Station, completing its historic mission of delivering cargo over a 1,000 mile surface traverse from McMurdo to South Pole. Join me in congratulating . . ." Etc., etc.

"Carol said this went out to everybody," Stretch explained.

I laughed. "Apparently, we're the last to know we've arrived."

We spread out after dinner, some to our bunks, some hanging out in the galley. But the bunkroom doors remained open. Our collective mood was to talk about going into Pole now, rather than waiting for tomorrow morning.

Tom and Greg had never been to Pole. Judy went to Pole once on a boondoggle flight in 1993. She was there for two hours. Russ had last been to Pole in 1983 as a heavy mechanic. Things would look and feel way different for him.

Stretch, Brad, and John V. had been to Pole more recently. We four were the most familiar with the place.

"We can expect a group to meet us at the hold-back line," I explained. "I've told them when we'll arrive. There'll be a *National Geographic* photographer among them, and he needs to capture video of our arrival. We're going to cooperate, but we'll find out exactly what he wants tomorrow."

Some eyebrows raised, and a voice or two repeated "*National Geographic…*"

I explained our discovery of the two-way radio problems. Stretch would lead the heavy tractors, but Greg would get to the hold-back line ahead of the rest of us to tell me what was going on. If there were any surprises in store, I needed him to be not just my eyes, but my ears as well. At least *our* radios could talk to each other. And we'd be met by a guide who'd lead us to our designated camping spot. Right after that, we'd get the Welcome-to-South-Pole-Station-Dos-and-Don'ts briefing. We'd change our living habits, too.

"We can't do our dishes, which means we can't cook. And we can't shower the way we've done it on the trail. We don't have a wastewater disposal setup that we can use there. And we don't dare use any of the station's snow in our own snow melter. It's too contaminated with diesel to risk in our system. So . . . we're going to depend on the station's sanitary facilities and their galley for these things."

The prospect of a change in our sanitary habits raised visible apprehension. Our collective speculations came to another awkward impasse, ending with mutual frustration: the crew with me that I had no immediate answers, and myself that I had none either.

"All I know is we're welcome at South Pole Station. As guests, we need to fit into their way of doing things. That's as much as anybody can hope for, until tomorrow when we actually get there."

We turned in to our bunks, left to our own thoughts of what tomorrow might bring.

I rose at 0400, dressed, grabbed some snack food, then stepped outside and started *Fritzy*. The tractor noise would stir some in their bunks, but none would start moving until 0600. I'd be back about then.

A cloudless blue sky and perfectly calm air, everywhere around, made splendid weather for a solitary trip to fetch the Pole tractor. Yesterday's tracks stretched out before me. Here were the D8's. Over there were the *Elephant Man*'s, coming and going twice. Farther still were Brad's and mine. Their braided patterns recorded our trials getting ourselves and our cargo across the Plateau swamp.

I arrived at the Pole tractor, recalling how the beast broke down four hundred miles out of McMurdo. We'd dragged the cripple over six hundred miles up the Leverett, across the sastrugi and the Plateau swamp. Now I backed *Fritzy* up to the spreader bar sled and stepped out to hitch that improbable rig to my tractor.

Camp at Pole minus 13 lay over the disk of my horizon now. Around the entire compass, only our tracks on the snow, and a line of green flags stretching due north and due south as far as the eye could see, gave any tangible sense of place. Heading back to camp, I added yet one more set of tracks to the lines we'd made.

From three miles out, our fleet was merely dots in the distance. From a mile, I could make out folks hitching tractors to sleds. By the time I pulled into camp, our tractors were already pointed south, idling in snuffy anticipation. The galley was still set up for breakfast and one last muster.

"Let's all switch to 143.00 MHz for comms today," I said. "Greg, you're way out in front. Let me know what's going on up there. I'll be riding drag and won't see or hear anything unless you relay it."

"Got it," Greg affirmed.

"Thank you. Stretch, you've got a track-packed road ahead of you today, and I hope it set up for you. If it didn't, and you have to get back on virgin snow, best go to the left of the green flags."

We'd give Stretch a head start. He'd radio back when he saw the first sign of the station on his horizon. That'd be in about four miles. The rest of us would catch up and go in staggered behind him. Judy first, Brad second, and me last. If it worked out, we'd all arrive at the hold-back line at about the same time. The *National Geographic* photographer might get a cool shot.

"No matter what happens, we're going to stop at the hold-back line, pulled up alongside each other. We'll get out of our tractors and gather in front of Stretch's blade for a confab, see what they have in mind. Anybody have anything to say?"

No questions or comments.

"Then there's just one more thing before we start. We've brought this American flag from my hometown of Silverton. This flag was flown at half-mast in Memorial Park on September 11, 2001. This same flag has traveled with us each year on this project. It's been with us at each farthest south. Let's secure the modules and set up our flagpole."

We were still erecting the flagpole on the living module's deck when an orange Twin Otter, belonging to the British Antarctic Survey, buzzed low over us against a deep blue sky. Once again, an aerial salute in several passes thrilled us. By their last pass, our Stars and Stripes were flying high. This was the beginning of our day.

Greg's team left straightaway. Stretch lumbered forward on his head start. The rest of us hung back, patiently at first, waiting for Stretch to get ahead. By the time he'd made two miles, the rest of us felt stupid just standing around. We climbed in our tractors and started creeping slowly forward.

We'd not caught up with Stretch when he radioed: "*Fritzy,* I see something on the horizon to our right. Looks like a white structure of some kind."

Stretch was passing Pole minus 9. Shortly we caught up, slowing our pace to match his, often stopping to give him more ground, then surging ahead again.

I wanted more than anything now to be with Stretch and Russ and Judy. I wanted to hear what they might be thinking, to share the joys they must be feeling. But I could only be happy for them and be alone with my own thoughts as South Pole Station again rose into clarity.

We came over the hill with our horizons in collision. South Pole Station by its mere structure took dominion over every sastrugi, over every compass point, over every space and orientation in our monotonous surroundings. The entire Plateau ordered itself around that station. Wallace Stevens's poem "Anecdote of the Jar" drifted into mind. Had Stevens been on the Polar Plateau, instead of on a mountaintop in Middle Tennessee, he might've written "Anecdote of the Pole."

"*Fritzy*, Feleppa here. We're at the hold-back line."

Visions of a close order, *en echelon* formation of tractors smartly approaching the hold-back line was the stuff of fantasy. We were coming in spread out, but coming in nevertheless.

"Copy that. Whatcha doing, Greg?"

"I am liaising . . . with numbers of people who have come to meet us."

"Very good. Who's there, and what do we know?"

"There're many of the same we saw yesterday. In addition, there's a fellow from NSF. . ."

Jerry Marty. I wonder if he is too busy to talk?

"There're several from station management. . ."

B. K. Grant and Jason, maybe Liesl Schernthanner.

"And there's the *National Geographic* photographer who'd like you to go on by. He wants moving video of the fleet pulling into the station."

"Copy that. Please inform our hosts our intention is to stop at the hold-back line as we discussed this morning." Things were about to get busy.

The D8, the *Elephant Man, Red Rider*, and *Fritzy* all parked shoulder to shoulder. Greg, Tom, and John V. met us in front of Stretch's blade.

The crowd, twice yesterday's size, waited at the five black panels. Jerry Marty stood among them, politely standing back, but I beckoned him over to join us. The sandy-haired fellow's eyes sparkled. He looked like a surfer on a good day at Long Beach. I put my arm around his lean shoulder and said simply, "I'd like you to be here right now. It'd mean a lot to me. To all of us."

"Thank you," he said as a grin spread under his brush moustache. "This is great!"

Then Jerry and I, our backs to the hold-back line, faced the crew. In this last moment of privacy I addressed them:

"Today we have done something remarkable. Each of us knows the struggle we've gone through, so this will not be a windy speech. But we're about to get into a whole lot of people, and a whole bunch of other stuff we don't even know what it is yet. Before all that happens, I want to congratulate each of you on our achievement, and offer my hand in thanks. Allow me this formality."

I sought Stretch first. "Thanks for everything, Stretch. You are the man who drove the D8 to Pole. How was your road today?"

"Umm . . . we made about three miles an hour. Pretty good, actually."

Then to Russ. "Congratulations. This has been on your mind for many, many years. And here you are!"

"Yes, sir. And here we are!" Russ smiled back.

"Judy, you're not for handshakes." I hugged her, saying, "Thank you for all your help," as she hugged me back.

"Brad, you're great to work with. Thanks for being part of this." We shook hands warmly, then I thought to ask: "Where's your girlfriend?"

"Ah, she had to work today. But she hears us. She works at South Pole Comms. She knows we're here."

"Good. Good," I smiled for Brad, and asked that he switch the milvan sled he'd just brought in for *Snow White*. That would make a better picture for the *Geographic* . . . going into Pole with its snow dump trailer.

I looked to Greg, Tom, and John V. "Think of it . . . a trail you've blazed across a continent! Simply magnificent!"

Jerry chimed in then. If he'd had a tail, it would've been wagging. "This is truly historic. This is a great day. My personal congratulations to all of you. We'll make it official at 90 degrees South when you can muster your tractors there. Can we do that? Would that be all right?"

"We wouldn't miss that picture for the world, Jerry." I laughed for all of us. "How about right now we just mingle a bit."

Our trail-worn travelers merged with the well-parka-ed group of Polies, mixing seamlessly and easily. B. K. Grant, the South Pole area director, was among the small crowd moving toward us. I'd always admired her competence. Though I'd little to do with her except on formal occasions, I identified her with South Pole Station itself. Now, I walked right up to the blonde boss-of-the-place. B. K. in turn approached me, bearing a sparkling smile and a hearty laugh. The formality I expected from her melted away the moment before we met. Both our arms, now suddenly outspread, clasped each other in warm embrace.

"B. K., I can't begin to tell you how much your holiday welcome means to our weary crew. Thank you so much for that," I choked.

"Oh sure! Your timing couldn't have been better!" She was a frontier ranch woman declaring the latch strings were out to a gang of trail busters.

✧ ✧ ✧

The crew joined me back at Stretch's blade with Jason.

"He's going to lead us into the station. There's no air traffic now, so we're cleared to go in. We've a quarter mile of virgin snow between here and Marisat. We don't want to get stuck in that snow right in front of the photographer."

As one, we rolled our heads back, nodding in understanding.

"Once we've rounded the corner at Marisat, we'll be on packed snow from then on. Greg, your Marine Corps flag looks mighty good flying from the back of our PistenBully. Stretch, follow Greg with the Stars and Stripes. Judy, Brad, and I will follow you in the same order. As soon as we get parked, shut down and plug in. They're going to show us where the bathrooms are, and then we'll get the orientation. We won't bother to refuel today. We won't think about work for the next two days. The day after Christmas we'll start our turnaround. Probably two days of that, and we'll head back to McMurdo the next morning."

That sounded strange.

Back in our tractors, each operator responded to my hail. No pedestrians lingered about our sleds. "Okay, Captain Feleppa, give Jason the go sign."

Our procession swung into line. We crossed the last quarter mile of snow swamp at the stately pace of two and a half miles per hour. Once we got to Marisat, the D8 leaped forward to four miles per hour.

Jason led us through long, organized rows of huge cardboard boxes and metal machine parts stacked on elevated snow platforms. This was the storage yard on the station outskirts. Pole denizens popped their heads over nearby berms to wave their welcome. The workers on station were men and women dressed just like us: brown overalls and grimy jackets, faces protected by fleece mufflers, eyes hidden by omnipresent glacier glasses and goggles. They cheered when our flags passed by.

Around the next corner, a large cardboard sign lay propped up against the end of a berm. It read:

CONGRATULATIONS SOUTH POLE TRAVERSE!
FROM YOUR FRIENDS IN SILVERTON, CO,
ELEVATION 9,318 FEET—AMERICAN LEGION POST 14

I lost it then. Scotty Jackson must've placed the sign that morning. Scotty, from my hometown, worked with me the last year of the tunnel project. He'd since stayed on at Pole with the cargo group. He knew we carried our hometown flag each of these years. He knew we brought it into Pole today, fulfilling my old promise to Post 14. Today, Scotty's sign brought home, and the remembrance of friends, to South Pole. Tears streamed down my face. I choked back sobs of thanksgiving.

Several hundred yards and a few twists and turns later, our fleet stopped in line at the base of a steep snow berm behind Summer Camp. Summer Camp above us was a collection of a dozen Jamesway tents: olive, canvas-covered Quonset huts just like the one we'd used at the Shear Zone that first year. Many of South Pole's seasonal workers berthed at Summer Camp. Bringing our own berthing, we'd be their downwind neighbors for a few days.

The PistenBully crawled up the berm first and disappeared from view. Stretch went next with the D8 and the module train bearing the Colors. *He* disappeared from view.

My radio squawked: "*Fritzy*, you have any preference for how we park up here?"

"Negative on that." I couldn't see a thing from down below. "Just make sure we can turn around."

Judy and the *Elephant Man* climbed the berm. She paused at the top, waiting for Stretch to settle into position. After Judy moved on, Brad and *Red Rider* climbed the hill.

In a few minutes, Greg radioed, "Come ahead *Fritzy*."

The platform above opened to a broad flat surface, big enough to hold a soccer field. Our modules and tractors lined up just ahead to my left. The refrigerator van sled, a pair of fuel tank sleds, and *Snow White* sat sidetracked, well off to my right.

"Show me where you need me to park," I requested over the radio.

John V. stepped out from behind the module train and motioned me forward. *Fritzy*, with Pole's tractor in tow, pulled ahead.

Six hundred miles dragging that deadweight cripple . . . delivered. Forty-three days out of McMurdo. Nineteen crossing the Plateau . . . all cargo here. Two three-thousand-gallon tank sleds . . . one full, one nearly empty. All souls intact.

I gave up on thinking.

John V.'s hand signals guided me to parking. Through my windshield, a crowd of faces looked back at me. I leaned over *Fritzy*'s steering wheel and switched off my engine. The entire world's noise stopped. I drew a deep breath, and rocked well back in my seat for a moment. Then I opened the cab door to my left. Slowly, I descended the side steps to the ground, making sure of my balance, making sure not to slip and fall when I touched down.

I managed two steps toward the crowd when a fellow with a wispy short beard and straight dark hair hanging chin-length stepped forward. He was fortyish, trim, half a head shorter than me and sported a McMurdo-issue red parka. "Do you mind?" the *Geographic* photographer asked.

"Uh, no. What?" I answered absently.

He shouldered his massive video camera and thrust a microphone to my face. "And how does it feel to be here at last?"

Had I been thinking about it, I would've predicted that question. But I wasn't thinking any more. Not until I realized he waited for my answer.

How does it feel? Fine, great . . . good trip, man?

I recalled my exchange with Trevor Griffiths some years back. Griffiths wrote the screenplay for *The Last Place on Earth*, a magnificent 2002 documentary drama of Amundsen's and Scott's race to the Pole. It *felt* like what his Amundsen said when he got to Pole. I grabbed for, and mangled, that speech:

"I have no great words for you. No grand emotions to share. This is a good day to be alive, and we are glad to be here."

|15| Christmas at South Pole

Dressed in our cleanest wrinkled clothes, we made our way to the new station a quarter mile from camp. The easy walking made my legs uncertain and wobbly. For a month and a half, in soft snow, I'd been compensating in advance for a fall I expected with each step. Now with firm snow beneath my feet, I *still* compensated in advance. Phantom pressures in the small of my back mimicked tractor vibrations. My brain surged forward looking for more trail to bust.

Across the snow-packed spacious campus, I passed over my tunnel and wondered what shape it was in now. The blue cargo office to my left had been located somewhere else a few years ago. To my right, stacks of refrigerator-sized cardboard boxes full of construction debris lay in long, neatly arranged rows. Future traverses would probably haul them back to McMurdo. The famous geodesic dome covering the 1970s station hadn't been torn down yet. It lay up ahead, nearly hidden by snowdrifts, and dwarfed by the immense elevated station.

The new two-and-a-half-story structure perched fifteen feet above the snow on massive steel pedestals. A temporary exterior wooden staircase led from the ground level to the first floor. Inside, other floors led to other stairs and down long hallways. Ultimately all paths led to the galley.

The galley was a high-ceilinged, airy room. Dining tables crossed its egalitarian space. Broad picture windows graced the long wall on the room's upwind side. From the sheltered comforts of the plush galley, one looked directly down on the Pole monument, planted at exactly 90 degrees South. The long wall opposite the picture windows held the buffet line where the galley staff laid out wonderful meals.

Our crew drifted into the galley on their own schedules and spread out to different seating. I found Scotty Jackson, my hometown neighbor who'd placed the welcome sign on the station's outskirts. Scotty was a bit older than me, my height, and wore a long black ponytail. He'd been a sheriff's deputy in my hometown for a number of years. Scotty was always calm in a crisis. I was about to confide my reactions to his sign when Megan Whitmore, a heavy equipment operator, joined us.

Megan was the first Antarctican I ever met. In 1993, I stepped off the plane at Denver's Stapleton Airport and wandered to a designated rendezvous prescribed to new hires. Finding no signage, no sign of anything that spoke of Antarctica to me, my eyes fell upon a diminutive female sporting a thick, auburn braid. She wore a combination of hiking and traveling clothes, and sat on a duffle bag. A backpack sat on the ground beside her. I had a duffle bag, too. Taking the chance, I asked, "Antarctica?"

She answered simply, "Yep."

When Megan joined us this evening, our dinner conversation turned to things new at Pole. A person could now get off the airplane, brave the cold walk to the new station, take up quarters, change into a t-shirt and jeans, and spend their entire season in its warm confines. Such wasn't the life chosen by most of the Polies, though. Scotty's job with cargo and Megan's job with heavy equipment required outside work. But the simple fact that one *could* come to Pole now and never venture outside portended a lifestyle change, a cushy environment for administrators and their ilk. Their numbers would grow.

After dinner, Scotty had business to attend to. So I asked Megan if she'd tour me around the elevated station, killing time before the evening's lecture.

Megan led me out of the galley and graciously walked me around the new building. On the galley level and down a central hallway she showed me a large community room equipped with a dozen personal computer stations. Farther down the hall we found a designated music room that had been commandeered as a smoker's room. Somewhere through what had become a maze of hallways and stairs, we entered a spacious gymnasium, equipped for half-court basketball. In another wing of the station, Megan led me through a high-ceilinged lounge, down another hallway, and into a dormitory section. Here she showed me her room. Like every other space in this new station, her room had a window . . . so different from the dark, windowless spaces of the older navy constructions. Megan's room had a telephone and a personal computer line.

For all the luxuries she showed me, what struck me most was not the contrast of today's conveniences to the dearth of them in days past. The legendary hardships of the earliest explorers to reach here, less than a century ago, belonged to another age. Nor was the contrast with the tamer life in the Jamesway Summer Camp particularly stark. We had seen this coming. Rather, the sheer volume of materials and supplies that went into building and furnishing this massive station, the realization that every bit of it had been flown in by LC-130 aircraft, awed me by the logistical audacity of it. Our proof-of-concept delivery was puny by comparison.

Megan led back to the galley where we parted company, she to find a seat and I to find Scotty-Bob Smith, captain of the South Pole plumbers. The large room was already filling up with people. At the far end of the room, recessed into the back wall, a saloon provided standing room for numbers of people. Along the sidewall, where the buffet line ran, folks took standing room there, too. Our crew sat scattered about the room, and I was glad they were there. I needed their support.

Scotty-Bob approached me, extending his hand in greeting. This was the first time we'd run into each other since our arrival. During the off season he and Jerry Marty hinted that an evening lecture on the traverse would be welcome, if we got to South Pole. I gave Scotty-Bob a disc then, containing a slide show covering the first three years of our project. He'd carry it to Pole by plane and set up the projection and audio systems in advance. In exchange, he gave me a shoebox to deliver back to him.

"This is the largest crowd we've ever seen, for any lecture." Scotty-Bob beamed through his whiskers. The smiling plumber was always up-beat, volunteering his time boosting station morale. "The community is really, really interested in your traverse."

"Well, it's all of ours, but we've a good story to tell, and some neat pictures to show. Do we have a way of blocking the light coming through the windows?" I asked. It was 7:30 at night on December 23rd at South Pole. Broad daylight streamed into the room.

"Yep. We'll get the blinds drawn."

After a thoughtful introduction from B. K. welcoming us once again to the station, I found the energy to turn on.

"Thank you, B. K. And thanks to all of you who have welcomed us to your holiday celebrations." I gazed around the full room. "We've been four years getting here. Tonight, let me tell you what that was like. Let me show you where we've been."

Entertaining pictures of mule trains, camel caravans, and ship convoys couched our project in the context of hauling cargo over trackless wastes. Text slides described our mission as "proof-of-concept," and introduced the idea of matching machine mobility to the peculiarities of the Antarctic terrain. Turning from concepts to progress, pictures showed finding and filling crevasses at the Shear Zone in Year One, slogging through the Ross Ice Shelf swamp in Year Two, and winning our way across the Shoals only to be turned around at the top of the Leverett in Year Three. Interspersed maps depicted our advancing route to Pole. Missing, however, were any pictures of our Plateau crossing.

I described what happened along the trail this year, and what we found for terrain between the top of the Leverett and Pole. They learned of Sastrugi National Park, and the Plateau swamp outside their back door. When I described adjusting to loss of tractors and the mind-numbing shuttling, trail weariness settled over me again.

One astute young man asked, "What efficiencies does the traverse offer over LC-130s?"

"That, of course, is the *big* question we hope to answer. Unfortunately, we can't answer it yet, because we haven't finished. Early feasibility studies suggested traversing could deliver twice the payload for the same fuel consumption as an LC-130. I've steadfastly refused revising those early conclusions, because we don't have solid data yet. But I don't see any reason why that projected performance, or better, shouldn't hold. Understand, this proof-of-concept project spent a lot of time finding the way here and breaking trail. Future traverses won't have to do that. We've not just been pointing our tractors south, and we've yet to make a real snow road out of this trail we *have* found."

The young man may have been asking about cost as well. I added, "As for dollar efficiencies, based on our lessons learned from this project we'll get a handle on the operating costs. Likewise we'll design the future traverse fleet.

All that must wait until we're done. As far as capital costs, three seven-tractor fleets complete with sleds might cost $25 million. One new LC-130 might cost $80 million. So the capital outlay encourages us to look at traversing.

"We're not sure that three traverse fleets based out of McMurdo are the best way to go. It may be that a single plateau fleet housed at Pole and a single ice shelf fleet based at McMurdo is a better way. That's about the best I can offer you now. If you like, I'd be happy discuss your very good question further. Why don't you catch me at one of your meals here?"

The bright young man accepted my invitation, and in the days to come we would have that discussion.

"Is there another question?"

A few followed, and I met each with the best answer I could. But the last question struck an emotional chord: "Did you ever doubt you'd make it here?"

I stared pensively at the floor, replaying all the days from the beginning when NSF announced its full support for traverse development. *When had there not been doubt?*

With a deep sigh, I looked up. "There is always a way. We didn't necessarily know what that way was. But if you're willing to invest the time and the money, then you will find the way. For us, it has never been easy. Not with time. Not with money. Not with terrain. Our route was mostly unexplored until we explored it. And plan though we might, we never knew what we were getting into until we got there. In October of this year, still at McMurdo, it was a question: could we make it? It is a question no more. We are here."

The community as one gave a prolonged, warming round of applause.

I added a post script: "We have brought 218,000 pounds of Christmas gifts to you, and we look forward to officially delivering those. Tonight we are proud to make our first delivery. Would Scotty-Bob please come to the front?"

Scotty-Bob worked his way around the tables and chairs and folks standing in the aisles. Looking beyond him to the audience, I announced with all the drama I could muster: "Ladies and gentlemen, the South Pole Traverse Proof-of-Concept Project proudly makes its first delivery." I held aloft a cardboard shoebox for all to see, a box Scotty-Bob recognized.

"The mail!" I cried. The box contained several hundred commemorative envelopes, stamped and cacheted "Delivered via Surface Traverse from McMurdo to South Pole."

Scotty-Bob accepted the prize to deafening renewed applause. He and Jerry Marty later distributed those decorated envelopes to every person at South Pole Station.

I closed by introducing our crew by name, one at a time. From scattered locations around the room, each stood and acknowledged the community with a smile and a wave. We invited the community to come by our digs downwind of Summer Camp.

"Consider it open house, and you're invited. If you've any more questions, do not hesitate to ask any member of this fine crew. They'll have better and more interesting answers than I. For now, I'm talked out. Thank you for having us as your guests."

Over Christmas Eve and Christmas we mixed happily with the Polies. Our open house found many takers at all hours. One evening Scotty Jackson dropped by with a bottle of Irish whiskey and shared it to the bottom with those who happened to be around. Another night a carpenter's helper from New Hampshire serenaded us with a medley of her old-time banjo music.

Polies, equally proud of their facilities, guided us through their changing environs: the new elevated station, the new power plant, and the old station under the dome. Scotty Jackson toured me, Judy, and Greg through the tunnel network we'd dug under the station several years before.

I found Scotty on Christmas Eve at breakfast and asked if he'd like to join me in *Fritzy*. I needed to retrieve the sleds still back at the hold-back line. He was all for it. We'd meet at his cargo office in an hour. But Brad, who happened to be eating breakfast with us asked, "How'd you like me to bring in the milvan sled?"

"Brad, you don't have to do anything today unless you want to. Scotty and I can get it."

Brad said, "Well, I was sort of thinking I'd go out there in *Red Rider . . .*"

"Gotcha, Brad. Scotty and I won't be out there for a while. You two have a good time and enjoy the views."

"Thanks." Brad left right away.

After dawdling over late coffee and rolls in the galley, I rendezvoused with Scotty and we strolled to the traverse camp.

"I missed seeing you when we came in. But I got to tell you, that sign you left in the berms . . . I completely lost it. I mean, I've been consumed with this traverse every minute of every day on the trail. I lay awake at night imagining what might happen, wondering what I've missed that might get somebody hurt. When we pulled into the station and I saw your sign . . . that was the first time it all got to me. I broke down."

"I know how you feel, John," Scotty confessed. "Sorry I couldn't be there either. But when I put up that sign . . . I got all choked up, too."

"Then I'm glad you weren't there! 'Cause then everybody at Pole would have seen two grown men bawling their eyes out!"

We rounded the corner of the Summer Camp Jamesway lounge into a full view of our parked fleet. *Red Rider* was back. The milvan sled was parked next to our two tank sleds. Above the living module, our hometown Stars and Stripes stretched out atop our flagpole. At the same time, we both noticed there was no wind. Yet our flag posed stiffly unfurled atop the pole, against a clear blue sky.

"Imagine that," Scotty laughed. It was frozen.

"Scotty, you ever run a Challenger tractor?" I asked, approaching *Fritzy*.

"Not yet."

"Well, walk around it with me and I'll show you the check out. I'll take her out to the hold-back line. You can sit beside me in the helper seat."

Fritzy's engine temperature rose quickly to 100 degrees Celsius after starting. It was a warm day by Pole standards. We drove back out toward Marisat and turned right to cross the skiway. Since no airplanes came on Christmas Eve, we crossed unannounced. Then passing the flat rack sled, we pulled up to the five black panels and climbed out onto the snow.

"Scotty, these panels were our target coming into Pole. Take a look out there to the north, along our tracks. Can you see the green flags to the right of them?"

Scotty squinted a moment, then exclaimed: "Oh, yeah! I see them."

"Standing here, and looking out there, I want you to understand. Starting at these black panels, a continuous line of green flags, planted no more than one quarter mile apart, leads all the way back to McMurdo, all 1,028 miles. You want to walk back to McMurdo? Those green flags lead the way."

Scotty got it. He'd been working when I gave my lecture. So I told him of the terrain we encountered from the top of the Leverett, about the extent of the Plateau swamp, and about shuttling our loads. We had just one more load to shuttle. The flat rack sled.

"How about you run *Fritzy* and bring the last load, the last mile into the station?"

On Christmas Eve, at the second of three seatings, we joined in the station's all-out dinner. The galley staff and a host of generous volunteers put on a culinary *tour de force* that would win raves from any gourmet. B. K. wore a black sleeveless dress, which was a killer combination for the slender, long-haired blond. She met us entering the room, and escorted us to a long table in the middle. Behind us sat a table from cargo. To their side sat fuels workers, fuelies. All these people worked hard with one another, day in and day out, and they still wanted to sit down to a holiday meal together.

We rose in orderly rounds to the buffet line. I halted before the meat selections. A long-standing promise to me had been kept. "Cookie" John, who'd been the head chef at South Pole for a number of years, promised me two years ago that he'd prepare a special meal for the traverse on our arrival, whenever that may be. Cookie asked me what I wanted. Without hesitation, I answered: beef wellington.

But Cookie John quit the Pole job six months ago. The day he walked out of the Denver office, he dropped by my cubicle to say so-long. He'd pass on my request, he'd said. Today, I stood before beef wellington in the buffet line, and softly spoke my thanks to Cookie John.

Jerry Marty caught up with us toward the end of the banquet and asked for assistance from the veterans among us. Pole tradition held that on Christmas Day a big Mantis crane moved out to the Pole marker, raised its boom to full extent, and hoisted the Stars and Stripes and the POW-MIA flags on its cable. Service veterans at Pole traditionally presided over that ceremony. Stretch, a Vietnam vet; Russ, who served in Korea; and Greg, our Iraqi Freedom marine, found Jerry later that evening. The next morning at breakfast we saw their handiwork through the galley windows.

After Christmas Day breakfast we entered our tractors in Pole's annual "Round the World Race." This was a colorful event in which runners, walkers, sledders, and skiers in zany costumes locomoted by their chosen means around the Pole monument. Three laps made a two and a half mile course. Mechanized entrants, such as our tractors and all manner of whimsical contraptions, took their laps outside the runners.

Liesl Schernthanner organized the start with the foot racers gathered around her. The ponytailed skier from Ketchum, Idaho pointed her megaphone over them. The contestants may have heard her instructions, but the hundred or so entrants were more interested in laughing and socializing. Liesl herself was seldom seen without a smile

I parked *Fritzy* to the side with the engine off and the side door open, listening as best I could. Liesl raised a starter's pistol into the air, the unmistakable signal the race was about to begin. Runners and walkers faced the starting line. The snow absorbed all the bang out of the shot. Liesl's gun poofed instead. The runners lurched forward with a cheer.

Fritzy crawled ahead. Dave Watson, a big lumbering miner who'd finished the tunnel with me and stayed on at Pole as a heavy equipment operator, rode with me. Judy ran behind me in the *Elephant Man* with a gang of joy riders. Brad brought *Red Rider* behind Judy. Somewhere in the crowd, John V. piloted the PistenBully, pulling a sled-load of Polies on a long rope tether. Tom and Greg both chose to run their laps with the ground-pounders. Stretch and Russ walked their laps.

In the chaotic fun that followed, the Round the World Race resembled more a comical scene from *Mad Max*. A fellow on the inside track took his laps on drywaller's stilts. Earnest skiers and joggers weaved around him. A tractor passed us on the outside dragging a lounge couch on a makeshift sled. Aboard the couch, half a dozen beer-swilling partygoers laughed and waved to everyone they passed.

"Here come the plumbers!" Dave called out when a snowmobile pulling a sled load of toilets passed us. A well-bundled body sat on each toilet seat, and each mittened hand held a shiny beer can.

We passed Greg and Tom, slowing our pace to match theirs, honking encouragement with *Fritzy*'s snow-muffled *beep-beep-beep*.

Checkers with clipboards kept track of each entrant's laps. The race took an hour to complete. Every face glowed with smiles and laughter the entire time. At the race's end, all participants gathered in the spacious galley for cocoa and cookies.

✧ ✧ ✧

December 26 was back to work for us, as for all the South Pole community. After another fine breakfast with them, we gathered in our own galley to divide our jobs for the day.

Russ and John V. would spend the next two days turning over with the Pole mechanics. Pole needed to know all about the D8 and the MT865 and what we did to repair *Snow White*. Jason explained Pole was shorthanded on mechanics, so Russ and John could help them out on their own projects.

"While you're both around the shop, please locate the spare parts for *Quadzilla*. We'll back-load them tomorrow."

"Roger that," Russ agreed.

Today, Stretch and Judy would move the bulldozer and the MT where Jason wanted them. Then they'd take *Red Rider* and a station loader to demonstrate the use of *Snow White*. Pole annually gathered drift snow from around the station and dozed it into enormous piles, some forty feet high. They pushed those piles well downwind of the station to get rid of the drift snow. These days, their push stretched to a half mile. That's why the USAP designed and built *Snow White* in the first place. That's why we brought it to them: to haul snow rather than push it. Stretch and Judy would finish their day hauling snow for Jason.

"Brad, you and Greg are with me. We're going to meet some folks from Cargo and off-load the Flat Rack while they officially receive the stuff. If you don't mind, Brad, start up *Fritzy*. I'll be along shortly. Tom, hang back a bit. I've got a couple assignments for you I need to explain."

To everybody I announced, "Meet back here at 1:00 p.m. We'll gather up our tractors, take them to the Pole marker, and stand for the picture. Jerry Marty will make the ceremonial welcome. The *National Geographic* photographer will be there. Scotty Jackson will bring his camera, too. Plan your day around it. Otherwise, that's all. Let's go."

Tom and I stayed back. As our mountaineer, Tom was our first-line emergency medical caregiver. I asked Tom to find out all he could about the medical facilities at Pole, and about their procedures for a medevac. I didn't know what they were, but wanted that knowledge traveling with us.

"Anybody here you can to point me to, where I might start?" he asked.

"The station Doc, or B. K., or Liesl. But as far as I'm concerned, you're on your own and you can go with this wherever you want. Let me know what new knowledge you come up with."

"Okay. In a medevac, don't most folks get flown out to McMurdo?"

"Yes, of course. But in a couple of days we'll be down the trail. My sense is as long as we're on the Plateau, any medevac will go first to Pole by Twin Otter, and then to McMurdo by LC-130. But picture us with an emergency in Sastrugi National Park."

I shared my concern that a fixed-wing aircraft couldn't find a safe landing in that region. As for preparing a landing surface in the rough stuff, our return traverse would be ill-equipped. We'd have only one twelve-foot blade on *Red Rider* and no D8.

"Maybe a Twin Otter pilot can give me some wisdom. What was the other assignment?"

"For some reason we don't have two-way VHF comms with South Pole."

That had been an unpleasant surprise . . . a two-year-old plan, then finding out we couldn't talk to each other. I'd be occupied off-loading cargo. I needed Tom to get to the bottom of it and fix it. Two-way VHF comms with Pole was essential to our mission safety.

"I'll start with South Pole Comms." Tom took on the job. "Brad's lady friend is on duty now. She may help."

At 1:00 p.m. we stood by our tractors at the Pole monument. There were actually two monuments at Pole. The ceremonial monument looked like the cartoon barber pole surrounded by flags of the Antarctic Treaty Nations. Nearby the geographical monument was a small, decorative brass cap, set on a slender metal pole planted upright in the snow. Next to it, a sign proclaimed: "Amundsen-Scott South Pole Station, 90° South." We gathered at 90 degrees South. Downwind, the station edifices dwarfed us. Upwind, the plateau snows looked more familiar.

Jerry Marty spoke the official words of welcome for NSF. We took turns displaying our flags: the Silverton American Legion Post 14 flag, of course, then Greg's U.S. Marines Corps flag, and finally a surprise flag. From my parka's pocket I pulled out the Canadian Maple Leaf. Master sled-maker Herb

Setz of Peace River, Alberta, sent it to me at my request. Herb made all our sleds and was deeply involved in our redesign as we sought to build the ideal fleet. He'd be pleased to get it back.

The photo session broke up. I quietly asked Jerry if we could meet the following morning. The risks associated with our return traverse, and how they might impact South Pole Station, needed to be well understood.

"Risks?"

"Yeah. We were nineteen days crossing the Plateau. If our return with three tractors is as rough as it was getting here with four—if anything goes wrong—you might be seeing more of us."

Jerry checked his book. "Tomorrow at 0930? Cheese Palace?"

Jerry Marty's office at South Pole Station was a heavily insulated, plywood building located close to Summer Camp. Jerry was a Green Bay Packers fan, a Cheese-Head. His digs had become known as the "Cheese Palace."

Jerry's Cheese Palace sat next to the fuel pits. On my way over, I checked the tank sled we'd positioned there. It'd not yet been filled. I entered Jerry's place and found B. K. and Jason there with Jerry. The *Geographic* photographer was also there with his big camera. They were all seated at a long plywood table bolted to the office sidewall. Overhead lights reflected yellow off the unfinished plywood into the room. It was warm inside. I took off my parka and tossed it onto the pile of parkas shed by the others.

"I hope you don't mind that *Geographic* is here," Jerry remarked after the good-mornings went around. "We're collecting footage for an NSF film we want to release for the International Polar Year. It's a couple of years out. Your traverse is of interest for that."

I greeted the *Geographic* photographer separately, then I turned back to Jerry. "I don't mind. But *you* might mind. I'm going to acquaint you with some of our weaknesses . . . you might not want *weaknesses* on film. And I don't want to mince words for the sake of a camera."

Jerry concurred. The camera would stay off for now. "What do you have for us, John?"

"The first thing is right outside your door: our fuel tank sled. There's a couple hundred gallons left in it. To fill it to capacity, we might need 2,500 to

3,000 gallons. If you can spare that much, naturally we'll be grateful. If less, we need to know how much you actually do put in."

Jason said, "We'll fill it. I'll get the fuelies to attend to that this morning."

"Thank you. Aside from fuel, if things go bad for us that could also impact your operations here. You know that we hoped to come into Pole with six tractors and leave with four. Instead we came in with four tractors and a cripple. We'll be leaving with three. Our fourth tractor is broke down on the Leverett. So even though we're dropping a lot of weight here, three tractors going back will still be loaded heavy. If one of them breaks down, the two remaining ones won't have a prayer of completing the Plateau crossing. And if that happens, we'd come back to Pole. That means wintering the fleet here, and the attendant drain on your resources."

"Understood. Anything else?" Jerry showed no particular expression.

"If our road-building effort across the swamp doesn't hold up for our return, then we'd certainly be forced again into shuttling. In that event, a return to South Pole for even more supplemental fuel is likely."

"Is there another?" Jerry asked.

The catastrophic loss of one fuel tank sled, or its contents, on the Plateau section could again force our return to South Pole. We'd not seen such a loss yet, but we could make no guarantees for getting back across the sastrugi without damage. None of us, none among my crew and none at South Pole Station, wanted to see the traverse limping back to the station. Our nearest source of cached fuel lay at the base of the Leverett Glacier, 370 miles away.

"What do you hope for, John? That is, what are your chances?" B. K. asked.

"If we can get near that depot," I answered, "then we're home free. Any unexpected support we might need after that would come from McMurdo."

Jerry opened his notebook, speaking aloud as he wrote. "Nearest fuel at Leverett base, 370 miles."

"I'll tell you what," I offered. "We're leaving tomorrow. I hope you won't hear from me with troubles on the trail. But when we do get to the Leverett, I'll drop you a line to say all is well."

"That's what we'll hope to hear, then," Jerry offered. "Anything else?"

"Jason, what do you say to topping off our tractors' tanks at the end of shift today? You know we've been using them around the station quite a bit. It shouldn't amount to too much."

"We can do that, John."

"That's most generous. Thank you, once again."

Our discussions now concluded, we re-created the meeting for *Geographic*.

The afternoon saw most of our crew at Summer Camp back-loading for the return traverse. I sat at the comms booth in the living module, finishing up Field Report #6, when our radio squawked.

"South Pole Traverse, South Pole Traverse, this is South Pole Comms."

It was an unfamiliar male voice. Apparently, Tom had solved our comms problems.

"Go ahead South Pole Comms, this is South Pole Traverse," I responded.

"South Pole Traverse, I need Magsig, Vaitonis, Van Vlack, and Wright to come to the South Pole Comms office immediately and sign some papers."

We'd just come from lunch in that same big building. Now we were back at work.

Magsig, Vaitonis, Van Vlack . . . the papers Dave brought out on the Twin Otter? Naw, can't be . . . and now me?

"Is this a joke?" I asked earnestly over the radio, while looking out the comms booth window. Stretch was craning gear into the flat rack. Russ and John V. were probably in the heavy equipment shop.

The voice came back: "I assure you this is no joke. Please send your men right away."

Looking queerly at the microphone, I asked back, "Right. Who is this?"

The voice gave a name I do not remember, then added: "I am the contractor's human resources representative for South Pole Station."

Enough! "And we are four, and scattered about your station. You are one. You may bring these papers to our camp yourself. Traverse clear."

I turned off the radio, now that it was working.

The papers arrived later that afternoon, brought by our friend Jason. They were identical to those we'd signed on the Ross Ice Shelf. The three signers had not initialed each page of the document.

Jason also brought a single page for me to sign. It was the last page of a document titled "Pre-Season Performance Expectations." That document normally contained several pages. The one page contained no text, no discussion, no expectations, no space to initial . . . just a line to sign and date.

16| Return to McMurdo

"It's been lovely here," Judy smiled. "And today is a fine day to go."

December 28 was a fine day: bright blue skies, a scattering of high cirrus, and not a breath of wind on the ground. Judy walked with me across the station's campus toward Summer Camp and our waiting fleet. We'd just enjoyed our last breakfast in the South Pole galley. Her mood was important to me, important to all of us.

She'd once commented back down the trail, "Sometimes I feel like I'm living in close quarters with seven husbands!" She spent a lot of time with Myers-Briggs analyses, seeking enlightenment on different personality types. However, Judy got along with each of us guys through her innate strength and goodness. But seeing her lady friends, faces without beards, had been a blessing. "We had Christmas gifts for each other. My friend showed me all around the new station. And we just talked and talked . . . We had the *best* time!"

Talking was a job requirement for me. The contractor mandated safety talks each day at the start of shift. These became our morning briefings. We held them while our tractors warmed up. Some were more useful than others, particularly those that laid out terrain intelligence. Now I wearied of the sound of my own voice. The others wearied of it, too.

As we neared our tractors, Judy peeled off to start the *Elephant Man. Red Rider* and the PistenBully were already running. I went to start *Fritzy*, making a mental note to stow the flagpole before we broke camp. Today our flag hung limp. Direct sun had vaporized the ice that froze it the other day.

The others were as ready to go as Judy, but in our galley their faces wore blank expressions, braced to endure another briefing. They knew what I was about to say. But I had to mark the moment of change.

"We have established and proved a heavy haul route to South Pole. We have delivered eleven LC-130 loads of cargo as evidence. We have one more task to perform, and that is: get back to McMurdo and get back safely. A safe and successful roundtrip completes our mission."

I added new information: "We're anxious to get home, although I can't imagine a meeting or an e-mail in McMurdo I regret having missed. But charging for the barn is when we get careless. That's when one of us gets hurt. So do build this into your thinking: we will make several planned stops."

We'd grab our sidetracked sleds on the move but take at least a full day back on the Leverett with *Quadzilla*. We'd make another stop at ASTER 2, rig for radar and prospect a shortcut to FORK. That might take a day or two. We'd stop at SOUTH where we stashed an old sled loaded with fuel drums last year. I'd decide whether to leave it or retrieve it to McMurdo then. Finally, we'd stop at the Shear Zone as usual and radar the crossing before bringing the fleet over.

"*Our* job is not yet done. Now let's go finish it."

One of my shorter briefings, it broke up immediately to the sound of stools scudding across the galley floor and feet shuffling out the door. Greg and I collided at the doorway.

"Hoo-ahh!" I mumbled. "Did I say it right?"

"That would be *Ooh-Rah*!"

From *Fritzy*'s cab, I spotted no stray legs wandering around *Red Rider* which was hitched to the module sleds. "Brad?" I radioed.

"Ready."

"PistenBully?"

"Two aboard and ready." Greg and John V. would bring up the rear this time. The PistenBully was now stripped of its radar boom. All of that was stowed in a sled behind me.

"Judy, what do you got?"

"*Elephant Man* has four on board and we are ready." Stretch, Russ, and Tom rode with her. She pulled the refrigerator van, a full tank sled, and the empty spreader bar rig. No stray feet around her train, either.

"Judy, anybody milling around behind me?" *Fritzy* and I hitched to the milvan sled, the flat rack sled, and the second full fuel tank sled.

"You're clear."

"South Pole Comms, South Pole Comms . . . South Pole Traverse."

"Go ahead, South Pole Traverse," Brad's friend acknowledged.

"South Pole Comms, South Pole Traverse is departing South Pole Station for McMurdo. Request permission to proceed across the extended center line of the runway."

"South Pole Comms copies all. Proceed as requested. Have a good trip."

"Thank you. Brad, take off!"

A small group of Polies at Summer Camp waved good-bye. Another work-day for us all.

We awoke the morning of January 3 in the Parade Grounds, under the headwall of the Leverett Glacier. A thick ice fog filled the basin. Wet snowflakes drifted tentatively through the still air. We saw nothing of the Plateau's rim. We could not see the stony faces of Mt. Beazley, nor Magsig's Rampart. We saw neither a flag ahead, nor a flag behind. A month's worth of new blown snow obliterated all signs of our outbound track. Thirty miles below sat *Quadzilla*, alone and waiting.

This foggy morning we weren't going anywhere. Stretch was already up and at his oatmeal when I rose. After one look outside, I whispered quietly at the bunkroom doors: "Fog. Sleep in."

"Odd," I mentioned softly to Stretch. "Coming down the Leverett last year we ran into fog and big wet flakes. Remember that?"

Stretch squinted into his memories on the galley ceiling. "Yep. It was fog-gy then. Real foggy. But it didn't last, once we got below it."

"Yeah, that's right. We did get below it. There's something weird about the weather around here that I just don't get. It's wet."

We'd seen the dry, katabatic dumps off the Plateau up here. But even last year we dragged our way through soggy stuff at the bottom. Those snows came from gyres off the Amundsen and Bellingshausen Seas and swept along the mountain fronts. This year we got into wet storms at CAMP 20. By the time we got to the base of the Leverett, our surface was crumbly ice, not snow.

Mike Roberts tipped me off last year to an ephemeral lake of liquid water he'd once seen at the base of the Shackleton Glacier. That was one of the big glaciers we drove past after turning at FORK. Mike's lake was a shallow ponding of melt water, perched on the ice. He hinted we might find something like that one day at the base of the Leverett. Liquid water in a shallow lake could hide a multitude of crevasses.

Hidden crevasses may be today's or tomorrow's problems. But liquid water around here, even just wet snow, portended something else: warmth. What did that mean for the Ross Ice Shelf? Two-thirds of our route crossed it. In March of 2000 the big B-15 iceberg broke off the Shelf's edge into the Ross Sea. It corked off McMurdo Sound, and among other things kept us from getting that extra fuel we needed last year. Calving off the seaward margins is the typical way ice shelves shed mass. But in February 2002, over on the Weddell Sea side of the continent, the entire Larsen B Ice Shelf completely disintegrated in three days. Glaciologists called that event *rapid ice melt*. I guess so. Climate folks were now talking about catastrophic impacts of whole ice sheets in Greenland and Antarctica melting rapidly.

If an ice melt was going on here, slow or fast, we'd see it first near the ice shelf margins: at the seaward edge and possibly at the continental shore, such as at the Leverett base. That'd be something, to find an open-water channel at the shore instead of ice. For that matter, I wondered, what good would McMurdo be if Ross Island on which it sat was surrounded by open water? Ross Island lay right at the seaward edge of the Ross Ice Shelf. The base of the Leverett might become the next southernmost deepwater port. Our modest effort to cross the Ross Ice Shelf would become a footnoted "so what?"

Last year's snow pits at the base of the Leverett had shown us thin lenses of blue ice. Liquid water had been there, but it was all a mystery to me. I called the region the Lake District. The D8R had spent nearly a year in it. I wish it could tell me what that was like.

I made coffee and posted a note on our whiteboard: "Next weather call at 0900." Nothing to do but wait. We had a good run up to this point.

Our return trip over Plateau had gone well. What took an exhausting nineteen days to cover on the outbound leg, took only six coming back. Our roadwork through the swamp held up. *Fritzy* and the *Elephant Man* wallowed only once. No shuttling. One broken sled: a sastrugi snagged a ski on our spreader bar rig. Picking up the sidetracked tank sleds added no noticeable burden. We hit SPT-18 at the top of the Leverett early enough on the sixth day to bail over the headwall and make camp in the Parade Grounds.

This morning's fog arrested our northbound momentum. I resorted to posting weather calls on the galley wall, and at 0900, I asked my *eyes* to join me for a recon. From thirty paces in the direction in which we thought lay the next green flag, Greg and I turned around to find the big red living module nearly invisible through the pea soup. Turning again to face down the trail, we stood several minutes peering for any sign of a green flag.

"Not for me. You?" I asked.

"I see nothing."

Our boot prints guided us back to the living module. We barely made those out in the flat light. I erased 0900 on the whiteboard, and replaced it with 1000.

At 1000 hours and at 1100 hours, our recon brought the same results: no flag, no go. We made an early lunch. If the weather lifted by noon, we stood a good chance getting to *Quadzilla* that evening.

Greg brought the binoculars for the noon recon. Again, we followed our boot prints to the end of our beaten path. Then we ventured another hundred feet farther. For five minutes we stared in a promising direction.

"If we can sneak forward and spot a flag through this stuff, we could lay a track out to it with the PistenBully. We could go flag to flag following the PistenBully tracks," Greg offered.

As long as we could spot a flag. A certain track ten feet in front was as good as a flag at a quarter mile. Trying it would break our frustrating idleness. "Good idea," I agreed. "You see a flag?"

Greg, the binoculars still at his eyes, said, "I see one out there that comes and goes. Take a look."

"Point," I asked, taking the binoculars.

For some time I looked in that direction. Then for a brief moment the fog thinned. The washed-out but unmistakable form of a stick of bamboo with a banner dangling from the top appeared.

"I see it!" Then it was gone again. "Greg, we don't have any black flags for at least the next mile, so that's a green one. I'm game. Let's go back and tell the others to start their engines and hitch up. Good eye."

✧ ✧ ✧

"If you lose sight of the vehicle in front of you, or the tracks you're following, stop right where you are. Radio the rest of us that you have stopped. We'll all stop then and wait until you can see. I'm going to ride with Greg in the PistenBully. I know this Leverett route best of any of us."

We'd not be steering by GPS. The crevasses we knew about were too close to the road to trust GPS with it usual position errors. We'd be looking for green flags, and they'd be hard enough to spot. Greg and I would make many stops.

"Brad, don't run over us, we're that little red thing in front of you. John V., bring up *Fritzy*, please. And Judy, you'll have four pairs of eyes. Have a good time. Now let's see what we can do."

Descending from the Parade Grounds, our fleet proceeded flag to flag, making lots of stops, and some of those lasted as much as ten minutes. Greg and I advanced as far as we dared, never losing sight of the flag behind us. Then we'd stop and wait, until Greg spotted one in front of us through foggy partings. We covered three miles that way, and lost quite a bit of altitude. As we pulled abreast of the next green flag, Greg announced he could see the one past it.

"Really?" I asked, surprised.

"Really." Moments later he said, "I can see two!"

I still couldn't see the first one.

"Are you following our tracks okay?" I radioed back to Brad.

"No problem," Brad answered.

"Take off and lay us some tracks, Greg!"

The second flag was actually a wooden post marking a turning point. Crevasses lay within two hundred feet of it. Jim Lever found one of them last year in a close encounter.

"We marked it with several black flags. They're off to our right. Stop at the post. The green flag line turns left there."

Greg stepped out of the PistenBully with the binoculars. The heavy tractors stood at idle behind us. In a minute, Greg popped back into the PistenBully: "Got it!"

We reached the new flag. From there we spotted the next three. Within a mile the snowy surface stretched out beyond the last flag that even Greg saw.

Ten miles and two thousand feet below our start, we broke through the bottom of the fog.

"Twenty miles to *Quadzilla*!" I radioed. We'd drop another thousand feet to get there. The fleet picked up speed to seven miles per hour.

The Leverett opened up, no longer constrained by the narrows at Mount Beazley. The glazed surface that a month before had borne our year-old tracks we now found covered with blistered snow, flaked into icy slabs half a foot thick. There was no glaze and no sign of our tracks. There had been heat here while we were on the Plateau. A quick freeze had raised the blisters. It looked like scablands. And frost rime was everywhere. Today's fog had brought that.

Such heat! One of these days we might really find a lake at the bottom.

The fog blanket overhead hid the distant crags familiar to us. We spotted a dark dot afloat in the gray where the horizon should be. We arrived minutes later. *Quadzilla*'s left front rested on a stack of wooden blocks. We'd left it standing straight up. Now it precariously tipped left, no doubt settling under the same heat that blistered the surface.

A month-old camp circle surrounded *Quadzilla*. Though we couldn't see the tracks marking that perimeter, we knew the circle was still safe. Russ wanted the energy module parked within an extension cord length of the disabled tractor, so Greg pulled past it while Brad moved in. Brad unhitched and cleared away the drift snow around *Quadzilla* with *Red Rider*'s blade.

"Interesting day," I remarked to Greg. "Good job, bringing us through that fog."

Before turning in, I wrote Jerry Marty and B. K. that we'd completed the Plateau crossing in good time and without incident. We had plenty of fuel and camped this night within forty miles of our depot at the Leverett base. I thanked them especially for topping our tractors' tanks before we left. That got us fifty miles down the trail for free. And I thanked them once again for their hospitality.

Under a cloudless sky in the morning, Russ and Greg went to work on *Quadzilla*'s drive track. John V. saw to oil changes and maintenance on the other tractors. Stretch and Judy looked after our sleds. Brad, Tom, and I filled in where we could.

By late afternoon, Russ fired up *Quadzilla* and paced her around the camp like a high-spirited pony. His grinning thumbs-up through the tractor's tinted windows proclaimed all was well. We finished the afternoon rearranging our sled trains, allowing now for the resurrected tractor.

At the evening meal, I remarked, "Thank you all for your good work today. Tomorrow's an easy day to the depot. But tomorrow is a special day for another reason: It's Russ's sixtieth birthday! Last year we celebrated it at the top of this glacier. Tomorrow, we'll celebrate it at the bottom . . . on our way *back* from Pole! That's a good excuse to sleep in. Breakfast at 0900. Engines on at 1000."

But next morning's weather wouldn't celebrate with us. Blue skies gave way again to fog and a moody, gray overcast. Our late breakfast satisfied our hunger cravings, but we'd have no sun-basking, and no spectacular views to incite our wonder. It was a day for leaning forward and getting down the trail.

We covered the downhill in good time, never losing quarter-mile visibility. The foot of the glacier held no lake, not even a puddle. Not this year, anyway. An hour's stop to gather the depot, then five more miles through the flat light footed us firmly on the Ross Ice Shelf once again. I grilled steaks that evening, John V. prepared shrimp and horseradish sauce, and Judy baked a chocolate birthday cake.

The Transantarctic Mountains vanished. We knew they were near, but we saw no horizon, and rarely a shadow. Only our green flags, ghosting about in flat light, gave us direction. Days dragged on as if we moved through a dream of uncertain consequence: neither good nor bad, neither joyful nor foreboding. The fog simply existed, and we drifted through it in straight lines.

Occasionally we passed a post that told us we had come to a turning, yet once we turned onto the new course, we faced again that same pervading white, dotted by dark green flags leading to a vanishing point. Our instruments informed us of record mileages: seventy-five to ninety miles a day. We were closing on McMurdo, fast. But it didn't feel like it.

We stopped at a post labeled ASTER 2. There, we quickly reassembled the radar to probe for a shortcut to FORK. If we could cutoff CAMP 20, the shortcut could shave fifteen miles off the whole route. Tom, Stretch, Greg, and I departed the main fleet and prospected the first ten of the shortcut's miles. We found eight crevasses. The time invested in drilling and certifying them for crossing would cost us two days. I thought that a bad trade for the four hours, two going and two returning, we might shave off the future route. Plus, we had no certainty those eight would prove safe, and there was a high probability of finding more crevasses beyond them.

I ran the radar on this foray. At ten miles I called it off. The easy shortcut wasn't there. We returned to the idled fleet at ASTER 2, resumed advance on our proven route, and still posted fifty miles that day.

January 9 we recovered our last depot of tank sleds where the Pole tractor had broken down, and we moved on through the flat light. By this time the *Elephant Man* towed the PistenBully behind its train, riding a pair of plastic recovery skis.

Tom developed what he believed were kidney stones, a painful medical condition. Tom, John V., and I raised the resident doctor in McMurdo by Iridium phone. His remote diagnosis confirmed Tom did have kidney stones, but he advised we make no extraordinary preparations for a medevac. The doctor prescribed medications that we had on hand, urging Tom drink plenty of fluids and get lots of rest.

The doctor's reluctance to standby a medevac surprised me. The USAP flew medevacs frequently. But that was a doctor's call. A medevac, in any event, would be difficult now. No day of the previous six offered weather when a fixed-wing aircraft could make a safe landing at our position. Overcast, low ceilings, total loss of horizon and surface definition . . . until that changed, an airborne medevac was not possible. We were then fifty miles north of RIS-1, Year Two's farthest south.

"We could have Tom back in McMurdo in seventy-two hours," Stretch offered.

He was right. Our road was giving us unimagined mobility. We might find the physical reserve to put three days back-to-back and get Tom to the doctor's care. But no matter how nobly intended, that kind of push heightened risk of injury or accident to the rest of us from shear fatigue. I offered the hurry-up option to the doctor, keeping my concerns for the crew to myself. We could *still* do it, no matter what.

"Not necessary. Just keep him as comfortable as possible, and let me know of any change in his condition," the doctor said.

"You okay with that?" I asked Tom, who'd overheard the doctor's advice.

"Oh yeah. I've had them before. You can't do anything with these stones except wait for them to pass. I can ride in my bunk, or here in the energy module. It won't be great, but it wouldn't be any better in McMurdo, either," Tom explained.

"John V., you are now our first medical caregiver. Are you okay with traversing?" I asked, thankful to have discovered his emergency medical expertise long after I hired him as mechanic.

"They both say it's okay, so I'm okay with it. But like the Doc says," John V. added, "notify him of any change in condition."

Our eyes strained through the flat light, mile after mile. I visited Tom midday and evenings. He suffered stoically.

On January 11, the weather cleared. A long line of low clouds lay off our southern horizon. That's where the fog went. Before us to the north, the brilliant blue sky bore a blazing yellow sun. Tom woke that morning, relieved from passing three stones during the night. Color had returned to his face. He smiled delicately at the breakfast table.

"Tom! You look better!"

He brightened. "I do feel a little better! I'm sore and I've lost a lot of sleep. But better. I still want to ride in my bunk today, though. I don't feel perfect."

"No problem. John V., that is a change in condition. Will you please call the Doc tonight?"

That evening we passed SOUTH and made camp a hundred miles from the Shear Zone. Tom took a turn for the worse during the day. Different kidney, more stones.

"John V., let me know what the Doc says. Tell him we're now in helicopter range from McMurdo. We've plenty of aviation-grade fuel with us if he wants to reconsider a medevac."

Then I took Greg and Brad, along with *Fritzy* and *Red Rider*, a quarter mile back to SOUTH. We dug out the cache of twenty-four fuel drums lashed atop the old navy sled I'd "stolen" from McMurdo last year. The cache insured our five tractors could get to the Shear Zone if we needed the fuel.

But Tom was ailing. If a medevac had come, here was aviation fuel at the limits of helicopter range. If we'd been another fifty or sixty miles south, a chopper could have refueled here, made the distance, come back and refueled again, and still got back to McMurdo. This depot was going to stay.

Red Rider pushed up a platform of snow three feet above the natural surface. Tomorrow morning, after that platform had set up and hardened, we'd park the sled on top of Brad's work. For now, Greg headed back to camp with Brad. I stayed behind for a solitary remembrance of reaching SOUTH that first year, and our wretched sojourn there the second. After a last look at the post, I climbed into *Fritzy*, turned my back on SOUTH, and gave it not another thought.

John V. met me outside the living module while I was plugging in. "Tom and I talked to the Doc," he said, "and we went over the changes . . . first better, then bad again. The Doc still says we should just bring him in. No medevac."

"All right, John. Thank you. How's Tom doing?"

"He hurts, but he's okay and understands."

Friday, January 13, was a good day. Tom was still ailing, but we crossed the dorniks and camped within striking distance of McMurdo. Unless something drastic happened, we'd be going in tomorrow. That evening, we off-loaded the PistenBully and rigged it for radar. It would run the last twenty miles to the Shear Zone under its own power.

The evening's e-mail brought a personal note from Rebecca Hooper. She expected our arrival and asked if I could give an ETA. She said that the director of the contractor's company "and others would like to meet you . . . if you don't mind."

I remembered the solitary laborer who cheered us from the cargo lines at Williams Field a year ago. I remembered the pickup truck passing us on Scott Base hill, its driver absently lifting his hand an inch or two above the steering wheel. Rebecca's note suggested a more generous reception. As for our crew, each was deeply tired, all were happy to finish, half were eager to get back, others less thrilled, and one of us who was in pain needed to get back.

"Becky," I wrote, "if all goes well, we'll pull into Williams Field mid to late afternoon. My first concern is getting the fleet safely back across the Shear Zone. Once we do that, we'll be three hours from Willy. I'll call you from the McMurdo side of the Shear Zone when we're clear and heading in. One among us needs to get to the doctor without lollygagging. Of the others who might be there, please keep their numbers smallish. But among them . . . we'd all be pleased to see you there, Becky!"

And I wrote, "If George Blaisdell and Dave Bresnahan are on hand, it would be nice to see them at the finish line. Those guys have stood by us from the beginning, through thick and thin . . . And if you could arrange for Carol to be there as a surprise for Stretch, that would be something special."

January 14 brought crystalline clear weather. Featureless horizons floating before us for days now washed onto the shores of familiar land. Yesterday brought us to the margins of the Ross Ice Shelf. We passed the rocky Minna Bluff to the west. Snow-covered Mount Discovery rose behind it, then Black Island and White Island. As we neared the Shear Zone, those landmarks do-si-do-ed into their McMurdo-bound perspectives. Mount Erebus to the north glistened in the bright sun, showing off every crevasse on its glaciered slopes. A plume of white steam rose vertically from its summit against the polar blue sky.

We gathered in our galley for one last briefing. The small space felt unusually crowded with half of us standing, half of us seated, and all fully dressed and ready to go.

"Indulge me please; I have some things to say. And I have been waiting, even hoping, for this moment to say them. I want to say them while it is still just us, before we get back to McMurdo and all those people."

They graciously, if reluctantly, gave me their patience.

"One day last summer, I enjoyed a cup of morning coffee with my wife. We talked about me going away one more time to finish this job. The strangest thought came to me as I gazed out our bay window, overlooking Memorial Park. I asked my wife: 'Do you suppose anyone has ever done this before? I mean, who has ever traversed from McMurdo to Pole and back?'"

The question hung for a moment. In our galley, the expressions were the same as my wife's: *Surely yes. Someone has done it.*

"We went through the list as best we knew, all the great ones: Amundsen, 1912? Started at Bay of Whales, not McMurdo. Shackleton, 1909? Started from McMurdo but turned back a degree and a half short of 90 degrees South. Lack of food. Survived, though. Scott, 1912? A McMurdo start, got to Pole. Died on the return with a couple hundred miles to go. Lack of food again. And cold."

Stretch sat at his customary end of the galley table. He interjected with a touch of cynicism, born of enduring yet one more briefing: "Hillary drove his tractor to Pole."

"That's right, Stretch. And my hat's off to him. But according to the New Zealand press, he doesn't think much of what we're doing now, though his particular gripe with us is not clear. Yep, he had a McMurdo start, Scott Base if you want. Got the first tractor to Pole with little gasoline to spare. But he *flew* back to McMurdo. Didn't bring his tractor home. We, meaning the United States Navy, flew it out for him a couple years later. Now it sits in a museum in Christchurch."

Looking to the others I continued: "As part of that same expedition, Fuchs brought his tractors across the continent from the Weddell Sea . . . again, not McMurdo. He crossed to Pole then retraced Hillary's route *back* to McMurdo. I think he was pissed that Hillary ran into Pole ahead of him. Hillary later flew back to the top of the Skelton Glacier to guide Fuchs down.

"Even the army-navy expeditions of the late fifties and sixties, they made it to Pole. Took them three years. Started at Little America, near Amundsen's Bay of Whales, made an end run around the Transantarctic salient. Little America ain't McMurdo, and they didn't drive their stuff back."

I hadn't spoken of these things. Such had no business distracting us from the vigilance we kept up to ensure our own success. Its mere mention might have jinxed us. But now, emboldened by the proximity of our goal, just tens of miles and a Shear Zone crossing away, I made my declaration.

"I researched it, and now I'm sure: *No one has ever traversed from Mc-Murdo to Pole and back.* And I reckon the last man to try it died in the attempt in 1912."

The pronouncement brought silence in its wake.

"What we are about to do today may be considered by some, even by us, a minor Polar record. But consider what we're doing for the United States. The support contractor was lucky it hired us. NSF's been alternately supportive, or retreating from the prospect of our failure.

"Think beyond all that: McMurdo has long been viewed as the best port site on the continent, strategically and logistically. Sir James Ross spied it, and much later the Brits sent Scott and Shackleton down here, as if it were British territory. But our U.S. Navy built a base here. We built McMurdo to support our construction and occupation at South Pole. Up to today, Pole's been supported entirely by airlift from McMurdo. Never before has a surface supply route from McMurdo to Pole been established."

Not even the wind whistled outside. The land itself hushed.

"Today we're poised to complete the roundtrip traverse from McMurdo to Pole. We're doing it in typical American fashion: big tractors, big sleds, heavy cargo. No one can ever take this achievement away from you. *You will be the first.*"

Heads nodded now, accepting and pleased with the truth. Those standing, leaning back against the kitchen counter, folded their arms proudly across their chests. Those seated remained deep in thought, staring at their clasped hands.

It had long griped me that the first three claimants to win the North Pole were all Americans and that each of their claims was clouded: Cook, Peary, and even Byrd whose bust was over there behind the Chalet. In truth, the first person to even *see* both poles was Amundsen. All those other guys were in the hero business. They had to be famous to win patronage. We were neither heroes, nor famous. We were unimportant working stiffs in the USAP scheme of things, and we were supported by the awesome power of the U.S. taxpayer.

"If anybody wants to question *our* achievement . . ." My tone rose defiantly. "They can start at that first green flag we planted, and follow the flags all the way to Pole and back."

"That's the end of *that* speech," I said. "I do have another one for you . . . *Thank you* for your help."

I started 'round the cramped room, shaking each one's hand, offering a personal word of appreciation.

"Okay. Let's go."

Before midday we reached Home Free South. Others switched sleds around for the narrow passage, while Greg and I went into the Shear Zone with the PistenBully. Greg steered. I sat next to him, operating the radar. In my lap lay the printed record of our October crossing.

"The place doesn't change *that* fast," I instructed Greg before we started. "But it's a small matter to spend an hour making sure there're no surprises. I'm thinking of what another marine once told me: 'Do not trust anything in that place.' He ought to know."

In four years, things here *had* changed, but we hadn't done a lick of maintenance. One day that'd catch up with us. I wanted Greg to learn where the worst problems were. "You might be back this way sometime. What you know might save somebody's life."

Greg's eyebrows knitted with the unspoken question: *are you going somewhere?*

"Let's go the first mile, then stop at the milepost. Three miles an hour. Stop if I holler," I told him.

"Right, Boss."

"Jeez . . ."

We crawled down the road and kept up a running dialog. Greg called out when we passed green flags and signposts. I flipped through the printed record and kept one eye on the radar screen. We found nothing new in the first mile. Greg stopped at GAW+2, while I arranged the printed file for the next mile.

We found nothing new in that mile, either. But I stopped Greg just short of Personal Space.

"Look at this picture." I showed him the radar screen with the printed record alongside it. "There's no change here *since October*. Notice these dipping surface layers this side of Personal Space. We filled Personal Space the first year. But these sagging lines just east it of tell me something's under here, too. We're parked on top of it now."

It had to be something big, and it probably had one hell of a thick bridge. CRREL gave us guidance that year on bridge strengths. But it was my decision to cross it. We had crossed it ever since then without incident. Greg studied the displays, raising an eyebrow.

"We drilled it and drilled it, and never found a void to blast into. But each year these sagging lines get saggier. Now . . . you see that black flag standing all alone, ten feet left of the road?"

"I see it," Greg confirmed, looking south.

"That first year, Rick Pietrek and I found a more thinly bridged crevasse right there. That's what the radar showed. Man, we were crevasse-finding fools! Tom went down in Personal Space up ahead of us, but never found the connection. Anyhow, I think the crevasse under that black flag is part of a monster right under us."

Greg captured the area in his mental map.

"We never drilled over there. It was off our road. But if we ever come back here to reinforce this crossing, make it wider—which would be very smart of us—you go over to that black flag and shoot an access hole. Send a mountaineer down to look around; you'll find out what this thing under us is. Now you know. Remember that black flag. Let's go on."

We came to GAW+1. I got out the last mile's worth of printed records. Within a hundred yards after starting again, I hollered, "Stop!"

Greg braked immediately. I froze the image on the computer screen. We'd just passed a green flag between Crevasse 7 and Strange Brew.

"See these weird, squiggly lines on the screen? Now look at this printed record," I pointed to where the same green flag beside us was marked on the printouts. "This thing on the screen wasn't here in October."

It didn't look like a new crack. But next year, it might grow up. I penciled a note on the printed record, and then we moved on.

At GAW, I radioed back to the fleet. "Judy, tell the others to stay in their cabs the whole way across. If anybody needs to get out for any reason, call. We'll come out and make sure their area's clear."

"Roger, copy."

"Brad, how much fuel do we have after last night?"

"We drained the tank we were using, John. We're pulling one more full tank."

"That must be South Pole's fuel. I guess we owe them now."

"As a matter of fact, it *is* the tank we filled at Pole. Fancy that," Brad replied.

We'd get to McMurdo on what's in our tractors, and never tap that tank. I never thought we'd cut it that close.

"Tom, got your radio on? How're you doing?" I asked. The approaching fleet was now a mile away. Tom rode in the living module with a walkie-talkie at the ready.

"I'll make it." Tom sounded whupped.

When the whole fleet passed by GAW and lined up in the Shear Zone Camp, I breathed a sigh of relief that was four years coming.

We stopped long enough to off-load our surplus flags. Brad and Greg would come back in a few days to dress up the Camp area. They'd cache our ten-footers, protecting them from larcenous McMurdo-ites.

Rebecca wasn't at her phone when I called, so I left a message on her answering machine. Outside, Stretch was antsy to get down the road, but I asked him for one last thing: "Please help me set up the flagpole."

"You bet I will," he said, reawakened to our purpose. Stretch imagined searching for Carol back in town, but I knew she'd be waiting for him at the finish line. Stretch would look mighty good coming in under that flag.

All set now, my thoughts turned to Tom. In three hours we'd have him at McMurdo General.

When the first of us arrived at the post marking the start of our road, the last of us trailed two miles behind—Russ, proudly bringing *Quadzilla* back to town.

From that post, another half mile on a well-established snow road took us to the Williams Field road at the city limits. Another nine miles led to Ross Island over snow roads that pickup trucks ran with ease. Two more miles ran over dirt roads into McMurdo.

As each tractor rounded the post, we gathered up to go in line together. One last stop. One last chance to stretch our legs. Tom joined us.

I started to climb back into *Fritzy* when he stopped me.

"John, would you mind if I rode in your cab with you?" Tom would not cross the finish line in the living module. I understood.

"Tom, I'd be honored."

In our cabs now, I radioed to Greg, "Proceed." Moments later, Brad started rolling. My hometown colors flew above him. Ahead, a small crowd waited for us on the Williams Field road.

At precisely 1514 hours on January 14, 2006, a Navstar satellite overhead signaled my GPS receiver. I grabbed my radio. "Mac-Ops, Mac-Ops . . . South Pole Traverse."

"Go ahead, South Pole Traverse, this is Mac-Ops."

"Mac-Ops, South Pole Traverse has arrived at Williams Field with all souls. The concept is proved. This will be our last transmission. Over."

"Copy all, South Pole Traverse. Welcome back. Mac-Ops clear."

"Traverse clear."

Fewer planes would fly to Pole now. United States Antarctic Program logistics would never be the same after our quiet victory.

There had been no other job. That was the job.

Behind us, one thousand miles of green flags led through crevasse fields, across snow swamps, over sastrugi and mountain ranges to South Pole and back . . . safely, because we proved it. East of us, *Linda*'s steely carcass drifted toward the Ross Sea.

INDEX

ABOUT THE AUTHOR

John H. Wright began his career in the underground mines of the American West as a mining geologist and hard rock miner. With the closing of the western frontier he headed south to Antarctica, serving first as an explosives engineer, then later driving a tunnel in the ice beneath the South Pole. Because of his record in service to the United States Antarctic Program executing dangerous, difficult jobs with an impeccable record for safety and achievement, he was selected to lead the historic South Pole Traverse Proof-of-Concept Project. He is honored to tell its story.